Great Britain Meteorological Office

A Discussion of the meteorology of the Part of the Atlantic being north of 30° N.

For the eleven Days ending 8th February 1870

Great Britain Meteorological Office

A Discussion of the meteorology of the Part of the Atlantic being north of 30° N.
For the eleven Days ending 8th February 1870

ISBN/EAN: 9783337107437

Printed in Europe, USA, Canada, Australia, Japan

Cover: Foto ©ninafisch / pixelio.de

More available books at **www.hansebooks.com**

A

DISCUSSION OF THE METEOROLOGY

OF THAT

PART OF THE ATLANTIC LYING NORTH OF 30° N.

For the Eleven Days ending 8th February 1870,

BY MEANS OF

SYNOPTIC CHARTS, DIAGRAMS, EXTRACTS FROM LOGS, REMARKS
AND CONCLUSIONS.

Published by the Authority of the Meteorological Committee.

LONDON:
PRINTED BY GEORGE EDWARD EYRE AND WILLIAM SPOTTISWOODE,
PRINTERS TO THE QUEEN'S MOST EXCELLENT MAJESTY.
FOR HER MAJESTY'S STATIONERY OFFICE.
PUBLISHED BY E. STANFORD, CHARING CROSS.

1872.

A DISCUSSION OF THE METEOROLOGY

OF THAT

PART OF THE ATLANTIC LYING NORTH OF 30° N.,

For the Eleven Days ending 8th February 1870.

INTRODUCTORY REMARKS.

BETWEEN the 29th of January and 8th of February 1870 various notices of extreme atmospherical disturbances were sent into this Office.

For instance, at Heart's Content in Newfoundland, between 1 and 10 p.m. local time of January 30th, the barometer fell from 29·51 to 28·53, "wind S. by W. strong."

Again, in the eight hours between 4 p.m. and midnight of the 29th, on board the S.S. "Delta," in about 40° N. and 64° 30′ W., the mercury fell 0·8 in., accompanied by a heavy gale shifting from south-east to west. This gale was afterwards experienced by several vessels to the north-eastward of the "Delta," and seemed to be connected with that which blew at Heart's Content on the 30th.

Then again, Capt. Murphy, of the "Tarifa," was keeping a log for this Office, and on February 5th his barometer (a standard instrument) was down to 27·33 in about 51° N. and 24° W. during a gale of hurricane force. This reading was afterwards proved to be correct by the logs of two other ships near her. These facts were referred to in the first Quarterly Weather Report for 1870, where it will be seen that the barometer at St. Petersburgh was at the same time 30·99! giving a difference of pressure of 3·66 inches! From February 5th to the 8th, in Norway and on the north-east coast of Scotland, very heavy south-east gales were experienced, with a sea which did much damage to the harbour works at Wick.

It will be remembered that the "City of Boston" left Halifax on the 28th of January, and was never heard of again.

On these grounds it was thought that Synoptic Charts of the weather over the Atlantic north of the 30th parallel during these days, would throw some light on its changes which might be useful to practical men.

The system followed has been to collect data from every available source, by which means we have the observations of more than 30 ships for most Charts, besides those from several land stations.

The following is a list of ships and stations, with the names of those persons who have kindly helped by sending data.

Ship's Number on the Charts.	Name and Nature of Ship.		Captain's Name.	Sender of the Data.	Hour of Observation.
1	"City of Antwerp"	S.S.	Robert Leitch	W. Inman, Esq.	8 a.m. G. T. &c.
2	"City of Cork"	S.S.	R. A. Allen	Do.	Do.
3	"Etna"	S.S.	George Lochead	Do.	Do.
4	"Prussian"	S.S.	J. E. Dutton	Captain Grange from Montreal Ocean S.S. Co.	Do.
5	"North American"	S.S.	W. Richardson	Do.	Do.
6	"Nestorian"	S.S.	D. Aird	Do.	Do.
7	"Minnesota"	S.S.	J. Price	Messrs. Guion & Co.	Do.
9	"Colorado"	S.S.	J. A. Williams	Do.	Do.
10	"Manhattan"	S.S.	W. Forsyth	Do.	Do.
11	"Iowa"	S.S.	John Hedderwick	Messrs. Handyside & Henderson.	Do.
12	"Dacian"	S.S.	James Laird	Do.	Do.
13	"India"	S.S.	R. D. Munro	Do.	Do.
14	"Europa"	S.S.	John McDonald	Do.	Do.
15	"Moravian"	S.S.	Robert Brown	Captain Grange from Montreal Ocean S.S. Co. and log for this Office.	
16	"City of London"	S.S.	Henry Tibbits	W. Inman, Esq.	Do.
17	"Helvetia"	S.S.	A. Thompson	National S.S. Co.	Do.
18	"Virginia"	S.S.	C. Thomas	Do.	Do.
19	"England"	S.S.	G. Grigs	Do.	Do.
20	"The Queen"	S.S.	W. H. Thompson	Do.	Do.
21	"Denmark"	S.S.	James Forbes	Do.	Do.
22	"Pennsylvania"	S.S.	W. Hall	Do.	Do.
23	"Atrato"	Paddle S.	G. Parkes	W. I. R. M. S. P. Co.	Do.
24	"Nile"	Paddle S.	R. Revitt	Do.	Do.
25	"Cuban"	S.S.	W. Robinson	W. I. and Pacific S. S. Co.	Do.
26	"Venezuelan"	S.S.	John Cavell	Do.	Do.
27	"Australian"	S.S.	Joseph Barker	Do.	Do.
28	"West Indian"	S.S.	John Millar	Do.	Do.
29	"Chatillon"	Sailing	T. De Lalande	Imperial Observatory, Paris	8 a.m. ship time.
30	H.M.S. "Orontes"	S.S.	H. Phelps, R.N.	W. W. Vine, Esq., R.N., Navigating Lieut.	8 a.m. G.T., &c.
33	"Cuba"	S.S.	E. R. Moodie	Captain observing for this office with Standard instruments.	Do.
34	"Duncairn"	Sailing	James Finlay	Do.	Do.
35	"Tarifa"	S.S.	Michael Murphy	Do.	Do.
36	"Palmyra"	S.S.	William Watson	Do.	Do.
37	"Austrian"	S.S.	James Wylie	Do.	Do.
38	"Nicoline"	Sailing	A. J. Heim	Herr Von Freeden	Do.
39	"Westphalia"	S.S.	N. Trautmann	Do.	Do.
40	"Deutschland"	S.S.	H. A. Neynaber	Do.	Do.
41	"Hammonia"	S.S.	E. Meier	Do.	Do.
42	"Swea"	Sailing	A. F. Hartmann	Do.	Do.
45	"Carl Georg"	do.	G. Stöver	Do.	Do.
46	"Nemesis"	S.S.	Edwin Billings	Captain Inglis, Cunard's Line	Do.
47	"Tripoli"	S.S.	W. H. P. Hains	Do.	Do.
48	"Calabria"	S.S.	Wm. McMickan	Do.	Do.
49	"Marathon"	S.S.	F. Le Messurier	Do.	Do.
50	"Hotspur"	S.S.	William Hetherington	Captain observing for this Office with standard instruments.	Do.
51	"Samaria"	S.S.	John Artis Martyn	Do.	Do.
52	"Delta"	S.S.	Gilbert Shaw	Do.	Do.
53	"Weser"	S.S.	G. Wencke	Herr Von Freeden	Do.
54	"Bremen"	S.S.	C. Leist	Do.	Do.
55	"Rhein"	S.S.	T. Meyer	Do.	Do.
56	"Perseverance"	Sailing	C. Davidson	Captain observing for this Office with standard instruments.	

Name of Land Station.	Name of the Sender of Data.	Hour of Observation.
Central Park Observatory, New York, data from self-registering instruments.	Professor Daniel Draper -	8 a.m. G. T., &c., &c.
Stykkisholm, Iceland -	Scottish Meteorological Society	10.30 a.m. G. T.
Reykjavik, Iceland -	Do. -	9 a.m. G. T.
Thorshavn, Faroe Islands -	Do.	Do.
North Unst, Shetland -	Do.	Do.
Lews Castle, Stornoway -	Do.	Do.
Monach, N. Uist -	Do.	Do.
Dunvegan, Skye -	Do.	Do.
Callton Mor, Argyleshire -	Do.	Do.
Ballabus, Islay -	Do.	Do.
South Cairn, Wigtown -	Do.	Do.
Sandwick Manse, Orkney -	Rev. C. Clouston, LL.D. -	Do. Wind continuous from anemometer belonging to the office.
Dublin -	Dr. J. W. Moore -	9 a.m. G. T.
Gibraltar -	Army Medical Department	Do.
St. John's, Newfoundland -	Do.	0.30 p.m. and 6.30 p.m. G. T.
Heart's Content, Newfoundland -	E. Weedon, Esq. -	0.30 p.m. G. T.
Halifax, Nova Scotia -	Army Medical Department	1.15 p.m. and 7.15 p.m. G. T.
Do. do.	F. Allison, Esq., through Captain D. Hunter.	Various hours.
Quebec, Canada -	Do. do.	1.45 p.m. and 7.45 p.m. G. T.
Belleisle, Strait of Belleisle -	G. Scott, Esq., Chief Officer S.S. "Nestorian."	4 p.m. G. T.
Forteau Point, Labrador -	Do. do.	Do.
Funchal, Madeira -	M. da Silveira, Director of the Lisbon Observatory.	10 a.m. G. T.
Terceira, Azores -	Do. do.	10.45 a.m. G. T.

In addition, the materials furnished by the self-recording observatories in connexion with the office, and those contained in the Daily Weather Reports, the Bulletin International, and the Norsk Meteorologisk Aarbog, have been used.

The work of extracting the data from the Logs and constructing the Charts has been carried out by Mr. Charles Harding, to whom I am indebted for many valuable suggestions.

A Chart* is drawn for 8 a.m. *Greenwich time* of each day, and when land observations are not available for this hour, those nearest to it are entered, and the Greenwich time is given. For instance, those of Madeira are for about 10 a.m. Greenwich time, whilst those of Terceira in the Azores are at nearly 11 a.m. Greenwich time. At Belleisle and St. John's, Newfoundland, we have only observations for the afternoon by Greenwich time, which reduces their value. In many ports the direction and force of the wind are so much affected by local influences that they are of little value. This is certainly the case with Madeira, where it is almost always nearly calm, and the reports from Harrison Point in Cumberland Sound (where the "Perseverance" whaler was wintering), and Newfoundland are from sheltered places.

The time of each quotation has been reduced to that of Greenwich, unless the contrary is specially stated; this makes it easy to compare the simultaneous observations

---

* Mercator's projection has been used in spite of its disadvantage in distorting the surface of the earth, and consequently the shape of the isobars; for, its meridians being parallel, it is the only method which affords so simple a means for comparing the direction of different winds on its various parts.

of different ships; and to avoid confusion, all extracts from logs given in the remarks on a given Chart lie between 8 a.m. Greenwich time of the given day and that following it, so that it will be understood that whatever is extracted took place between what appears on the Chart of the given day and that of the next. This rule is broken in the extracts accompanying the Chart for January 29th. As this is the first day it has been thought right sometimes to quote the weather, &c. of the 28th. Again, as the Chart of February 8th is the last, it has been thought right sometimes to extract data after 8 a.m. Greenwich time of the 9th, in which case a line is drawn to show that the 24 hours are passed, and then running extracts extending over several days are frequently taken, with the object of discovering when the various ships met the East wind which was pressing itself to the westward over the Atlantic.

The time at Greenwich for each extract has been found by applying the longitude in time of the *previous* noon to the given local time. This method has been followed because it is the custom on board most ships only to alter the clocks (showing local time) for the effect of change of longitude at noon of each day.

The data given on the Charts are the true direction and force of the wind, the latter by Beaufort's scale.* The direction is shown by an arrow supposed to fly with the wind, having its point in the position of the station or ship†; the force by the number of feathers on the arrow, 1 being a light air, 12 a hurricane; a calm is represented by a small circle thus ☉. The figures at the feathered end of each arrow are the ship's number according to the list given on page 4, so that her name may be found if required.

In a convenient place near the wind arrow are given,—
1st. The barometer reading corrected as near as possible.
2nd. The temperature of the air.
3rd. The temperature of the sea enclosed in a circle for distinction.
4th. Beaufort's letters for the state of the weather.*
5th. The state of the sea.

When any one of these data is not available a line is drawn in its place; for instance, if none were given there would be five lines thus ≡.

In cases where several ships are very near each other, it has sometimes been requisite to precede the data of one or more by the number of the ship, thus (51).

The most trustworthy barometer readings have been used for drawing isobaric lines for each tenth of an inch, and although they do not always take that curved shape which it is probable they really have, it has been thought best not to modify them; in their present state their irregularities show the great need for more observations, standard instruments, and careful observers; they are as correct as it is possible to make them from the data, and their general direction is sufficient to show the relation between the height of the barometer and the direction and force of wind.

---

* Beaufort's scale for expressing wind-force and weather is given on each chart.
† A variable wind is shown by a curved arrow.

The practice of drawing them at equal distances between the given observations supposes that the barometrical difference is equally distributed over the intervening space. The difference in the force of the wind experienced by each ship shows that most probably this is not the case, but no allowance has been made, so that there is little doubt but that in some cases the lines ought to be closer in one part and further separated in another part of an intervening space.

At Terceira the 11 a.m. Greenwich time observations have been combined with those of 8 a.m. from ships, for drawing the isobars. Nothing nearer could be obtained, and the oscillations of the barometer are much less at Terceira than they are further north; for instance it was never below 30·00 or up to 30·40 during the eleven days with which we are dealing, so that the change of three hours is not likely to cause an important error.

On certain parts of the charts, "probable higher pressure," or "probable lower pressure" have been written, where the direction of the wind and trend of the isobars indicate that observations in those parts would have proved this to be the case. Reference has also been made on the charts to the plates of the Quarterly Weather Report, published by this office, when they prove certain facts.

Isotherms of the surface temperature of the sea have been drawn. No doubt more observations would modify them, but they are sufficient to show what sudden changes are experienced between 35° W. and New York, also the north-easterly course of the isotherm of 50°.

It frequently happens that between 8 a.m. of one day and 8 a.m. of another, a ship has had very important changes in the wind, weather, barometer, &c. which changes may have passed to another ship, but may not be shown on the Chart of either day; for this reason copious extracts have been made from the logs. These extracts, as we have already stated, generally begin with the 8 a.m. (Greenwich time) data from which the Chart is constructed, and give any important change which has taken place before 8 a.m. (Greenwich time) of the following day, so that it may be possible for the reader to trace out any change in which he may be interested, even though no remark may have been made on it.

In the margin of each extract are given,—

    1st. The number by which the ship is distinguished on our list, and which is given at the feathered end of the wind arrow on the Chart.
    2nd. The ship's name.
    3rd. Her position at 8 a.m. Greenwich time of the given day.
    4th. The true direction in which she is steering (to the nearest point).
    5th. Her position at 8 a.m. Greenwich time of the following day.

A few remarks are sometimes given after an extract to call attention to any important fact.

The extracts for each Chart are commonly preceded and followed by remarks, and at the end some conclusions have been drawn from the whole series of Charts.

It will be noticed that the extracts begin with the most *eastern* ship, irrespective of her latitude, and work to the *westward*. The reader has only to notice the longitude at 8 a.m. of the given day in the margin of the extract, then by running his eye along that meridian until he comes to her latitude he will soon find the ship's position on the Chart.

Three Charts have been drawn for intervening hours, at times when something remarkable seemed to require them, viz., at 6 p.m. of the 30th January and 3 p.m. and 8 p.m. of February 5th.

Diagrams 1–5, of which the last two are copied from Plate A. published in the Quarterly Weather Report, give the continuous range of all the meteorological data for certain ships' tracks across the Atlantic. They are given to illustrate the general change, and to show important gales. No. 1 illustrates the gale of the 30th January, whilst Nos. 2 and 3 show how two ships bound contrary ways experienced the same gale, the one meeting and the other being overtaken by it. Nos. 4 and 5 give the remarkable case of a falling barometer experienced by a ship bound west with a northerly wind blowing. An explanation of the diagrams is given with the first.

It may be well to explain that the term "gradient," which is frequently used in this paper, relates to the amount of barometer difference (or difference of atmospheric pressure) in a given distance, and is fully explained in the Barometer Manual published by this Office.

The extracts from logs and remarks on each Chart have been made with the idea that the reader will go carefully through them, so that the general remarks at the end do not go into particulars which have been already given.

HENRY TOYNBEE,
Marine Superintendent.

EXTRACTS FROM LOGS, AND REMARKS.

Extracts and Remarks to accompany the Chart for January 29th, 1870.

WITH this Chart allusion will sometimes be made to the wind and weather experienced on the 28th.

It will be seen that a southerly gale is blowing in the south of Ireland and in the Hebrides.

A gale blowing throughout the day veering to S.S.W. at 3 p.m., and to W.S.W. at 7 p.m.

At midnight wind unsteady S.W. by W. 8. 2 a.m., 30th, it backed to S.E. by S. 9. 4 a.m. wind was again S.W. by W. 7, with heavy squalls and rain and a high confused sea. The barometer seemed to be unsteady, varying its action with the changes in the direction of the wind.

No. 4.
S.S. "Prussian."
In { 55° 14′ N.
     10° 39′ W.
     8 a.m. G.T. 29th.
Bound Westerly.
To { 54° 8′ N.
     16° 32′ W.
     8 a.m. G.T. 30th.

Comes the next in longitude, though much further south. She is experiencing an ordinary west-north-west gale with much sea.

This northerly tendency in the westerly wind, whilst it is southerly further north, is interesting as being common in this latitude.

Her barometer rose as she went south.

No. 29.
"Chatillon."
In { 40° 17′ N. 16° 7′ W.
     8 a.m. G.T. 29th.
Bound South.
To { 37° 33′ N.
     16° 48′ W.
     8 a.m. G.T. 30th.

At 9 p.m. the wind had veered to S. by W., and increased to a fresh gale with a rising sea.

11 p.m. A strong gale from W. by S.

Like No. 4 she experienced an ordinary southerly gale veering to west.

No. 17.
S.S. "Helvetia."
In { 51° 24′ N.
     17° 5′ W.
     8 a.m. G.T. 29th.
Bound Wly.
To { 50° 48′ N.
     21° 44′ W.
     8 a.m. G.T. 30th.

No. 10.
S.S. "Manhattan."
In { 50° 56′ N.
     18° 46′ W.
     8 a.m. G.T. 29th.
Bound Westerly.
To { 50° 14′ N.
     23° 51′ W.
     8 a.m. G.T. 30th.

8 a.m. Variable westerly 4.
2 p.m. South-south-easterly 5, and increasing. Heavy south-westerly swell.
9 p.m. West-south-westerly 6, heavy squalls.
3 a.m. 30th. Westerly 7, heavy hail squalls.
No barometer or thermometer readings given.

No. 51.
S.S. "Samaria."
In { 51° 16′ N.
     19° 8′ W.
     8 a.m. G.T. 29th.
Bound East.
To { 51° 43′ N.
     12° 27′ W.
     8 a.m. G.T. 30th.

No. 51 had standard instruments from this office.
Wind backing from S.W. 6 to S.E. 8. During the time it was doing this the barometer slightly rose for eight hours, then fell for eight hours, and eventually rose for eight hours. During the last four it rose more than ·2 in. This seems to have been due to her easterly course.
Nos. 4 and 17 bound west had the falling barometer and shift to West, which are common to land stations or ships bound west.
No. 51 seems to have steamed into the south-east wind and left the south-west wind astern of her, as if these winds were blowing round an area of low pressure which was nearly stationary.

No. 55.
S. S. "Rhein."
In { 49° 45′ N.
     28° 58′ W.
     8 a.m. G.T. 29th.
Bound West.
To { 48° 44′ N.
     34° 12′ W.
     8 a.m. G.T. 30th.

After 6 p.m. blowing with the force of a gale in the squalls from west. Lowest barometer at 2 p.m. (29·25), rising steadily afterwards.
2 a.m. of the 30th. The wind drew W.N.W. force 5 to 8, afterwards freshening into steady 8.
The permanence of this westerly wind, changing but little as the ship goes to the west, looks as if the wind were blowing round the southern end of a large, fixed area of low pressure to the north of her.
The remark on No. 51 alludes to the same thing.

No. 11.
S.S. "Iowa."
In { 52° 21′ N.
     32° 38′ W.
     8 am. G.T. 29th.
Bound South-westerly.
To { 50° 49′ N.
     35° 10′ W.
     8 a.m. G.T. 30th.

At 6 a.m. of the *28th*, No. 11 was in about 53° 30′ N. 30° 18′ W. with a strong gale from west and heavy sea which moderated, and by 10 p.m. of *28th* the wind and weather were unsettled.
At 8 a.m. of 29th the wind was west 4, as given on the Chart. This freshened into a strong gale from N.W. with passing showers of hail and a heavy sea by 3 a.m. of the 30th.
This ship seems to have been on the south-western side of the area of low pressure, with which the winds experienced by all the previous ships alluded to seem to have been in relation.

No. 5.
S.S. "North American."
In { 50° 55′ N.
     36° 7′ W.
     8 a.m. G.T. 29th.
Bound E.N.Ely.
To { 52° 56′ N.
     29° 49′ W.
     8 a.m. G.T. 30th.

At 7 a.m. of the *28th*, No. 5 was in about 47° 26′ N. 43° 49′ W. with an unsteady fresh, and at times very squally west-north-westerly wind which had been stronger. She and No. 11 passed each other at about 5.20 p.m. of the 29th. No. 5 had not had such strong winds as No. 11, but both had them westerly, showing the great extent of this wind, which seemed to be blowing round the more permanent low pressure in the centre of the Atlantic. The difference of force may be partially accounted for by their different routes.

No. 5 experienced a steadily *falling* barometer from 7 a.m. of the 28th until 8 a.m. of the 30th, it having changed from 29·95 to 29·27, the wind being *north-westerly* the whole time. This fall, with a north-westerly wind, seems to have been caused by her easterly course, indicating that she was going to the eastward faster than the area of low pressure, or that she was travelling down the western slope of an area of low pressure, which was nearly stationary.

Wind backed from N.E. 4 at 7 a.m. to N.N.W. 5 at 11 a.m., and increased to N.W. 8 by 10.30 p.m. Her wind continued N.W. 9 for the remaining part of the 24 hours.

Nos. 54 and 55 were in about the same longitude at 4.30 a.m. of the 30th. No. 54 bound east, and a degree to the southward reports the wind W.N.W. 10. No. 55 bound west and a degree northward gives the wind W.N.W. 7. Now, as the ship bound east would feel the wind least, it looks as if the wind really was much stronger to the southward than to the northward.

No. 54.
S.S. "Bremen."
In { 46° 25′ N.
     39° 30′ W.
     8 a.m. G.T. 29th.
Bound E. by Nly.
To { 47° 29′ N.
     32° 15′ W.
     8 a.m. G.T. 30th.

Her 8 a.m. westerly wind freshened into a gale by 11 a.m, and she kept a brisk north-westerly gale for nearly two days, with the barometer oscillating a little and eventually rising.

She seems to have met No. 55, and both experienced the same north-westerly gale, but the barometer on board No. 55 was steadily rising until the wind backed to S.W. Here the different action of the barometer in ships bound in opposite directions is striking.

No. 14.
S.S. "Europa."
In { 48° 47′ N.
     40° 0′ W.
     8 a.m. G.T. 29th.
Bound E.N.Ely.
To { 50° 48′ N.
     33° 31′ W.
     8 a.m. G.T. 30th.

Wind increased to a fresh westerly gale by 3 p.m. with heavy snow squalls and high sea. At 4 p.m. the snow squalls were violent. The barometer rising; it rose ·2 in. between 3 and 7 p.m., when the snow squalls were most violent. At 4 a.m. of 30th had strong wind from W. by N. with heavy sea.

No. 46.
S.S. "Nemesis."
In { 48° 50′ N.
     41° 42′ W.
     8 a.m. G.T. 29th.
Bound W.S.Wly.
To { 47° 19′ N.
     45° 38′ W.
     8 a.m. G.T. 30th.

Wind changed from N.N.E. 2 at 3 a.m. to S. 2, with lightning in the W. and S.W., accompanied by a high but falling barometer, which continued to fall with the wind changing to S.W. and W. and freshening. At 7 a.m. of the 30th it was W. 6 with rain squalls.

No. 45.
"Carl Georg."
In { 38° 7′ N.
     44° 53′ W.
     8 a.m. G.T. 29th.
Bound E. by N.
To { 38° 56′ N.
     41° 26′ W.
     8 a.m. G.T. 30th.

No. 37.
S.S. "Austrian."
In { 45° 26' N.
     48° 48' W.
     8 a.m. G.T. 29th.
Bound W. by Sly.
To { 44° 19' N.
     54° 17' W.
     8 a.m. G.T. 30th.

No. 37 had standard instruments from this Office.
At 5 a.m. wind variable from N. to W.N.W., settling into N.W. 6 until 2 a.m. of the 30th, when it backed to S.E. and the barometer fell rapidly.
At 7.30 a.m., 30th, the wind was E. by S. 4, and increasing.
No. 37 had the surface temp. 32° when No. 22, about 20 miles north of her, had it 46°. In eight hours No. 22 had it 34°.
Diagram 1 contains a continuous record of this ship's observations during her passage from England to America. (See the explanation preceding the diagram.)

No. 22.
S.S. "Pennsylvania."
In { 45° 48' N.
     48° 54' W.
     8 a.m. G.T. 29th.
Bound W.S.Wly.
To { 44° 49' N.
     52° 36 W.
     8 a.m G.T. 30th.

A strong gale from W.N.W and N.W., moderating about 5 p.m., but continuing a fresh gale for the remainder of the day. Her barometer seems to have been much too low, it was only read to tenths. The temperature of the sea fell 12° in eight hours.
Notice how No. 22 makes no mention of the south-easterly wind experienced by No. 37 at 2 a.m. of the 30th, though they were both bound to the westward.

No. 16.
S.S. "City of London."
In { 43° 50' N.
     55° 4' W.
     8 a.m. G.T. 29th.
Bound W.S.Wly.
To { 42° 26' N.
     61° 20' W.
     8 a.m. G.T. 30th.

Light north and north-westerly winds with a rising and afterwards steady barometer until 9 p.m., when the wind shifted to S.S.E. and freshened with a falling barometer, which amounted to a strong gale by 4 a.m. of the 30th.
No. 37, about 2° N. and 7° E. of No. 16, did not get this shift to S.E. until 2 a.m. of the 30th, or five hours later. Both were bound westerly. This indicates the north-easterly route of the area of low pressure accompanying the gale.

No. 30.
H.M.S.S. "Orontes."
In { 43° 15' N.
     55° 19' W.
     8 a.m. G.T. 29th.
Bound Easterly.
To { 43° 35' N.
     49° 53' W.
     8 a.m. G.T. 30th.

Light north-north-easterly and north-easterly winds until about 2 a.m. of the 30th, when the wind commenced to veer to S.E. and the barometer to fall.
7 a.m. 30th, wind E. by S. 2.
No. 37 bound west would be in about the same longitude as No. 30 bound east at 2 a.m., and they got the change at the same time, but up to this change the former had north-westerly whilst the latter had north-easterly winds.

No. 25.
S.S. "Cuban."
In { 34° 52' N.
     55° 25' W.
     8 a.m. G.T. 29th.
Bound N.Ely.
To { 36° 49' N.
     51° 56' W.
     8 a.m. G.T. 30th.

No. 25 was far south. She had a freshening wind from S.W. by W., which amounted to a moderate gale by 4 a.m. of the 30th. Her barometer seems to have been steady, but it was only read to tenths.
The area of low pressure experienced by Nos. 30 and 37, &c., seems to have passed to the N.W. of No. 25, moving in a north-easterly direction.

A brisk breeze from N.N.W., as shown on the Chart, which lasted until 8 p.m., when the wind veered to N.N.E. fresh, and gradually fell light, with a rising barometer, up to 11.30 p.m.

At 3.30 a.m. of 30th the wind was light E.N.E., with falling barometer.

At 7.30 a.m. the wind was east, a gentle breeze.

No. 48 bound fast to the eastward was not caught by the gale until p.m. of the 30th. By referring to the margins or to the Chart for the 30th it will be seen that at 8 a.m. of the 30th No. 48 was 5° *east* of No. 37, which accounts for No. 37's getting the south-easterly wind first, though on the Chart of the 29th she (No. 37) appears as the most easterly ship.

No. 48.
S.S. "Calabria."
In { 42° 51' N.
    { 56° 18' W.
    { 8 a.m. G.T. 29th.
Bound E.N.Ely.
To { 44° 21' N.
   { 49° 10' W.
   { 8 a.m. G.T. 30th.

No. 26 was far south. She had a steady southerly wind and fine weather, barometer falling slightly.

Nos. 25 and 26 seem to have had the wind which prevails round the west and north-west sides of the area of high pressure, which is common at the northern verge of the north-east trades, between which and the American coast, over the hot water of the Gulf Stream, the waves of low pressure seem to drift to the north-eastward. Before closing this paper we propose saying a few words on the cause of the waves or areas of low pressure and revolving winds which are experienced here in the winter months.

No. 26.
S.S. "Venezuelan."
In { 30° 42' N.
   { 60° 32' W.
   { 8 a.m. G.T. 29th.
Bound E.N.E.
To { 32° 46' N.
   { 56° 31' W.
   { 8 a.m. G.T. 30th.

A moderate north-easterly wind, rising barometer, and fine clear weather, until 4 p.m., in latitude 42° 9' N. 60° 2' W., when the wind drew E.N.E.

At 2 a.m., 30th, it was increasing from E.S.E., with a fast falling barometer.

At 8 a.m., 29th, the temperature of the sea was 54°, at 4 p.m. 61°, and at 4 a.m. of 30th it was 44°.

No. 20 seems to have got the changes to E.N.E. and E.S.E. from 10 to 12 hours earlier than No. 48, and she was 5° further west.

No. 20.
S.S. "The Queen."
In { 41° 56' N.
   { 61° 32' W.
   { 8 a.m. G.T. 29th.
Bound E.N.Ely.
To { 43° 6' N.
   { 57° 23' W.
   { 8 a.m. G.T. 30th.

Moderate to light northerly winds, drawing to east with clear weather.

At 4 p.m. in 42° 37' N. 63° 45' W. the wind was E. by S. freshening, and the barometer falling briskly.

At 5·30 a.m. of the 30th the wind was S.E. by E., a fresh gale, and gloomy with heavy rain.

At 7.30 a.m., 30th, the wind shifted to N.W. by W., hard gale, with heavy rain.

No. 47.
S.S. "Tripoli."
In { 43° 3' N.
   { 61° 37' W.
   { 8 a.m. G.T. 29th.
Bound Wly.
To { 42° 28' N.
   { 67° 20' W.
   { 8 a.m. G.T. 30th.

No. 47 seems to have got the change to S.E. several hours before No. 20, she was going west, whilst No. 20 was going E.N.E.

No. 47 had the temperature of the sea 38°, whilst No. 20, a degree farther south, had it 54°.

No. 12.
S.S. "Dacian."
In { 40° 26′ N.
63° 52′ W.
8 a.m. G.T. 29th,
Bound Ely.
To { 40° 22′ N.
61° 10′ W.
8 a.m. G.T. 30th.

A fresh north-east wind from 8 a.m. of *28th* to 6 a.m. of 29th.
At 8 a.m. wind drew east and freshened.
At 4 p.m. in 40° 23′ N., 62° 35′ W. the wind was E.S.E. 7.
At 3 a.m., 30th, wind S.E., force 10.
At 5 a.m., wind variable, force 10, with heavy squalls and lightning.
No barometer observations were given.

No. 12 was passing to the southward of No. 47 where she seems to have had the north-easterly wind stronger, though its effect may have been estimated differently by the two ships which were going in opposite directions.

These ships had the shift to the south of east at much the same time in nearly the same longitude.

No. 52.
S.S. "Delta."
In { 42° 5′ N.
64° 10′ W.
8 a.m G.T. 29th,
Bound South.
To { 39° 16′ N.
64° 30′ W.
8 a.m. G.T. 30th.

No. 52 left Halifax at about 3.39 p.m. of the *28th*, within half an hour of the time that the "City of Boston" left the same port. It will be remembered that we are using Greenwich time, which makes these ships to have left Halifax a little before noon, and about noon local time respectively.

This we learn by comparing the log of No. 52 with a letter in the "Times" dated March 10th, 1870, saying that the "City of Boston" sailed at noon, local time, of Friday the 28th, but Capt. Hunter, a careful observer for this office, says in his letter forwarding Mr. Allison's observations:

"I was in Halifax and saw the 'City of Boston' sail on the 28th January 1870; it was a very fine day for that season of the year. A.M. of the 29th it began to breeze up from the southward and eastward; P.M. it blew a very heavy gale from the same quarter, the barometer falling very rapidly. A.M. of the 30th the barometer in my house had fallen to 28·35, which is much lower than I ever knew in this locality. The barometer is a marine one, 200 feet above the sea level, and I think will range ·2 lower than a standard one.

"The 'Delta' sailed from here about two hours before the 'City of Boston' sailed for England, and that ship's journal may give you some information about the weather."

Now the Delta's log states, "Sailed from Halifax at 11.25 a.m." (3.39 p.m. G.T.) Hence, according to Capt. Hunter, the "City of

Boston" sailed about 1.25 p.m. (5.39 p.m. G.T.), which is probably more correct than the letter in the "Times."

The "Delta," from the time of leaving port, had a moderate north-westerly wind veering to north, with a smooth sea. The barometer, a standard instrument from this office, rose until the wind veered east of north at noon of the 29th, when it fell, and the wind veered more easterly with a turbulent sea. This change in the state of the sea came on with a rise of 11°, and eventually of 21° in its temperature.

At 8 p.m. in about 40° 24' N. 64° 30' W. the wind was freshening from E. by S., force 7, the barometer having fallen ·2 in. in four hours, and the sky overcast.

At midnight the barometer was about 29·65, having fallen ·4 in four hours, and there was rain.

At 4.18 a.m. of the 30th in 39° 38' N. and 64° 30' W. the wind was S.E. by E. 8, and between this and 8 a.m. shifted to west 11 in a heavy squall, the barometer having continued to fall a tenth per hour until this shift, when there was a heavy cross sea and lightning in the S.W.

A moderate easterly wind and clear weather until 4.20 p.m. in 41° 17' N. 65° 5' W., when the wind freshened and drew to the south of east with a falling barometer.

At 4.20 a.m. a strong E.S.E. breeze, and squally with rain.

7.20 a.m. Wind E.S.E., no change having been recorded since 4 p.m. of the previous day. The following remark is given in this log. "Indicating a gale with a heavy southerly sea rising."

No. 49.
S.S. "Marathon."
In { 40° 57' N.
66° 38' W.
8 a.m. G.T. 29th.
Bound E. by Nly.
To { 41° 59' N.
62° 10' W.
8 a.m. G.T. 30th.

At 1 p.m. the wind changed from N.E. 3 to E.S.E. 2 with a falling barometer, it then veered to south, keeping moderate, but at 9 p.m. in 31° 40' N. 73° 48' W., it suddenly shifted to west, force 8, when the barometer commenced rising.

No. 38 was very far south, and seems to have been caught up by an area of low pressure, travelling to the north-eastward. The wind freshening into a gale from west after the lowest pressure had passed, looks as if the steepest gradient was on the south side of this area of low pressure, as in the case of the "Delta" (No. 52.)

By looking further on in this log, other indications of the same kind are visible.

It seems probable that this was the same area of low pressure which afterwards swept over the ships to the north-eastward of No.38. If so, it seems to have increased in intensity before arriving at No. 52.

By the kindness of Professor Draper we have been supplied with copies from the curves of self-registering instruments at the New York

No. 38.
"Nicoline."
In { 30° 40' N.
73° 24' W.
8 a.m. G.T. 29th.
Bound Nly.
To { 32° 48' N.
73° 40' W.
8 a.m. G.T. 30th

New York Observatory, 8 a.m. 29th, to 8 a.m. 30th.

Observatory, I therefore propose to quote them for each day after recording the ships' observations.

Wind N.N.E. ¼ E., 5 *miles per hour**, barometer 30·23, air 33°. The barometer had fallen ·13 since 5 a.m., when the wind was N.W., the change to N.N.E. ¼ E. having taken place at 7 a.m. The barometer continued falling until 1 a.m. 30th, when it was 29·69; it then rose gradually.

The wind veered gradually to S.E. by E. at 3 p.m., from which time it gradually backed through N. to W.N.W. by 1 a.m. 30th, the time of lowest pressure. It continued from this direction (though oscillating considerably) until 8 a.m. 30th.

Hence we may conclude that the area of low pressure which was S.W. of Halifax at 8 a.m. of 30th was nearest to New York about 1 a.m. of that day.

GENERAL REMARKS ON CHART FOR 29TH JANUARY.

The logs of 26 ships have been consulted.

There is a southerly wind over the British Islands, amounting to a gale in Ireland and the Hebrides.

The wind is south-east in Norway, a south gale is blowing in Iceland, and a light north-west wind in Cumberland Sound.

---

* The following approximate proportion of miles per hour for each figure of Beaufort's scale has been provisionally adopted in this office, but more data are required.

Beaufort's Scale.			Velocity in miles per hour.
0	-	-	0 to 2
0·5	-	-	3 ,, 5
1	-	-	6 ,, 10
2	-	-	11 ,, 15
3	-	-	16 ,, 20
4	-	-	21 ,, 25
5	-	-	26 ,, 30
6	-	-	31 ,, 36
7	-	-	37 ,, 44
8	-	-	45 ,, 52
9	-	-	53 ,, 60
10	-	-	61 ,, 69
11	-	-	70 ,, 80
12	-	-	above 80

⚡ (Obtained from 620 comparisons of estimation and anemometrical results at Holyhead in 1869–70.)

The arrow representing the wind at New York will be known from those of ships by its not being numbered.

It is N.W. fresh at Heart's Content, and the p.m. observations at Belle Isle are westerly. From Halifax we have the following remark :—Midnight, 29th (4.15 a.m. 30th, Greenwich time) "Wind was very high "from S.S.E., with rising temperature and barometer rapidly falling."

The wind is light N.W. at Terceira, and a light westerly air prevails at Madeira, whilst a north-east gale is reported at Lisbon.

The north-east gale at Lisbon does not seem to have a barometric gradient to account for it. It must, however, be remembered that if every partial strong wind has a corresponding steep gradient, that gradient is likely also to be partial, and requires delicate observations in the same locality to detect it; otherwise by merely comparing the observations at distant stations a gradient, which is steep in some parts, is spread out over a great distance, and seems to contradict the fact that strong winds have steep gradients.

The isobars run curiously off the coast of Portugal; more observations would have been very useful, still they indicate that the air branches off to the right and left as it closes with the land.

Unfortunately there are no correct observations from Bermuda available for these Charts.*

This day there seems to have been a large area of low pressure in the central part of the Atlantic, round which the neighbouring winds circulated. The gradient seems to have been steepest on the south-western side of this area of low pressure, and to have been steeper at some distance from the lowest pressure than it was nearer to it.

There are also indications of travelling areas of low pressure, especially one experienced by No. 52 to the southward of Halifax, which was accompanied by a heavy gale as it passed over her on its north-eastern route, and on the following day over several ships which were to the eastward.

Diagram 1 shows how No. 37 approached this gale on the 29th, with a fast rising barometer, north-west wind, and fine weather; also that she passed through another area of low pressure before she got to Portland, Maine.

Isobaric curves have been drawn; they tend to show the general relation between the pressure and wind, but the observations are not sufficiently numerous to make them so complete as we would wish.

It is a significant fact that No. 38, near the coast of America, has a northerly wind, whilst No. 26, 15 degrees to the eastward, has it

---

* Since the Charts were lithographed we have received through the kindness of Major-Gen. Lefroy, R.A., Governor of Bermuda, some observations from that station which are embodied in the remarks.

Extracts and Remarks to accompany the Chart for January 30th, 1870.

No. 2.*
S.S. "City of Cork."
In { 52° 23′ N.
5° 54′ W.
8 a.m. G.T. 30th.
Bound S.W. by W.
To { 51° 42′ N.
8° 29′ W.
8 a.m. G.T. 31st.

No. 50.
S.S. "Hotspur."
In { 47° 13′ N.
7° 29′ W.
8 a.m. G.T. 30th
Bound South.
To { 46° 14′ N.
7° 55′ W.
8 a.m. G.T. 31st.

No. 39.
S.S. "Westphalia."
In { 49° 28′ N.
9° 14′ W.
8 a.m. G.T. 30th
Bound West.
To { 49° 15′ N.
14° 58′ W.
8 a.m. G.T. 31st.

No. 51.
S.S. "Samaria."
In { 51° 43′ N.
12° 27′ W.
8 a.m. G.T. 30th
Bound East.
To { Cork.
2 a.m. G.T. 31st.

No. 4.
S.S. "Prussian."
In { 54° 8′ N.
16° 32′ W.
8 a.m. G.T. 30th.
Bound West.
To { 53° 17′ N.
22° 24′ W.
8 a.m. G.T. 31st.

southerly. Although there are but few ships in this neighbourhood, the proximity of northerly and southerly winds there is shown on 11 of the 14 charts.

A cursory examination of the Chart is sufficient to show that a strong southerly gale is blowing over part of the British Isles.

Had a fresh southerly gale and high sea, barometer steadily falling; lowest reading 29·20 at midnight, where it hung for some hours, the ship being at anchor at Queenstown, and the wind having decreased.

7.30 a.m., 31st. A fresh south-west wind and rising barometer, with the wind drawing more westerly.

8 a.m., S.S.E., 6, with heavy rain and a falling barometer. A high southerly sea.

8.30 p.m. S.S.E., 7, heavy rain and squally.

	Air.	Bar.	Sea.
8 a.m. S., 9. Sky looking threatening	51°	29·55	51°
8.40 p.m. W. by S., 8—9	50	29·17	50
4.40 a.m., 31st. W., 9	46	29·32	50

Diagram 4 gives a continuous record of this ship's observations, copied from Captain Trautmann's log, and shows a section of the depression through which she passed on the 30th inst.

Had a gale from S.E. by S., with an increasing southerly swell. Barometer rose ·22 in. in four hours. This seems to have been the effect of her easterly course, for No. 2, going to the S.W., had a falling barometer for the same time.

The wind continued steady, S.W. by W., 6, with a high confused sea and steady barometer until

3 p.m. Wind variable from S.W. by W., to W. by N., 5 to 7.
8 p.m. it was N.N.E., 6.
11 p.m. N.N.W., 6.

---

* The figure 2 has been omitted at the feathered end of the arrow on this day's 8 a.m. Chart. The steamer was on the S.E. coast of Ireland.

2 a.m. 31st, W.N.W., 6, where it remained steady with a rising barometer.

No. 4 had a curiously changeable wind, backing from N.N.E. to W.N.W., as if she had steered into the north-western side of an area of low pressure travelling to the northward.

It will be noticed that at all stations to the eastward of No. 4, from latitude 47° to 63° N., the wind is south-easterly or southerly, whilst to the westward of her it is westerly or north-westerly, and eventually she had it N.N.W. Then, again, Iceland has an east gale, hence it seems probable that an area of low pressure extended in a north-westerly direction from No. 4, getting lower to the N.W., and seen to be higher to the S.E. of her. The easterly gale in Iceland seems to be blowing round the northern end of this area of low pressure.

The barometer of No. 4 is doubtful; no attached thermometer was given, and an estimated error of $+ \cdot 25$ in. has been used.

The barometers at Madeira, Lisbon, and Tarifa, indicate that the isobar of $30 \cdot 2$ trends to the southward along the coast, and the wind follows it.

Had a strong westerly wind with heavy hail squalls, the wind gradually going to N.W.

5.30 p.m. Fresh gale with hard squalls and high sea. The barometer rising.

5.30 a.m. 31st. N.W. by W., 6, with hail squalls.

No. 17.
S.S. " Helvetia."
In $\begin{cases} 50° 48' \text{ N.} \\ 21° 44' \text{ W.} \\ 8 \text{ a.m. G.T. 30th.} \end{cases}$
Bound West.
To $\begin{cases} 50° 14' \text{ N.} \\ 25° 38' \text{ W.} \\ 8 \text{ a.m. G.T. 31st.} \end{cases}$

Had a strong increasing wind from W.N.W., amounting to a gale at 9.30 a.m. with frequent squalls of hail. No. 17, two degrees further east, did not get a gale until 5.30 p.m.

7.30 a.m. 31st. Gale moderating and wind backing to the south-westward.

No barometer observations were recorded. The backing of the wind to the south-westward at 7.30 a.m., 31st, indicates that she was then entering the area of low pressure, which at 8 a.m. of the 30th was south of Newfoundland. This gives it a rate of progression of more than 30 miles an hour to the eastward.

No. 10.
S.S. " Manhattan."
In $\begin{cases} 50° 14' \text{ N.} \\ 23° 51' \text{ W.} \\ 8 \text{ a.m. G.T. 30th.} \end{cases}$
Bound Westerly.
To $\begin{cases} 49° 30' \text{ N.} \\ 28° 10' \text{ W.} \\ 8 \text{ a.m. G.T. 31st.} \end{cases}$

This ship does not log more than a fresh breeze, chiefly W. by N.; but it must be remembered she was going east, with the wind.

At 8 a.m. 31st, No. 5 passed about a degree north of No. 4, and they had similar weather.

No. 5.
S.S. " North American.
In $\begin{cases} 52° 56' \text{ N.} \\ 29° 49' \text{ W.} \\ 8 \text{ a.m. G.T. 30th.} \end{cases}$
Bound Easterly.
To $\begin{cases} 54° 12' \text{ N.} \\ 22° 30' \text{ W.} \\ 8 \text{ a.m. G.T. 31st.} \end{cases}$

No. 54.
S.S. "Bremen."
In { 47° 29' N.
32° 15' W.
8 a.m. G.T. 30th.
Bound Easterly.
To { 48° 17' N.
24° 47' W.
8 a.m. G.T. 31st.

8 a.m. Wind N.W., 9, squalls had been very violent, barometer very gradually rising. After 10 p.m. the gale commenced to decrease, being N.W., 7, but the direction was still north-westerly until 8 a.m. 31st.

Nos. 17 and 10, bound to the westward, seem to have steamed into this gale, whilst No. 5, bound to the eastward and several degrees further north, escaped it.

No. 14.
S.S. "Europa."
In { 50° 48' N.
33° 31' W.
8 a.m. G.T. 30th.
Bound E. by Nly.
To { 52° 23' N.
26° 32' W.
8 a.m. G.T. 31st.

Had a brisk west-north-westerly gale with heavy squalls, which moderated by 10 p.m., but continued west-north-westerly until 8 a.m. 31st. The barometer only read to tenths; it seemed to be rising.

No. 55.
S.S. "Rhein."
In { 48° 44' N.
34° 12' W.
8 a.m. G.T. 30th.
Bound W. by S.
To { 47° 37' N.
39° 9' W.
8 a.m. G.T. 31st.

Had a west-north-west gale with a steadily rising barometer until 10 p.m., when the wind lulled and backed to west, and eventually at about 1 a.m. of the 31st to S.W. with a falling barometer, when it blew a hard gale, veering again to the westward between 2.30 and 6.30 a.m. of the 31st, with a rising barometer.

No. 11.
S.S. "Iowa."
In { 50° 49' N.
35° 10' W.
8 a.m. G.T. 30th.
Bound W.S.Wly.
To { 49° 46' N.
37° 10' W.
8 a.m. G.T. 31st.

8 a.m. Strong north-westerly gale.
At 2 p.m. moderating and clearing up.
At 11 p.m. the wind backed to the south-westward, previous to the setting in of a fresh gale.
4.30 a.m. 31st. Wind southerly, increasing rapidly, and sea rising.
No barometer readings are given.

No. 11 seems to have got the moderating of the gale some hours before No. 14, a ship further east and steering east. Her weather resembled that of No. 55, a ship two degrees to the south of her.

It will be remembered that No. 10, a ship 12° to the eastward of No. 11, did not get the backing of the wind to S.W. until 7.30 a.m. of the 31st, whilst No. 11 got it at 11 p.m. of the 30th. The exact hour of these changes is not always given, but there is enough to show the easterly course and great speed of some of these changes.

No. 45.
"Carl Georg."
In { 38° 56' N.
41° 26' N.
8 a.m. G.T. 30th.
Bound E.N.Ely.
To { 39° 55' N.
38° 35' W.
8 a.m. G.T. 31st.

8 a.m. Wind W., 6, drawing to W.N.W., 6, by 1 p.m., with a rising barometer, from which time it drew more northerly and decreased.

It will be noticed that No. 45 is far south, and the area of low pressure represented on the Chart seems to have swept between her and Newfoundland without affecting her wind or weather.

8 a.m. W. by N., 6, heavy sea, rolling and pitching heavily, air 29° barometer 30·24, sea 37°.

By 11 a.m. the wind was light north-westerly, and fine clear weather, barometer fallen slightly.

From this time to 3 p.m. in 46° 52′ N. 46° 48′ W. air 31°, barometer 29·82, sea 33°; the barometer had fallen a tenth per hour, and the wind at 3 p.m. is given strong from E.S.E., but the exact hour of the shift is not given.

At 6.30 p.m. there was a heavy fall of snow, and at 11 p.m. she had a fresh gale apparently from S.E. with heavy rain.

From midnight until 7 a.m. of the 31st "variable" is given for the direction of the wind, though at 3 a.m. we have "strong gale and cloudy, "with a heavy confused sea, ship labouring heavily and shipping large "quantities of water."

At 7 a.m. of 31st "Strong W. by S. gale with violent squalls and very "heavy sea," the exact time of the shift is not given.

No. 46 seems to have steered into the north-eastern side of an area of low pressure and come out on its south-western side.

By referring to the Chart it will be seen that ships to the S.W. of her had a south-east wind at 8 a.m., whilst her north-west wind continued until 11 a.m., and probably later.

No. 46.
S.S. "Nemesis."
In { 47° 19′ N.
     45° 38′ W.
     8 a.m. G.T. 30th.
Bound W.S.Wly.
To { 45° 55′ N.
     48° 56′ W.
     8 a.m. G.T. 31st.

At 8 a.m. she had a gentle easterly breeze and clear weather; air 28°, bar. 30·43, sea 31°.

At noon it was freshening from S.E. and cloudy, barometer falling.

At 3 p.m. in 44° 49′ N. and 47° 6′ W. air 37°, bar. 30·06, sea 49°, there was a fresh gale from S.S.E., the barometer having fallen ·27 in. in four hours.

At 7.30 p.m. the gale increased from S.S.E. with rain, barometer 29·50, having fallen ·56 in four and a half hours.

At 1 a.m., 31st, wind lulled and shifted to W.S.W.

At 6.45 a.m. increasing gale from S.W. by W. with heavy squalls and a rising sea. Barometer at its lowest, viz., 29·22.

It seems quite clear that No. 48 got the shift of wind to E. and S.E. before No. 46, indicating that the change was travelling to the eastward.

No. 48.
S.S. "Calabria."
In { 44° 21′ N.
     49° 10′ W.
     8 a.m. G.T. 30th.
Bound E.N.Ely.
To { 46° 30′ N.
     42° 10′ W.
     8 a.m. G.T. 31st.

8 a.m. Wind freshening fast from E. by S. and drawing more southerly; air 29°, bar. 30·80, sea 33°.

1 p.m. Blowing a gale from S.E., air 39°, bar. 30·00, sea 38°.

3 p.m. In 43° 44′ N. 48° 38′ W., wind S.E., 9, air 45°, bar. 29·81, sea 45°.

No. 30.
H.M.S. "Orontes."
In { 43° 35′ N.
     49° 53′ W.
     8 a.m. G.T. 30th.
Bound Easterly.
To { 43° 24′ N.
     47° 29′ W.
     8 a.m. G.T. 31st.

7 p.m. Wind S. by W., 9, barometer fallen ·4 in. in four hours, being 29·44, air 56°, sea 57°.

3 a.m. 31st. Wind W., 10, air 51°, bar 29·40, sea 54°, barometer just on the rise; this force continued until 5 a.m., when it decreased to 8–9.

At 3 p.m. 30th, the "Orontes" hove-to on the starboard tack. Her lowest barometer was about 29·32 at 1 a.m. 31st.

It seems clear that No. 30, lying hove-to, got the shift to west before No. 48, steaming to the eastward.

No. 25.
S.S. "Cuban."
In { 36° 49′ N.
51° 56′ W.
8 a.m. G.T. 30th.
Bound E.N.Ely.
To { 38° 37′ N.
47° 48′ W.
8 a.m. G.T. 31st.

8 a.m. Had a moderate south-west gale.

At 4.20 p.m. Wind shifted to W. by S.; a moderate gale.

Midnight. Wind N.W. by W., blowing hard, with heavy rain.

At 7 a.m., 31st. Gale and sea moderating; barometer only read to tenths; it seemed to be steady.

No. 25 was far to the southward, and seems to have been on the south-eastern side of the area of low pressure, which had Nos. 30 and 48 on its north-eastern side.

No. 22.
S.S. "Pennsylvania."
In { 44° 49′ N.
52° 36′ W.
8 a.m. G.T. 30th.
Bound West.
To { 44° 2′ N.
55° 19′ W.
8 a.m. G.T. 31st.

8 a.m. Had a moderate west-north-west gale, which "freshened up hard" by 11.30 a.m.

At 8.30 p.m. the wind had backed to west, blowing a heavy gale, with terrific squalls and a high sea. Put the ship on the starboard tack, head S.S.W., going 2½ knots an hour.

11 p.m. Shipped a heavy sea, carrying away boats' chocks, knocking donkey-funnel down, and carrying away wheel chains.

At 2.30 a.m., 31st, gale veered to W.N.W., with heavy hail squalls, but moderating a little. From this time the barometer rose.

No. 22 gives no change of wind to the southward. This seems very improbable, considering the winds of other ships near her. (See also the Chart for *6 p.m.* of the 30th, where it seems most probable that the wind was E.S.E., instead of W.N.W.)

Between 4.40 p.m. of 30th, and 1.40 a.m. of 31st, Greenwich time, the barometer at Heart's Content (in 47° 50′ N., 53° 20′ W.) fell from 29·51 to 28·53, wind S. by W. strong. This was sent to us by telegram on the 31st January. It will be seen that the "Austrian" (No. 37) in about 43° 56′ N., and 56° 34′ W., got the lowest pressure about 5.45 p.m. of the 30th, or about eight hours earlier, and they were about 269 miles apart, giving a speed of about 34 miles an hour to the area of lowest pressure; but until the shape of the area is known, its speed can only be approximately estimated.

8 a.m. Wind E.S.E. 5; from this time the barometer fell ·62 in. in four hours.

At 11.45 a.m. the wind was E.S.E., 11.

At 3.45 p.m., in 44° 1' N., 56° 9' W., wind S.S.E., 9.

At 5.45 p.m. the wind was S.S.W., 11, in 43° 56' N., 56° 34' W., air 40°, barometer at its lowest, being 28·49, having gone down ·57in. in two hours; sea 43°.

At 7 p.m. Wind W.S.W., 11, air 40°, barometer 28·56, rising, sea 42°.

At 10.45 p.m. Wind W.N.W., 10, barometer rising ·4 in. in two hours.

7.45 a.m., 31st. W.N.W., 8—9, clearing, in 43° 40' N., 57° 53' W., air 36°, barometer 29·78, sea 46°.

```
                              No. 37.
                           S.S. "Austrian."
                          ⎧ 44° 18' N.
                       In ⎨ 54° 17' W.
                          ⎩ 8 a.m. G.T. 30th.
                            Bound West.
                          ⎧ 43° 39' N.
                       To ⎨ 58° 16' W.
                          ⎩ 8 a.m. G.T. 31st.
```

The following extract from the remarks is important.

11.45 a.m. "Blowing a heavy gale, with furious squalls and high "confused sea; ship labouring and rolling excessively, and shipping "much heavy water, with much force, over all." . . . .

"4.45 p.m. Gale increasing, with terrific squalls; tremendous sea "rising.

"5.45 p.m. Blowing a hurricane.

"7.45 p.m. Wind still veering to the westward, and blowing a per- "fect hurricane; spoondrift flying like smoke along the surface, and sea "running in liquid mountains.

"11.45 p.m. Gale inclining to moderate, wind W.N.W., 10.

"7 a.m., 31st. Weather improving, W.N.W., 8."

The fall of the barometer amounted to 1·7 in. in 10 hours.

Diagram 1 of the action of the barometer, &c., has been copied from Captain Wylie's log kept for this office; to it I have added the direction and force of wind and curves of the air and sea temperatures. It gives a continuous record of her instruments, &c., during the whole passage, and shows how she came into this gale with a fast rising barometer.

Here, then, at 8 a.m. of the 30th (see the Chart), about 40 hours after the "City of Boston" left Halifax, we have No. 37 about 400 miles to the eastward of that port, and steaming to the westward into a very severe gale, which blew with hurricane force, first from the eastward and then from the westward.

The force of the gale is confirmed by the action of the standard barometer supplied to the "Austrian," as well as by the remarks in her log. Hence it is pretty clear that there was weather bad enough to founder a well-conditioned ship, which might have been taken at a disadvantage by a sudden change of wind, or a stroke from such a sea; for as the "Austrian" was labouring and rolling excessively, nobody can say that such straining might not start an unknown weak point and cause a ship to founder. Still there is reason to suppose that a gale which one good vessel can weather may be equally well dealt with by another, and it is right to remember that the opinion of those men who have the most experience is that the "City of Boston" must have run upon heavy ice during this gale.

In considering this day's Chart it is well to remember that No. 30 left Halifax about 24 hours, and No. 52 about two hours, before the "City of Boston;" the former bound east to England, the latter south to Bermuda. Both got a tremendous gale.

By referring to Diagram 1 it will be seen that a steep ridge of high pressure was experienced on the 29th, with a north-westerly wind, continuing so long as the barometer rose; but at 3.30 a.m. of 30th the barometer had fallen slightly, and the wind drew east-south-easterly. At this time it seems as if the ship was entering the north-eastern edge of an area of low pressure. It seems not improbable that a wave of low pressure passed over her going to the north-eastward and shaped somewhat like the following woodcut:—

Here the decrease of pressure is represented by increase in shading. Now if several ships passed through such a wave of low pressure, decreasing its pressure in a north-westerly direction, then all the ships would experience similar changes of wind, whilst its force would depend upon the gradient in different parts of the wave.

It is worthy of notice that, at 7.30 a.m., when the "Austrian's" barometer commenced falling more rapidly, the sea temperature went up 8° in four hours, pointing to the disturbing influence of hot and cold water in close proximity.

The Chart shows that Halifax had an east gale at 8 a.m., and from Mr. Allison's data we know that the wind backed to N.E. with snow. Hence, according to Buys Ballot's law, the lowest pressure must have been over the sea, but it must also have been close to the land, for all the ships on that part of the sea which extends several degrees to the S.E. of Halifax had the change of wind from S.E. to S.W., W., and N.W., so that we may fairly suppose that the above woodcut represents what took place.

8 a.m. Steady S.S.W. wind and fine weather. Barometer falling gradually, wind freshening.
5.40 p.m. Wind S.S.W. fresh, weather fine.
4.30 a.m. 31st. Wind S.W. by W., fresh with heavy rain, barometer rising.
6.30 a.m. Wind W. by N., moderate, with thick weather and rain.

No. 26.
S.S. "Venezuelan."
In { 32° 46′ N.
56° 31′ W.
8 a.m. G.T. 30th.
Bound N.Ely
To { 34° 55′ N.
52° 32′ W.
8 a.m. G.T. 31st.

No. 26 was far to the S.E. of the area of lowest pressure, and seems to have experienced the ordinary changes of wind and pressure which are common to these latitudes when a slight wave of low pressure passes over a ship; it seems to have gone to the eastward faster than she did, as the barometer fell with a south-south-westerly and rose with a westerly wind.

It will be noticed that No. 25, to the N.E. of No. 26, and bound the same way, was experiencing similar changes, but more intense; both their winds seem to have been part of the system accompanying the area of low pressure to the N.W. of them, though being at a great distance from its lowest point they seem to have had only slight gradients.

At 8 a.m. strong gale with heavy squalls from E.S.E. and a heavy sea, the barometer (about 29·30) had fallen ·75 in. in four hours.
11.45 a.m. Heavy east-south-easterly gale and sea, with thick weather and rain.
1.15 p.m. Wind hauling to the westward.
3 p.m. in about 43° 34′ N. 56° 3′ W., wind S.S.W., heavy gale and sea, barometer steady for two hours.
11.45 p.m. Wind W.S.W., heavy gale, squalls, and sea; lost main-topsail.
5.30 a.m. 31st. Wind W., gale more moderate, barometer rising.

No. 20.
S.S. "The Queen."
In { 43° 6′ N.
57° 23′ W.
8 a.m. G.T. 30th.
Bound E.N.Ely.
To { 44° 22′ N.
52° 0′ W.
8 a.m. G.T. 31st.

At 11.45 a.m. 30th, the sea temperature was 48°, whilst at 11.45 p.m. it was 38°.

The sudden great fall of the barometer and veering of the wind, although the ship was going to the eastward, indicate the great speed of the area of lowest pressure in that direction.

At 8 a.m. wind S.E., force 10.
At 10 a.m. S.E., force 11, a very heavy cross sea.
1 p.m. Wind S.W., 12, blowing a hurricane and doing considerable damage, mizen blew away, main sheet block carried away, also main boom and sail; ship making very bad weather and washing everything off the decks. Got a tarpaulin in mizen rigging and a large hawser with 30 fathoms of chain for a sea anchor. Boatswain and two seamen disabled.

No. 12.
S.S. "Dacian."
In { 40° 22′ N.
61° 10′ W.
8 a.m. G.T. 30th.
Bound Ely. very slowly.
To { 40° 20′ N.
60° 17′ W.
8 a.m. G.T. 31st.

4 p.m. hove-to in 40° 21′ N. 60° 40′ W., wind N.W., hurricane force, which continued till 8 p.m.

9 p.m. Wind W., 10.

1 a.m. 31st. Wind S.W., 9–10, and continued so to 8 a.m.

No. 12 gives no barometer or thermometer observations.

It seems clear that she got the changes about five hours before No. 37, which ship was about 4° N. and 5° E. of her.

Nos. 12, 47, and 52 have given the hours at which the shift from a south-easterly to a westerly direction took place, they are as follows, in the order of Greenwich time:—

No. 52, 4 a.m. 30th, in 39° 38′ N. and 64° 30′ W., air 59°, barometer 29·23, sea 58°, wind shifted from S.E. ½ E., 8, to W. ½ S., 11.

No. 47, 7 a.m. 30th, in 42° 28′ N., 67° 20′ W., air 42°, barometer 29·13, sea 42°; wind shifted from S.E. by E., 8, to N.W. by W., 9.

No. 12, 1 p.m. 30th, hove-to in 40° 21′ N. 60° 40′ W.; wind shifted from S.E., 11 to S.W., 12.

By plotting these vessels' positions, and drawing a line, representing the area of lowest pressure which accompanied the change of wind, in such a direction that it would take three times as long to go from No. 52 to No. 12 as from No. 52 to No. 47, it runs in a north-westerly direction, giving a north-easterly track of about 18 miles an hour for the area of lowest pressure. All endeavours to give a track to these gales point to the north-eastern quarter as their usual route.

Such a method for estimating the speed with which the area of low pressure passed to the north-eastward is far from satisfactory, and other attempts make it much greater.

It is worthy of notice that although No. 12 was about 320 miles E.S.E. of No. 47, whilst No. 52 was about 213 miles S.E. by S. of her, all ships had the wind from S.E. or S.E. by E. before the shift to the westward, indicating that the front of the area of low pressure was a line extending N.W. and S.E. Both Nos. 52 and 12 got the wind northwesterly a few hours after the shift to the westward. None of the ships speak of a calm between the shift from S.E. to N.W. No. 47 speaks of it as instantaneous during heavy rain. No. 30 says it took place in a heavy squall with lightning to the south-westward. No. 12 remarks at the time of the shift "Gale still increasing," and an hour afterwards "Blowing a hurricane."

No. 16.
S.S. "City of London."
In { 42° 26′ N.
61° 20′ W.
8 a.m. G.T. 30th.
Bound Westerly.
To { 41° 37′ N.
64° 10′ W.
8 a.m. G.T. 31st.

At 8 a.m. wind S.E. by E., strong gale, very heavy squalls and rain, high beam sea. Barometer had fallen · 48 in two hours.

At 10 a.m. S.S.W. gale. Ditto weather. 2 p.m. lowest barometer, about 28·7 ins. in 42° 10′ N. 62° 13′ W.

At 3 p.m. wind S.W., same force, and high south-westerly sea, barometer rising.

At 5 p.m. wind W. by N., barometer had risen ·46 in two hours.

At 8 p.m. gale moderating.

At 9 p.m. wind N.W. by W., and decreasing fast.

7.15 a.m., 31st, wind W. by S., light breeze.

It will be seen that No. 16 also got the changes of wind about 5 hours before No. 37; her lowest barometer was about 2 p.m., whilst that of No. 37 was about 6 p.m.

At 10 a.m. " wind hauling to the westward." It seems to have been E.S.E. before this time, but its direction is not clearly given.

At 2 p.m. " heavy sea struck No. 3 boat, doing damage."

At 4 p.m. " hard gale with a heavy sea running." In 42° 20′ N., 60° 39′ W., barometer at its lowest, 28·35. At this time the wind shifted to W., and is logged from that direction for forty hours.

At 8 p.m. " moderating with less sea."

No. 49.
S.S. "Marathon."
In { 41° 59′ N.
62° 10′ W.
8 a.m. G.T. 30th.
Bound E.N.Ely.
To { 43° 11′ N.
56° 30′ W.
8 a.m. G.T. 31st.

It will be noticed that No. 49 got the lowest barometer about 4 p.m., whilst No. 16, 70 miles to the west of her got it about 2 p.m. plainly indicating its rapid movement to the eastward. In Halifax the wind backed from S.E. to E. and N.E., accompanied by snow; therefore the *lowest* pressure must have passed between this place and ships to the southward. At Halifax the barometer was down to 28·6 between 0·30 p.m. and 1·15 p.m., and supposing the mean of these hours to be that of the passage of the area of lowest pressure, it must have taken place a few minutes before 1 p.m. of the 30th, or nearly an hour before it passed No. 16, and she was about 160 miles S.S.E. of Halifax.

A wave of low pressure extending in a north-westerly and south-easterly line, and passing to the N.E., would fulfil these conditions.

8 a.m. Wind W., 11, having continued so since 4 a.m.; barometer rising, her lowest barometer (29·15) was about this time.

At 4.20 p.m. in 38° 28′ N. 64° 30′ W., wind W. by N., 10, barometer having risen ·4 in four hours, from this time the wind lulled.

At 4.20 a.m. 31st. W. by S., 7, with a heavy N.W. sea.

At 8.20 a.m. surface temperature 56°, at 0.20 a.m. 31st it was 70°.

No. 52.
S.S. "Delta."
In { 39° 16′ N.
64° 30′ W.
8 a.m. G.T. 30th.
Bound South.
To { 36° 30′ N.
64° 30′ W.
8 a.m. G.T. 31st.

No. 52 bound south steamed out of the influence of the low pressure, travelling to the N.E., through which she had passed, and went into the ordinary wind of the neighbourhood.

D 2

No. 47.
S.S. "Tripoli."
In { 42° 28′ N.
67° 20′ W.
8 a.m. G.T. 30th.
Bound West.
To { Boston outer light.
1.30 a.m. G.T. 31st.

8 a.m. Hard N.W. by W. gale, with heavy squalls and a high confused sea. The lowest barometer given is at 8·30 a.m., but it was no doubt lower before the shift to N.W.
4·30 p.m. strong N.W. by W. gale, high confused sea, ship labouring heavily.
5.30 p.m., fine clear weather with fresh N.W. by W. gale and a head sea.
7.30 p.m. Less wind.
Wind north-westerly, weather fine until she arrived at Boston.

No. 13.
S.S. "India."
In { 40° 21′ N.
70° 45′ W.
8 a.m. G.T. 30th
Bound East.
To { 40° 42′ N.
64° 50′ W.
8 a.m. G.T. 31st.

8 a.m. Strong N.W. by W. wind and very cloudy, barometer rising gradually.
6.20 a.m. 31st. Light northerly breeze and cloudy.
No. 13 left New York on the 29th with a N.E. wind, changing at 1 a.m., 30th, to N.W.; it blew a gale at 4 a.m. 30th from N.W. She seems to have felt the north-west wind of the south-western side of the wave of low pressure to the N.E. of her, but as the wave seems to have been going fast to the N.E., and No. 13 slower to the east, her wind became light and drew northerly, which is the prevailing wind near the coast at this season of the year.

No. 1.
S.S. "City of Antwerp."
In { 40° 24′ N.
70° 54′ W.
8 a.m. G.T. 30th.
Bound East.
To { 40° 16′ N.
64° 45′ W.
8 a.m. G.T. 31st.

8 a.m. Strong N.W. by W. wind and high following sea.
3.20 a.m. 31st. Light N.W. by N. wind and clear weather.
No. 1 seems to have had similar weather to that of No. 13; her barometer fell with the north-easterly wind on leaving New York, until the change came to N.W., when it rose.

No. 53.
S.S. "Weser."
In { 40° 34′ N.
71° 5′ W.
8 a.m. G.T. 30th.
Bound East.
To { 40° 49′ N.
63° 56′ W.
8 a.m. G.T. 31st.

8 a.m. Wind N.W., 8, with high sea, barometer steadily rising.
Between 4.15 a.m. and 8.15 a.m. of the 31st (exact time not given), the wind drew to N.N.W., 3. This agrees well with the experience of Nos. 13 and 1.
Diagram 2 gives a continuous record of this ship's data.

No. 21.
S.S. "Denmark."
In { 40° 31′ N.
71° 10′ W.
8 a.m. G.T. 30th.
Bound E. by N.
To { 41° 19′ N.
65° 41′ W.
8 a.m. G.T. 31st.

8 a.m. Fresh breeze from N.W. by W., dark cloudy weather.
5.36 p.m. Fresh gale from W. by N., barometer rising slowly.
4.30 a.m. 31st, N.W. by W. wind moderate and fine.
No. 21 seems to have had the gale a little stronger than No. 1, and she made a more northerly course.

These gales seem to be always followed by north-westerly winds, which would be expected, according to Buys Ballot's law, if an area of low pressure, having a north-easterly route, has passed over any place.

8 a.m. Wind N.W. by N., 6, drawing northerly and decreasing with a rising barometer.
5 p.m. Wind N. by W., 2. The temperature of the sea was 66° with a remark " strong ripples, limit of Gulf stream."
5 a.m. 31st. Wind S.E. by S., 2, barometer falling.
At 5 a.m. No. 38 seems to have been experiencing the north-eastern side of another wave of low pressure just advancing upon her.

No. 38.
"Nicoline."
In $\begin{cases} 32° \ 48' \text{ N.} \\ 73° \ 40' \text{ W.} \\ 8 \text{ a.m. G.T. 30th.} \end{cases}$
Bound North slowly.
To $\begin{cases} 33° \ 16' \text{ N.} \\ 73° \ 52' \text{ W.} \\ 8 \text{ a.m. G.T. 31st.} \end{cases}$

By referring back to the extracts from No. 38's log on the 29th, it will be seen that she did not get the strong south-easterly gale, changing to N.W., which was afterwards experienced by the ships to the north-eastward of her; but she had a light southerly wind and falling barometer, which shifted suddenly to W., 8, at 9 p.m. of the 29th. This looks as if the area of low pressure which accompanied this gale had not arrived at it greatest intensity when it swept over No. 38. Most probably its breeding place was where the hot and cold waters meet near the "strong ripples and limit of the Gulf stream," spoken of by Captain Heim. We hope to say more about the cause of these gales at the end of this paper.

8 a.m. 30th. Wind W. by N. ¼ N. 20 *miles per hour*, barometer 29·83, air 39°. The barometer continued rising until 2 p.m., from which time till 8 a.m. 31st it was pretty steady at about 30 ins.

New York Observatory.
8 a.m. G.T. 30th.
to
8 a.m. G.T. 31st.

The maximum temperature was 45°·5 at 11 p.m.
The wind continued W.N.W. until 1 a.m. 31st, when it shifted suddenly to N.E., between which point and E. it continued until 8 a.m., 31st.

GENERAL REMARKS ON CHART FOR JANUARY 30TH.

The logs of 31 ships have been consulted.
Plate VI. of the Quarterly Weather Report shows that all our self-registering barometers were falling rather quickly on this day, and a hard southerly gale was blowing at our western stations, whilst there was a strong south-easterly wind in Shetland, at Skudesnaes, and also in

Iceland. Corunna reports a strong northerly wind, which seems doubtful, especially as they give the wind fresh from S.W. at 6 p.m. 29th, and again at 6 p.m. 30th.

In Cumberland Sound the wind is light S.E.

At Halifax there was a gale from the eastward. Thanks to Mr. F. Allison's careful observations and remarks forwarded to us by Captain David Hunter, we have data for 8.15 a.m., Greenwich time of this day. He says, "30th 4 a.m., local time (8.15 a.m. Greenwich time), wind had "backed to E.* and blew a strong gale, thermometer 34°·8, barometer "29·272, rain showers began, temperature now decreasing, while baro- "meter still fell and wind backed to N.E., still a gale. Rain changed "to snow at 5.45 a.m. (10 a.m. Greenwich time), which fell until noon "to the depth of 3·8 ins. Strength of gale diminished before 8 a.m. "(0.15 p.m. Greenwich time), but wind remained very high till 4 p.m. "(8.15 p.m. Greenwich time), gradually working to N., temperature "continued to decrease slowly all day. From 8¼ to 9 a.m. (0.30 to "1.15 p.m., Greenwich time) barometer stood at remarkable minimum "28·60 ins., whence it rose quickly. Between noon 29th and 8.15 a.m., "30th (4.15 p.m., 29th, and 0.30 p.m. 30th, Greenwich time), pressure "decreased 1·09 ins. Total precipitation 30th = ·95 in. Sky cleared "suddenly before 10 p.m. 30th, (2.15 a.m. 31st Greenwich time), and a "well defined auroral arch appeared."

At Terceira there was a fresh north-west wind, whilst at Madeira there was a light southerly air.

Commencing on the eastern side of the Chart, it will be seen that there was a fresh southerly gale over our western coasts, which seemed to hang there.

No. 51, steering to the eastward, had a rising barometer; whilst No. 2, steering west, had it falling, proving that the area of low pressure to the westward, if moving at all, was not coming so fast towards the coast as No. 51.

Taking the ships in their order to the westward, we find that the south wind changes to W. in 20° to 23° W., and to N.W. and N. in 30° to 35° W. This system of wind seems to prevail round a large area of low pressure to the north.

No. 5, in 53° N. and 30° W., bound east; got no gale. This seems to show that the gradient to the north was less, and there seems to be a

---

* It will be remembered that at 4.15 a.m. Greenwich time the wind was very strong from S.S.E. See the remarks which accompany the Chart for the 29th.

common opinion that the westerly winds are generally not so strong north of 50° as between 40° and 50° N.

Passing on to 40° W., we come to a space which seems to lie between two systems of wind and areas of low pressure, where there were very few ships. We then come to No. 46 east of Newfoundland, and No. 22 south of that island. They have a moderate N.W. wind, whilst all the vessels to the S.W. of them seem to be experiencing the wind, accompanying a wave of very low pressure, having its greatest depression S.W. of Halifax, the lowest barometer was that experienced by No. 49, viz., 28·35 ins., whilst No. 37 had it down to 28·49 ins., and No. 16 to 28·70. The direction of wind experienced by various ships leads to the supposition that it was elongated in a north-westerly and south-easterly direction, and the hours at which the various ships got the change of wind from a south-easterly to a south-westerly and westerly direction seem to prove that it was moving very fast to the north-eastward.

Nos. 37 and 16, the ships which got very low readings of the barometer, lie about E.N.E. and W.S.W. of each other. As the exact hour of the change of wind is rarely given, it is difficult to estimate the speed at which the area moved; but it most probably amounted to from 30 to 40 miles an hour, *i.e.*, supposing it to have been in 65° W. (to the west of No. 49) at 8 a.m., and with No. 37 in 57° W. at 6 p.m. of the same day. The times of lowest pressure passing the "Austrian" and Heart's Content give about the same speed.

The shape, extent and track of the area of lowest pressure so modify any calculations as to its speed, that until we know more of these data we can only get rough approximations, as in the case of the remark following the extracts for No. 12 for this day. For instance, it seems probable that these areas are sometimes elongated in a north-westerly and south-easterly direction whilst they travel to the north-eastward, in which case their line of lowest pressure might cross ships lying N.W. and S.E. of each other at the same moment, though they might be hundreds of miles apart. Still, all evidence goes to prove that they move quickly to the north-eastward; or, if the opinion expressed further on in this paper be correct, they re-form quickly along a north-easterly line.

I have already remarked on the possibility that the "City of Boston" got the very worst part of this gale, as it seems to have travelled right in her track.

By comparing this day's Chart with that for 8 a.m. Greenwich time of the 29th, it will be seen that there were no signs of the south-east gale of the 30th at 8 a.m. of the 29th. On referring to the extracts it will be seen that No. 38. (the most south-western ship) did not get the first of a south-east wind until 1 p.m. of the 29th, whilst Nos. 49 and 12, several degrees to the north-eastward, did not get it until 4 p.m. of that date.

It has already been remarked that No. 38 (the most south-western ship) had only a moderate south-easterly wind, and after the change to W. it only increased to force 8. This leads to the supposition that the gale increased in intensity as it went to the north-eastward.

An extra Chart has been constructed for 6 p.m. Greenwich time of the 30th, which is the hour when No. 37 (the "Austrian"), with standard instruments from this office, was experiencing the lowest pressure (see Diagram 1).

This 6 p.m. Chart only needs careful inspection to show that the area of lowest pressure on the western side of the Atlantic had moved quickly to the north-eastward. Nos. 20 and 37, which had a south-east wind at 8 a.m., have it now south-west, and the south-east wind has extended to No. 48 in about 46° W. It is probable that it extended still further east, but observations in that direction are wanting.

Extracts and Remarks to accompany the Chart for January 31st, 1870.

A fresh southerly wind prevails over the British Islands, amounting to a gale at some places. This has continued for three days.

No. 50.
S.S. "Hotspur."
In { 46° 14′ N.
7° 55′ W.
8 a.m. G.T. 31st.
Bound S.S.Wly.
To { 44° 48′ N.
8° 54′ W.
8 a.m. G.T. 1st
Feby.

8 a.m. Had a south wind, force 5, weather squally and high south-westerly sea.

Noon, wind shifted to N.W. by N. in a heavy squall with hail.

8 p.m., wind had backed to W. by S., 2; weather fine. During the last 12 hours the barometer rose from 29·67 to 30·06.

The Quarterly Weather Report for this date (Plate VII.), shows that Valencia got a similar veering and backing of the wind between 9 a.m. and midnight, with a rising and falling barometer. The 8 a.m. Chart shows this ridge of highest pressure lying to the westward of Valencia and No. 50. These facts seem to prove that it moved quickly to the eastward.

33

8 a.m. Wind W., 8.
1 p.m., in 49° 11' N. and 16° 10' W., wind N.W., 9 to 7; barometer having risen ·17 in. in four hours.
9 p.m., in 49° 10' N. and 18° 12' W. Wind had backed to S.W., 6; the barometer falling again.
1 a.m., 1st February, S.W., 9; barometer falling fast.
No. 39 (the "Westphalia") seems to have passed from the western side of one wave of low pressure to the eastern side of another. See Diagram 4, which gives a section of the ridge of high pressure between the depressions.

No. 39.
S.S. "Westphalia."
In { 49° 15' N.
14° 58' W.
8 a.m. G.T. 31st.
Bound West.
To { 49° 6' N.
20° 55' W.
8 a.m. G.T. 1st.

8 a.m. W.S.W., no force given. Considerable swell. No other entry for 24 hours.

No. 29.
Ship "Chatillon."
In { 34° 46' N.
16° 58' W.
8 a.m. 31st.
Bound S.S.Wly.
{ 32° 52' N.
17° 43' W.
8 a.m. 1st.

8 a.m. Wind W. by N., 7, heavy head sea, with mist and hail squalls; barometer rising.
4.35 p.m. (in about 53° 3' N. and 24° 31" W.), wind S.W., 7, and barometer falling.
6.35 p.m. Wind S.S.E., 7; squally with rain, barometer still falling.
10.35 p.m. Wind S.W. by W., 7, squally with rain; barometer steady, but low (about 29·20).
4.35 a.m. of 1st, wind S.W. by W., 8, heavy squalls with passing showers and a heavy head sea; barometer steady.
No. 4 seems to have got the backing to S.W. 4½ hours before No. 39, she being in 24° 30' W., whilst No. 39 was in 18° W. Diagram 4, already referred to, helps the eye in judging of this change.

No. 4.
S.S. "Prussian."
In { 53° 17' N.
22° 24' W.
8 a.m. G.T. 31st.
Bound West.
To { 52° 45' N.
27° 33' W.
8 a.m. G.T. 1st.

8 a.m. Wind N.W. by N., fresh breeze, barometer 29·51, steady.
1.20 p.m. in 54° 28' N. 20° 48' W., light variable breeze, clear and fine; barometer rising a little.
4.20 p.m. Light variable airs.
7.20 p.m. Light easterly breeze.
10.20 p.m. Wind veering south of east, barometer falling.
5.20 a.m. of 1st. Wind south-easterly, fresh with rain, barometer gradually falling.
This light easterly wind looks as if No. 5 (being far north) had

No. 5.
S.S. "North American."
In { 54° 12' N.
22° 30' W.
8 a.m. G.T. 31st.
Bound East.
To { 55° 9' N.
15° 6' W.
8 a.m. G.T. 1st.

steamed to the northward of an area of low pressure, where there was very little gradient, and passed out on its north-eastern side, where the gradient was greater. We find frequent disturbances of this kind as ships approach the west coast of Ireland.

No. 54.
S.S. " Bremen."
In { 48° 17′ N.
24° 47′ W.
8 a.m. G.T. 31st.
Bound Easterly.
To { 49° 13′ N.
17° 36′ W.
8 a.m. G.T. 1st.

8 a.m. Had the wind N.W., 5 ; barometer falling.
1.30 p.m. in 48° 27′ N., 23° 4′ W., wind S.W., 3, and unsteady; barometer still falling.
9.30 p.m. Wind S., 5, with heavy rain.
5.30 a.m., 1st. Wind W., 5. barometer 29·53, fallen a little.
It seems probable that at 5.30 a.m., 1st., No. 54 was experiencing the wind of the southern side of the area of low pressure, which gave No. 5 a south-east wind on its north-eastern side. Both ships were bound to the eastward.

No. 17.
S.S. " Helvetia."
In { 50° 14′ N.
25° 38′ W.
8 a.m. G.T. 31st.
Bound Westerly.
To { 49° 48′ N.
28° 14′ W.
8 a.m. G.T. 1st.

8 a.m. Wind W. by N., strong and squally with passing hail showers, barometer rising.
2.45 p.m. Wind S. by W., strong breeze, thick rainy weather ; barometer falling.
6.45 p.m. Wind W. by S., strong breeze and squally, with rain ; sea rising.
2.45 a.m., 1st. Strong W. by S. gale with very heavy squalls and high sea.
No. 17 seems to have had a stronger gale than No. 4, also steaming to the westward, but three degrees to the north of her.
It will be seen that at 2.45 p.m. No. 17 got the south-south-westerly wind experienced by No. 10 at 8 a.m. The wind felt by No. 10 had been variable westerly.
This southerly wind seems to have been related to the area of low pressure which was to the S.W. of Newfoundland at 6 p.m. of the 30th, which indicates its easterly motion.

No. 14.
S.S. " Europa."
In { 52° 23′ N.
26° 32′ W.
8 a.m. G.T. 31st.
Bound E.N.Ely.
To { 53° 54′ N.
19° 54′ W.
8 a.m. G.T. 1st.

8 a.m. Wind W. by N. 4—5 ; barometer falling.
Noon. Wind backing to S.W., barometer falling ; a heavy N.W. swell.
5.30 p.m. Wind S.E. by S., 5 ; barometer still falling.
10.30 p.m. Wind E.S.E., 6 ; barometer still falling.
5.30 a.m. 1st. Wind W.S.W., 4 ; barometer ceased falling.
At noon, No. 14 seems to have been caught up by the area of low pressure shown on yesterday's Chart S.W. of Newfoundland, which was

travelling faster to the north-eastward than herself. No. 10 had the southerly wind of its eastern side at 8 a.m.

9 a.m. Wind S. by W., increasing; no barometer given.
3 p.m. Wind S. by E., increasing strong wind and heavy rain.
5 p.m. Wind S.W. by S., increasing gale and rising sea.
9 p.m. Wind W. by S., strong gale and heavy sea, filling decks with water.
4 a.m., 1st. Wind W. by S., increasing gale and high breaking sea.

No. 10.
S.S. "Manhattan."
In { 49° 30′ N.
28° 10′ W.
8 a.m. G.T. 31st.
Bound Westerly.
To { 48° 57′ N.
31° 13′ W.
8 a.m. G.T. 1st.

Nos. 10, 17, and 54, show how near a strong southerly wind may be to a light north-westerly one. (See this day's Chart.) Buys Ballot's law seems to require that there should be a ridge of higher pressure between them.

No. 10 seems to have passed from the eastern to the central part of a wave of low pressure between 3 p.m. 31st and 4 a.m., 1st. Her position at 8 a.m. of the 31st seems to have been on the eastern edge of the area of low pressure which was S.W. of Newfoundland on the 30th. She gives no instrumental readings.

8.30 a.m. Wind veered from S. to S.S.W., and increased to a gale.
11.30 a.m. Violent gale from S.W., with terrific rain squalls, slowed the engines and put her head to the southward; ship drifting about 1¼ knots per hour.
2.30 p.m. W.S.W. gale.
7.30 p.m. Stove No. 3 boat.
10.30 p.m. W.S.W. gale continuing with terrific hail and rain squalls.
3.30 a.m., 1st. Heavy W.S.W. gale with hail and rain squalls and heavy sea.

No. 11.
S.S. "Iowa."
In { 49° 46′ N.
37° 10′ W.
8 a.m. G.T. 31st.
Bound West, *but drifting East.*
To { 49° 24′ N.
36° 38′ W.
8 a.m. G.T. 1st.

No. 11 gives no barometer readings. At 8.30 a.m. she seems to have been on the eastern side of a wave of low pressure, which gradually passed over her, causing the wind to veer. She seems to have had a stronger gale than No. 10, which makes it probable that the worst passed some distance to the N.W. of No. 10, taking a north-easterly course, perhaps inclined more in that direction by the ridge of high barometer to the eastward of it.

At 10.30 a.m. Wind N.N.E., 4, barometer 30·41.
2.30 p.m. Calm and fine, barometer 30·39.
At 10.30 p.m. Wind S.S.W., 4, barometer 30·32.
At 6.30 a.m., 1st. Wind W., 6; barometer 30·16; violent squalls with rain.

No. 45.
"Carl Georg."
In { 39° 55′ N.
38° 35′ W.
8 a.m. G.T. 31st.
Bound N.Ely.
To { 41° 25′ N.
36° 10′ W.
8 a.m. G.T. 1st.

No. 45 seems to have only slightly felt the influence of the low pressure, which passed at some distance to the N.W. of her.

No. 55.
S.S. "Rhein."
In { 47° 37' N.
39° 9' W.
8 a.m. G.T. 31st.
Bound Westerly."
To { 46° 49' N.
42° 0' W.
8 a.m. G.T. 1st.

10.40 a.m. Wind W., 9, and high sea.
2.40 p.m. in 47° 27' N. and 40° 18' W., wind W.S.W., 10; high sea.
6.40 p.m. Wind W., 10.
2.40 a.m., 1st. Wind W.N.W., 10, heavy snowstorm; barometer steadily rising since 10.40 a.m. 31st.

No. 48.
S.S. "Calabria."
In { 46° 30' N.
42° 10' W.
8 a.m. G.T. 31st.
Bound E.N.Ely.
To { 48° 47' N.
34° 44' W.
8 a.m. G.T. 1st.

10.40 a.m. Blowing a terrific gale from S.W. by W. with hurricane squalls; very heavy sea; ship rolling heavily and taking much water on board.
11.40 a.m. Wind W.S.W., 10; same weather and sea.
7.30 p.m. Similar wind and weather; shipped a sea in starboard waist, breaking in the smoking-room doors, and glass of engine-room skylight.
2.30 a.m., 1st. Hard W. by S. gale with terrific squalls, and very heavy sea; ship labouring and taking much heavy water on deck. Barometer slightly risen, but oscillating; lowest 29·24 at 7 a.m. of the 31st.
6.20 a.m., 1st. More moderate from W. by S. with heavy squalls and very heavy sea. Barometer risen ·11 in four hours.

Note.—Lloyd's list for March 7th, 1870, says that on the 31st the "Calabria" lost a steward overboard, lost three boats, and shipped a sea in the saloon.

It looks as if the "Calabria" had gone along with but was gradually passed by the area of low pressure which swept over so many ships to the westward of her on the 30th.

No. 30.
H.M.S. "Orontes."
In { 43° 24' N.
47° 29' W.
8 a.m. G.T. 31st.
Bound Easterly.
To { 43° 52' N.
43° 57' W.
8 a.m. G.T. 1st.

At 8 a.m. Wind W., 8, 9; aneroid barometer 29·62, rising half a tenth an hour.
Noon. Wind W.N.W., 8.
Midnight. Wind N.W. by W., 6 to 5; barometer 30·05, still rising slowly.
3.10 a.m., 1st. N.W., 5—6, air 45°; barometer 30·08, sea 49°.

By referring to the remarks of the 30th it will be seen that Nos. 30 and 48 were near each other on that day, but that No. 48 kept steaming to the eastward, whilst No. 30 hove-to, and it seems clear that on the 31st No. 48, being 292 miles to the N.E. of No. 30, had to a certain extent kept company with the area of lowest pressure and corresponding weather, whilst No. 30 had just lost it. The 6 p.m. Chart of the 30th shows that No. 48 had then the wind south-easterly, whilst No. 30 had got the change to south-south-westerly.

37

By comparing the log of No. 30 with those of ships which kept on their route to the eastward it is clearly shown that in a southerly gale the wind may be expected to veer more quickly and the gale to moderate sooner with a ship hove-to than with one steaming or sailing fast to the eastward, whilst the vessel bound to the westward will get the changes quicker than the one hove-to.

10 a.m. Moderate W.N.W. wind with a dark windy appearance to the north-westward.
3 p.m. in 39° 8′ N. 46° 31′ W. same wind, confused sea, ship knocking about much.
8 p.m. Light baffling airs and cloudy.
4 a.m., 1st. Light north-north-westerly airs with a heavy west-north-west sea.

No. 25 seems to have (so to speak) seen the heavy north-west gale which was raging to the north-westward of her, and experienced its sea, whilst her wind remained moderate. This north-westerly sea of distant gales is very commonly experienced by ships that have just passed through the north-east trades, though they may not get the wind.

No. 25.
S.S. "Cuban."
In { 38° 37′ N.
47° 48′ W.
8 a.m. G.T. 31st.
Bound E.N.Ely.
To { 40° 7′ N.
44° 2′ W.
8 a.m. G.T. 1st.

8 a.m. Strong W. by S. gale, with violent squalls, and very heavy sea.
3.20 p.m. in 45° 30′ N. and 49° 51′ W. Strong W. by S. gale and heavy sea.
4.20 p.m. Strong W.N.W. gale and heavy sea.
7.20. p.m. Wind moderating, sea going down.
5.20 a.m., 1st. Fresh W.N.W. wind and fine.
Barometer rose until 11.30 p.m., when it was steady at 30·00.

No. 46.
S.S. "Nemesis."
In { 45° 55′ N.
48° 56′ W.
8 a.m. G.T. 31st.
Bound Westerly.
To { 44° 35′ N.
53° 23′ W.
8 a.m. G.T. 1st.

At 11.20 a.m. Fresh west gale; set upper maintopsail.
3.20 p.m. in 44° 43′ N. 50° 9′ W. Moderate W.N.W. gale, sea going down.
11.20 p.m. Decreasing W.N.W. wind and fine weather. Heavy sea.
4.20 a.m., 1st. Strong west-north-westerly wind and heavy sea, all possible sail set.
Barometer rising gradually throughout.
No. 20 was following in the rear of the gale which swept over her on the 30th.

No. 20.
S.S. "The Queen."
In { 42° 22′ N.
52° 0′ W.
8 a.m. G.T. 31st.
Bound E.N.Ely.
To { 45° 39′ N.
46° 17′ W.
8 a.m. G.T. 1st.

No. 26.
S.S. "Venezuelan."
In { 34° 55' N.
52° 32' W.
8 a.m. G.T. 31st.
Bound E.N.Ely.
To { 35° 58' N.
49° 24' W.
8 a.m. G.T. 1st.

11.30 a.m. Light unsteady breeze from the westward.
3.30 p.m. in 35° 36' N. 51° 25' W. Light N. W. by W. breeze and heavy north-west swell. Barometer risen slightly since 8 a.m.; now 30·20.
0.30 a.m. of 1st. Light variable winds, clewed up all sails.
7.30 a.m. of 1st. Light south-easterly wind. Barometer steady. At this time No. 26 was just experiencing the south-easterly wind of an area of low pressure coming over her from the westward. It will be noticed that she was far south.

No. 22.
S.S. "Pennsylvania."
In { 44° 2' N.
55° 19' W.
8 a.m. G.T. 31st.
Bound W.S.Wly.
To { 43° 0' N.
59° 11' W.
8 a.m. G.T. 1st.

8 a.m. Wind W.N.W., gale gradually moderating; barometer ?? 29·14.
11.40 a.m. Wind W.N.W., more moderate, cloudy with hail, high sea; barometer 29·70.
5.40 p.m. Wind W.N.W., moderate breeze, barometer 30·20.
10.40 p.m. Wind N.N.W., light with rain, barometer 30·00, falling.
2.40 a.m. Wind north, light; barometer 29·80, falling.
6.40 a.m. Wind N.E., freshening, with heavy rain; barometer 29·60, falling.
It will be remembered that No. 22 recorded no south-easterly wind on the 30th, when all ships in her neighbourhood got it. Her 8 a.m. barometer on this day seems to have been much too low.

No. 49.
S.S. "Marathon."
In { 43° 11' N.
56° 30' W.
8 a.m. G.T. 31st.
Bound E.N.Ely.
To { 44° 36' N.
50° 9' W.
8 a.m. G.T. 1st.

8 a.m. Wind W. by S., strong breeze with a high sea; barometer ? 29·24, and rising.
3.40 p.m., in 43° 35' N. 54° 33' W. Wind strong from W. by S. and confused sea, barometer 29·76, having risen ·36 in four hours.
3.40 a.m., 1st. Wind still W. by S., moderate, with a northerly swell; barometer 30·00, and continued so till 8 a.m. of 1st.

No. 37.
S.S. "Austrian."
In { 43° 39' N.
58° 16' W.
8 a.m. G.T. 31st.
Bound West.
To { 43° 10' N.
63° 26' W.
8 a.m. G.T. 1st.

8 a.m. Wind W.N.W., 8, still moderating and sea going down, stars showing out at intervals; barometer 29·79, rising.
4 p.m., in 43° 23' N., 59° 19' W. Wind W.N.W., 6; barometer 30·08, and rising.
4 a.m., 1st, in 43° 13' N. and 62° 27' W. Wind E., 3, overcast with clouds from S.W.; barometer 30·02.
8 a.m., 1st. Wind E., 7, barometer 29·87; hail, snow, and mist.
At 4 a.m. of the 1st we have No. 37 just entering on the north-eastern side of another wave of low pressure the lowest point of which passed to the south of her as the wind veered from E. to N.E. and N.W. See Diagram 1 for a section of it. Ships to the south of her got the change of wind to the S. and S.W. See Diagram 2 for the changes experienced

by No. 53. It will be seen that the action of the barometer was quicker with No. 37 bound west than with No. 53 bound east, the one meeting, the other going with the area of low pressure.

9 a.m. Moderating from S.W., force 11, clearing away wreck and getting all ready to keep ship away.
1 p.m. Wind S.W., 6; kept ship away, went full speed and set close-reefed square sails.
8 p.m. Wind S., 5.
Midnight. Variable, 3.
5 a.m. East, 6, increasing wind and gloomy, with heavy rain.
The wind reported by this ship at 8 a.m. differs from all near her; but I have thought it right to give it with a query. There are no instrumental observations.

No. 12.
S.S. "Dacian."
In { 40° 20′ N.
     60° 17′ W.
     8 a.m. G.T. 31st.
Bound E.N.E.
To { 40° 56′ N.
     58° 13′ W.
     8 a.m. G.T. 1st.

8 a.m. N.N.W., 3; decreasing sea.
Noon. Wind N.E., 2; barometer rising.
4 p.m., in 41° 2′ N., 61° 33′ W. Wind N.E., 2.
8 p.m. E.N.E., 2.
4 a.m., 1st, in 41° 40′ N., 58° 49′ W. Wind E.N.E., 4; barometer 30·06.
See Diagram 2 for a continuous record of the observations of this ship during the passage home. A comparison of Diagrams 1 and 2 is given in the remarks on No. 53 for February 1st.

No. 53.
S.S. "Weser."
In { 40° 49′ N.
     63° 56′ W.
     8 a.m. G.T. 31st.
Bound E.N.E.
To { 42° 6′ N.
     57° 51′ W.
     8 a.m. G.T. 1st.

8 a.m. Wind light W. by S. and cloudy; barometer about 30·03, rising.
5.24 p.m. Wind S.E. by S., light breeze and clear; barometer falling.
9.30 p.m. Wind E.S.E., moderate breeze and cloudy; light snow had fallen.
5.30 a.m., 1st. Wind southerly, moderate breeze and cloudy.
6.30 a.m., 1st. Wind S.W., light breeze and misty with drizzle.

No. 16.
S.S. "City of London."
In { 41° 37′ N.
     64° 10′ W.
     8 a.m. G.T. 31st.
Bound Westerly.
To { 40° 43′ N.
     70° 22′ W.
     8 a.m. G.T. 1st.

Standard instruments.
8.20 a.m. Wind W., 5, with a turbulent sea; barometer 30·13 steady.
4.20 p.m., in 35° 28′ N., 64° 30′ W. Wind
  S., 4, with rain - - - - ,, 30·07 falling.
0.20 a.m., 1st. Wind S.E., 5, with rain - ,, 29·92 ,,
4.20 a.m. In 34° 22′ N., 64° 35′ W., S.E., 7,
  with rain - - - - ,, 29·82 ,,
Temperature of sea generally 67° throughout.
This is the 2nd area of low pressure which No. 52 experienced since leaving Halifax on the 28th. Notice how her wind went to S.E., and on the 1st at noon to S.W. and W., whilst No. 37 had the change to N.E.

No. 52.
S.S. "Delta."
In { 36° 30′ N.
     64° 30′ W.
     8 a.m. G.T. 31st.
Bound South.
To { 34° 1′ N.
     64° 36′ W.
     8 a.m. G.T. 1st.

and N.W., proving that the lowest part of an area of low pressure passed between them.

No. 13.
S.S. "India."
In { 40° 42′ N.
     64° 50′ W.
     8 a.m. G.T. 31st.
Bound E.N.Ely.
To { 42° 0′ N.
     59° 55′ W.
     8 a.m. G.T. 1st.

8 a.m. Light N. by W. breeze and cloudy; barometer steady at ? 30·11.*

2 p.m. Light variable airs, with fine, clear weather.

4 a.m., 1st., in 41° 46′ N., 60° 40′ W. Stiff E. by S. wind, and gloomy, with heavy rain; barometer ? 30·02, falling.

No. 1.
S.S. "City of Antwerp."
In { 40° 16′ N.
     64° 45′ W.
     8 a.m. G.T. 31st.
Bound E.N.E.
To { 41° 42′ N.
     58° 59′ W.
     8 a.m. G.T. 1st.

8.20 a.m. Wind N.W. by N., light breeze and clear, sea temperature 42°.

10.20 a.m. Wind N. by E., light airs and cloudy.

Midnight. Wind E.N.E., light breeze, with rain.

4 a.m., 1st. Sea temperature 60°.

7. a.m., 1st. Wind E.N.E., strong increasing breeze, with rain.

After this the barometer fell rather quickly, and the wind veered to the southward.

After 7 a.m. No. 1 seems to have been just about to experience the south-easterly wind, which had been blowing with No. 52 for several hours.

No. 21.
S.S. "Denmark."
In { 41° 19′ N.
     65° 41′ W.
     8 a.m. G.T. 31st.
Bound E.N.Ely.
To { 42° 34′ N.
     61° 14′ W.
     8 a.m. G.T. 1st.

8 a.m. North-westerly wind, light breeze and fine.

Noon. Moderate easterly breeze and gloomy.

At 11.15 a.m., the wind shifted suddenly from the north-westward to the eastward, at which time she passed the "City of London" (No. 16), bound west; No. 16 seems to have kept a light westerly wind until 5.30 p.m. Probably the opposite courses led to a different estimation in the direction of this light wind.

No. 38.
Ship "Nicoline."
In { 33° 16′ N.
     73° 52′ W.
     8 a.m. G.T. 31st.
Bound N.Wly.
To { 34° 13′ N.
     74° 36′ W.
     8 a.m. G.T. 1st.

8 a.m. Wind S.W., 3. Barometer 30·08 falling, sea temperature 66°.

9 a.m. to noon. Continuous heavy lightning in N.W. and N.

5 p.m. In 33° 48′ N., 74° 12′ W., wind W., 3, squally, barometer 29·92, sea temperature 66°.

1 a.m., 1st. Wind S.W., 6, with rain squalls, barometer 29·72.

3 a.m. Wind shifted suddenly to W.N.W. in a heavy thunderstorm, squalls, and terrific lightning, night very dark, and sea phosphorescent.

5 a.m. In 34° 15′ N., 74° 35′ W. Wind W.N.W., 8. Very gloomy, with lightning, barometer 29·56; from this time the barometer seems to have risen; sea temperature 66°.

By referring to the data of No. 52, it will be seen that at 4.20 a.m. of 1st February, in 34° 22′ N. and 64° 35′ W., she had the wind S.E. 7, with rain;

---

* A note of interrogation means that the observations are uncorrected or otherwise doubtful.

hence at nearly the same time and in the same latitude, but 10 degrees of longitude apart, these ships had strong winds from opposite directions. Now such a state of things would exist if a wave of low pressure were between them, extending in a north-westerly and south-easterly direction, and travelling to the N.E. along the American coast line, thus:—

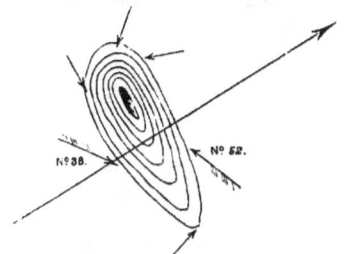

No. 38 had a light S.E. wind at 5 a.m. of the 31st, whilst No. 52 does not seem to have got a southerly wind before 4 p.m., which indicates an easterly track for the wave.

Diagram 1 shows that on February 1, No. 37 (near Halifax) got the change of wind from E. to N.E. and N.W., as a wave of low pressure passed over her. These changes are represented by the arrows on the north side of the area of lowest pressure in the accompanying figure. The changes of wind at Halifax were similar to those experienced by No. 37.

It is not supposed that this figure represents the exact shape of one of the areas of low pressure which travel along the coast of North America, but if the lowest pressure were at the darkest spot, and it increased outwards, having Halifax and No. 37 to the northward and Nos. 38 and 52 to the southward, then Buys Ballot's law tells us that similar winds to those experienced by the above-named ships and Halifax would be observed. The rapidity with which the wind generally shifts from S.E. to N.W., from which last point it blows for many hours, leads to the supposition that the part of the wave where the wind would be south-westerly and westerly must be narrow, as shown by the figure.

8 a.m., 31st. Wind N.E. by E. ½ E., *15 miles per hour*, barometer 30·03, air 34°. The barometer rose very slightly, reaching 30·08 at 2 p.m., when a fall set in, which continued until 8 a.m., 1st February, at which time it was 29·69.

New York Observatory.
8 a.m. G.T. 31st.
To 8 a.m. G.T. 1st Feby.

The thermometer fell until, at 2 p.m. (the time of maximum barometer) it was 30°, and continued so until 8 a.m., 1st.

The wind gradually backed through N. to N.N.W. This again seems to show that an area of low pressure passed along the coast to the south-eastward of New York, and that it was nearest to that place at 8 a.m. 1st. See the Chart for that date.

NOTE.—It will be remarked throughout this paper that the speed of the wind at the New York Observatory does not indicate so great a force by Beaufort's scale as we get from ships in that port.

GENERAL REMARKS ON CHART FOR 8 A.M., GREENWICH TIME, JANUARY 31ST, 1870.

The logs of 30 ships have been consulted.

A strong southerly wind is still blowing at several stations in the British Isles, and a S.E. gale at Shetland, whilst there is a fresh breeze from the same quarter in Norway.

In Iceland there is a southerly gale, and the barometer has fallen slightly.

In Cumberland Sound there is a light S.W. wind.

At Heart's Content and St. John's Newfoundland, at 0.30 p.m., the wind is N.W. and calm, with a great difference between their barometers. As a rule, there is very little agreement between the observations at these places; they seem to be affected by local circumstances.

At Terceira the wind is light S.W., and at Madeira there is a light westerly air.

By referring to the Quarterly Weather Report for this period, Plate VII., which contains January 31st and February 1st, shows that a wave of high pressure passed all the self-registering instruments, affecting the more westerly stations first.

This wave seems to be the same which lies to the westward of Ireland on our 8 a.m. Chart; with it the wind veered more westerly at all stations and ships, backing again after the passage of its crest.

Diagram 4 gives a section of it as experienced by No. 39 on the 31st.

We have, therefore, three different representations of this wave of higher pressure, viz., Plate VII. in the Quarterly Weather Report, Diagram 4, and our Chart; and it seems clear that the southerly wind on the western side of its crest, experienced by No. 10 in about 28° W. at 8 a.m., Greenwich Time, of the 31st, was blowing at Valencia by midnight of the same date, so that it probably travelled nearly 40 miles an hour. We may suppose it to have been a mere undulation, but carrying with it a change of temperature, pressure, and corresponding winds, in accordance with Buys Ballot's law.

By a rough estimate of the hours at which the crest of this wave passed the various self-registering observatories, we are led to suppose that it had a north-easterly track of nearly 40 miles an hour over the land.

Since 8 a.m. of the 30th, the system of wind, which then prevailed round an area of low pressure in about 20° W., seems to have travelled to the north-eastward. (See the 8 a.m. Charts of the 30th and 31st.)

The isobars on this day's Chart seem to show that there is a wave of low pressure extending from the west coast of Ireland to the west coast of Iceland, which deepens as it extends to the north-westward, and somewhat resembles the figure on page 24.

At the same time the very deep and sudden wave of low pressure experienced on the 30th by so many ships to the S.W. of Newfoundland, and also at Heart's Content, has passed to the north-eastward.

Then, again, the most westerly ships, in the later extracts from their logs, show signs of another wave or area of low pressure travelling to the eastward. It is not exhibited on the Chart, because it appeared later in the day. See the remark accompanying the extract from the log of No. 38, showing what was taking place at 4.20 a.m. of the 1st.

Extracts and Remarks to accompany the Chart for February 1st, 1870.

A fresh southerly wind, amounting to a gale at some stations, still prevails on the western coasts of these islands, having continued for four days.

8 a.m. Wind W.S.W., 4; barometer 30·16, falling.

8 p.m. A fresh gale, no direction given, but apparently from the south-westward; very heavy rain with a high sea. Ship put her stern under water suddenly, after which she was lying-to under a close-reefed main topsail.

No. 50.
S.S. "Hotspur."
In { 44° 48' N.
     8° 54 W.
     8 a.m. G.T. 1st.
Bound South.
To { 44° 8' N.
     9° 6' W.
     8 a.m. G.T. 2nd.

8 a.m. More moderate from W.S.W.; had been a strong increasing gale from south-westward.

2 p.m. Unsteady breeze, with hail showers; barometer gradually falling.

7 a.m., 2nd. Moderate southerly wind, with heavy westerly swell; barometer 29·11.

No. 2.
S.S. City of Cork."
In { 51° 33' N.
     12° 37' W.
     8 a.m. G.T. 1st.
Bound Westerly.
To { 51° 30' N.
     17° 8' W.
     8 a.m. G.T. 2nd.

No. 5.
S.S. "North American."
In { 55° 9' N.
      15° 6' W.
      8 a.m. G.T. 1st.
Bound East.
To { 55° 25' N.
     7° 9' W.
     8 a.m. G.T. 2nd.

8 a.m. Fresh south-easterly gale, high sea getting up; barometer 29·10, and falling ·05 per hour.
9 a.m. Increasing gale.
11 a.m. Wind shifted suddenly to S.W., with strong breeze; barometer at its lowest 29·00.
3 p.m. Strong S.W. breeze and clear weather; barometer 29·07, rising.
1.30 a.m. of 2nd. Wind S., fresh, with mild pleasant weather; barometer 29·35.
No. 3 seems to have first experienced a S.E. wind on the N.E. side of an area of low pressure, and then the S.W. wind on its south-eastern side, indicating that it swept over her on its north-eastern route. These small areas of low pressure seem common to the westward of Ireland.

No. 54.
S.S. "Bremen."
In { 49° 13' N.
      17° 36' W.
      8 a.m. G.T. 1st.
Bound Easterly.
To { 49° 42' N.
     10° 28' W.
     8 a.m. G.T. 2nd.

8 a.m. Wind W.S.W., 5; barometer 29·51, falling slightly.
5 a.m. of 2nd. Wind S.S.W., 3, with rain; barometer 29·55, steady.
Her easterly course seems to have caused the barometer to remain steady with a southerly wind.

No. 29.
"Chatillon."
In { 32° 52' N.
      17° 43' W.
      8 a.m. 1st.
Bound S.S.Wly.
To { 32° 7' N.
     18° 36' W.
     8 a.m. 2nd.

8 a.m. Wind N., 3; fine, sea smooth. No further entry for the 24 hours.

No. 14.
S.S. "Europa."
In { 53° 54' N.
      19° 54' W.
      8 a.m. G.T. 1st.
Bound E. by Nly.
To { 54° 57' N.
     12° 40' W.
     8 a.m. G.T. 2nd.

8 a.m. Wind W.S.W., 4, moderate with showers; barometer 29·1, rising slightly, but only read to tenths.
7 p.m. Wind S.W. by S., 5, showers; barometer 29·2.
2 a.m., 2nd. S. by W., 5; barometer 29·2, heavy westerly swell.
No. 14 seems to have steamed into a more southerly wind as she closed with the land, and her barometer *rose*.

No. 39.
S.S. "Westphalia."
In { 49° 6' N.
      20° 55' W.
      8 a.m. G.T. 1st.
Bound West.
To { 49° 3' N.
     25° 11' W.
     8 a.m. G.T. 2nd.

8 a.m. Wind W., 8; squally, frequent lightning in E., high wild sea; barometer 29·39 and falling.
5.30 p.m. Wind W., 10 to 11; very heavy rain squalls; barometer 29·26.
9.30 p.m. W. by S., 11, a hurricane, sea very high and wild; barometer 29·15.
1.30 a.m., 2nd. W., 10; lightning in S.W. and N.W.; a bright aurora. Lowest barometer 29·12.
See Diagram 4 for the continuous record of this ship's observations.

8 a.m. S.W. by W., 8; heavy squalls, with passing showers and heavy head sea; barometer 29·18, fallen.
4 p.m. W. by N., 8; ditto weather and sea.
6 p.m. N.W. by N., 7; barometer steady.
6 a.m., 2nd. N.W. by N., 7; barometer 29·55 rising.
At 4 p.m. No. 4 seems to have got the north-westerly wind, which the Chart shows to have been blowing to the westward of her at 8 a.m.

No. 4.
S.S. "Prussian."
In $\begin{cases} 52° 45' \text{ N.} \\ 27° 33' \text{ W.} \\ 8 \text{ a.m. G.T. 1st.} \end{cases}$
Bound W. by Sly.
To $\begin{cases} 51° 30' \text{ N.} \\ 32° 5' \text{ W.} \\ 8 \text{ a.m. G.T. 2nd.} \end{cases}$

8 a.m. W. by S., hard gale, with violent squalls and very high sea. Shipped a sea which carried away the chocks from under the four forward boats, and stove Nos. 8 and 5. Barometer 29·15, falling.
2 p.m. Ditto wind and weather with hail and rain, a very high sea; barometer falling slightly.
6 p.m. W. by N., heavy gale, with same weather; barometer fallen ·16 in 4 hours, and at its lowest.
Midnight. N.W. by W., heavy gale; barometer rising.
2 a.m., 2nd., gale slightly moderating; barometer rising.
No. 17 seems to have had stronger winds than No. 4., a ship about 3° north of her.

No. 17.
S.S. "Helvetia."
In $\begin{cases} 49° 48' \text{ N.} \\ 28° 14' \text{ W.} \\ 8 \text{ a.m. G.T. 1st.} \end{cases}$
Bound W. by S. slowly.
To $\begin{cases} 49° 16' \text{ N.} \\ 30° 4' \text{ W.} \\ 8 \text{ a.m. G.T. 2nd.} \end{cases}$

8 a.m., increasing gale from W. by S., high breaking sea, filling decks fore and aft.
4 p.m. Shipped a heavy sea on port beam, doing much damage.
10 p.m. Tremendously heavy gale, still W. by S., and high breaking sea.
No. 10 seems to have also had the gale stronger than No. 4, a ship more than 3° north of her.

No. 10.
S.S. "Manhattan."
In $\begin{cases} 48° 57' \text{ N.} \\ 31° 13' \text{ W.} \\ 8 \text{ a.m. G.T. 1st.} \end{cases}$
Bound S.Wly. very slow.
To $\begin{cases} 48° 7' \text{ N.} \\ 32° 22' \text{ W.} \\ 8 \text{ a.m. G.T. 2nd.} \end{cases}$

8 a.m. Strong gale W. by S., with heavy squalls and sea.
2 p.m. In 49° 22' N. and 32° 46' W., strong gale W. by S., with very heavy squalls; barometer (29·22) falling slightly.
6 p.m. Gale abating, with very high sea; barometer falling.
10 p.m. W. by N., squally, with less sea; barometer (29·23) rising.
2 a.m., 2nd. W. by N. More moderate; sea going down.
6 a.m. N.W. by W., fresh gale with heavy squalls; barometer 29·45 and rising.
This rising barometer and shift to N.W. looks as if she experienced the western bank of a wave of low pressure passing to the eastward faster than she was steaming.

No. 48.
S.S. "Calabria."
In $\begin{cases} 48° 47' \text{ N.} \\ 34° 44' \text{ W.} \\ 8 \text{ a.m. G.T. 1st.} \end{cases}$
Bound Ely.
To $\begin{cases} 49° 14' \text{ N.} \\ 25° 54 \text{ W.} \\ 8 \text{ a.m. G.T. 2nd.} \end{cases}$

No. 45.
Ship "Carl Georg."
In { 41° 25′ N.
36° 10′ W.
8 a.m. G.T. 1st.
Bound E.N.Ely.
To { 43° 9′ N.
32° 36′ W.
8 a.m. G.T. 2nd.

8 a.m. West, 7; barometer 30·14, falling.
2.20 p.m. West, 7; barometer 29·98; violent increasing wind and high wild sea.
10.20 p.m. N.W., 9; barometer 30·16.
6.20 a.m., 2nd. N.W., 10; barometer 30·12.

No. 11.
S.S. "Iowa,"
In { 49° 24′ N.
36° 38′ W.
8 a.m. G.T. 1st.
Bound W.S.W. very slowly.
To { 48° 58′ N.
37° 45′ W.
8 a.m. G.T. 2nd.

8 a.m. Heavy gale from W. by S., with heavy sea running, hail and rain squalls.
3.30 p.m. W. by N., heavy gale.
6.30 p.m. N.W. by W., heavy gale.
8.30 p.m. N.W. by N., moderating, squalls less violent; went on "half speed."
4.30 a.m., 2nd. N.W. by N. to N.W. by W., moderate and gloomy.

No. 11 seems to have been nearly stationary for two days, and to have experienced a very heavy gale, gradually shifting from W.S.W. to N.W. by N.

No. 55.
S.S. "Rhein."
In { 46° 49′ N.
42° 0′ W.
8 a.m. G.T. 1st.
Bound W. by Sly.
To { 45° 53′ N.
46° 55′ W.
8 a.m. G.T. 2nd.

8 a.m. W.N.W., 9. Barometer 29·79, rising.
3 p.m. in 46° 38′ N. 42° 18′ W., N.W., 8; barometer 30·04, rising, wind and sea decreasing.
7 p.m. N.W., 5; barometer 30·20, rising.
11 p.m. W.N.W., 5; barometer 30·23. Wind drawing southerly.
3 a.m., 2nd. S.E., 5; barometer 29·87, falling rapidly. In 46° 6′ N., 45° 38′ W.
7 a.m., S.E., 5 to 7. Barometer 29·27. Heavy rain.

No. 55 seems to have got the southerly wind about seven hours sooner than No. 11. She also got the moderating of the north-westerly gale about six hours before No. 11, indicating an easterly movement in the weather. Nos. 26 and 52, far to the S.W. of No. 55, had a southerly wind and falling barometer at 8 a.m. of this day. (See Chart for February 1st.) This was most probably the same which No. 55 experienced at 7 a.m. of the 2nd? Diagram 1 seems to show that at midnight G.T. (8 p.m. local time) of the 31st No. 37 was just entering the northern part of the depression which was the nucleus of this system of wind, she got easterly and north-easterly winds, whilst ships to the southward and eastward had them south-easterly and south-westerly.

No. 30.
H.M.S. "Orontes."
In { 43° 52′ N.
43° 57′ W.
8 a.m. G.T. 1st.
Bound E.N.Ely.
To { 45° 39′ N.
39° 32′ W.
8 a.m. G.T. 2nd.

8 a.m. N.W. by N., 5; barometer 30·16, rising; fine weather.
6.45 p.m. N. by W., 3; barometer 30·24, steady; fine weather.
10.45 p.m. Calm, barometer 30·25, steady; fine weather.
4.45 a.m., 2nd. S.E. by S., 2; barometer falling, overcast with rain.
6.45 a.m. S.E. by S., 6; barometer 29·90, falling; overcast, squally, with thunder.

47

No. 30 seems to have had less force in the north-westerly wind than No. 55, and she was 3° S. of her at 8 a.m.

8 a.m. Light N.N.W. airs and gloomy; heavy north-westerly sea, barometer falling.
9 a.m. Light N.N.W. breeze and gloomy.
4 p.m. Light E.N.E. wind and gloomy; barometer fallen ·3 in 12 hours.
8 p.m. Moderate E.S.E. wind, with drizzling rain.
11 p.m. Moderate S.E. wind.
3 a.m., 2nd. Strong S.E. breeze and cloudy.
4 a.m. Fresh S.S.W. breeze and cloudy.

No. 25.
S.S. "Cuban."
In { 40° 7' N.
44° 2' W.
8 a.m. G.T. 1st.
Bound E. by Nly.
To { 41° 21' N.
39° 39' W.
8 a.m. G.T. 2nd.

No. 25 is nearly 4° due S. of No. 30, and keeps in the same longitude throughout the 24 hours, but increases the difference of latitude a little. She seems to get the changes before No. 30, indicating a northerly movement in the system of weather.

8 a.m. West-north-westerly strong wind, heavy sea; barometer 30·14, rising.
3 p.m., in 46° 2' N., 44° 41' W. Fresh north-westerly wind, and fine, clear weather.
4 p.m. N.W. by N., moderate and fine, heavy north-westerly sea.
10 p.m. Easterly, light and cloudy.
11 p.m. Easterly, light and cloudy; exchanged signals with a German steamer, (most probably No. 55,) which ship got the wind drawing southerly with a falling barometer at the same hour.
3 a.m., 2nd. E. by S., fresh breeze and cloudy; barometer falling.
4 a.m. S.E. by E., fresh breeze and gloomy; barometer falling.
7 a.m. S.E. by E., increasing gale and thick drizzling weather; barometer fallen ·5 in four hours.

No. 20.
S.S. "The Queen."
In { 45° 39' N.
46° 17' W.
8 a.m. G.T. 1st.
Bound E.N.Ely.
To { 47° 9' N.
41° 8' W.
8 a.m. G.T. 2nd.

No. 20 seems to have had the decreasing N.W. wind, and shift to the eastward much earlier than 55, indicating a north-easterly motion in the system of weather.

8.20 a.m. Light S. by E. wind, barometer 30·19.
2.15 p.m. Brisk S. by W. wind and fine; barometer fallen slightly.
11.15 p.m. Strong S. by W. breeze and gloomy; barometer 30·08
4.15 a.m., 2nd. Moderate S.W. gale and thick weather.

No. 26.
S.S. "Venezuelan."
In { 35° 58' N.
49° 24' W.
8 a.m. G.T. 1st.
Bound N.Ely.
To { 38° 35' N.
45° 32' W.
8 a.m. G.T. 2nd.

No. 26 was several degrees S.W. of Nos. 20 and 25. She had the south-easterly wind some time before them.

No. 49.
S.S. "Marathon."
In { 44° 36′ N.
50° 9′ W.
8 a.m. G.T. 1st.
Bound E.N.Ely.
To { 46° 19′ N.
44° 55′ W.
8 a.m. G.T. 2nd.

8 a.m. W. by S., moderate and gloomy; barometer 30·00.
11.40 a.m. Variable and cloudy.
7.20 p.m. Fresh breeze and overcast.
9.10 p.m. South-easterly fresh breeze and overcast.
11.10 p.m. Brisk south-easterly gale with heavy **southerly sea.** Shipping heavy water; barometer 29·42.
4.10 a.m., 2nd. Strong S.W. by W. gale. Heavy southerly sea.
No. 49 got the south-easterly wind some hours before No. 20, which ship was east of her and bound the same way.

No. 46.
S.S. "Nemesis."
In { 44° 35′ N.
53° 23′ W.
8 a.m. G.T. 1st.
Bound W. by Sly.
To { 43° 7′ N.
57° 24′ W.
8 a.m. G.T. 2nd.

8 a.m. W. by N. Moderate breeze and fine.
9.30 a.m. E.S.E., apparently moderate.
1.40 p.m. Increasing east-south-easterly breeze with snow; barometer falling.
4.40 p.m. Moderate east-south-easterly gale, with heavy squalls, rain, and an increasing sea.
9.40 p.m. Wind variable.
11.40 p.m. W.S.W. Fresh breeze. A south-east swell with heavy rain; barometer 29·61.
3.40 a.m., 2nd. Strong W. gale and squally; heavy confused south-west and north-west sea.
7.40 a.m. Strong W. gale and squally; heavy confused south-west and north-west sea.
No. 46 had the changes before No. 49, which ship was to the eastward of her.

No. 53.
S.S. "Weser."
In { 42° 6′ N.
57° 51′ W.
8 a.m. G.T. 1st.
Bound E.N.Ely.
To { 44° 13′ N.
51° 56′ W.
8 a.m. G.T. 2nd.

8 a.m. E.N.E., 5.
3.44 p.m. S.E., 8; in 42° 36′ N., 56° 5′ W.; barometer 29·64, fallen ·24 in 4 hours. High sea.
7.44 p.m. South, 8; barometer 29·38, fallen ·26 in four hours. Less sea.
11.44 p.m. S.S.W., 7; barometer 29·26, fallen.
3.44 a.m., 2nd. West, 4; barometer 29·33, rising. High east-north-east sea.
7.44 a.m. West, 8; barometer 29·43, rising. Less sea.
No. 53 had the easterly wind before No. 46, which ship was to the eastward of her. See Diagram 2 for a continuous record of this ship's data. By comparing Diagrams 1 and 2 it seems clear that the lowest pressure of the area of low pressure (of which both show a section on

February 1st) passed between Nos. 37 and 53, for the former had a backing, whilst the latter had a veering wind. It will be seen that No. 37, the most westerly ship, had the lowest pressure at noon (local time), whilst No. 53 had it at 8 p.m. (local time). These Diagrams run in opposite directions, one ship being outward, the other homeward bound.

Supposing the lowest pressure to have travelled from the one to the other in this time, it must have had a speed of 63 miles an hour, but as these vessels were N.W. and S.E. of each other, and the lowest pressure passed to the southward of No. 37 and to the northward of No. 53, it is most probable that the southern part of the wave of low pressure was not very far from 53 when its northern part was passing No. 37.

The S.E. wind which came upon No. 53 at about 4 p.m. of the 1st, in lat. 42° 36′ N. long. 56° 5′ W., seems to have reached No. 55 at about 3 a.m. of the 2nd, in lat. 46° 0′ N. 45° 38′ W., giving a speed to the E.N.E. of about 45 miles an hour. As the entries of wind in the logs sometimes relate to the previous four hours, and at others only give the direction and force of wind which exists at the time of entry, it is very difficult to calculate the speed of these waves, but there seems to be no doubt that they go fast to the eastward.

8 a.m. Variable, 7. A very heavy cross sea, engine going slow.	No. 12. S.S. "Dacian."
11 a.m. S.W., 8. Set close-reefed square canvas.	In { 40° 56′ N. 58° 13′ W. 8 a.m. G.T. 1st.
11.40 p.m. West, 8. Strong gale and clear with very high sea.	Bound E. by Nly.
4.40 a.m., 2nd. N.W., 8. Moderate N.W. gale and very high sea.	To { 41° 43′ N. 53° 51′ W. 8 a.m. G.T. 2nd.
No readings of instruments are given.	

By referring to the extract from No. 12 for the 31st it will be seen that at 5 a.m. she had the wind E., 6; so that during the following 24 hours a wave of low pressure, having its point of lowest pressure to the northward, must have passed over her from a westerly towards an easterly direction to bring about the changes of wind which she experienced.

	Air.	Bar.	Sea.	
10 a.m. E. by N. Strong increasing breeze	41°	29·91	54°	No. 1. S.S. "City of Antwerp."
Noon. East. Fresh gale with heavy head sea	42	29·81	53	In { 41° 42′ N. 58° 59′ W. 8 a.m. G.T. 1st.
2 p.m. E.S.E. Strong gale with heavy head sea	45	29·67	55	Bound E.N.Ely.
4.45 p.m. East (? S.E.) Strong gale with heavy head sea. 42° 25′ N. 57° 9′ W.	56	29·33	56	To { 43° 49′ N. 53° 4′ W. 8 a.m. G.T. 2nd.
7.45 p.m. South. Moderate breeze, heavy head sea	56	29·28	57	
9.45 p.m. South. Increasing breeze	55	29·23	56	

	Air.	Bar.	Sea.

10.45 p.m. S.S.W. Increasing breeze, 42° 59' N. 55° 31' W. - - - - - - 54° 29·31 52°

7.45 a.m., 2nd. W. by S. Fresh breeze, sea going down - - - - - - - 42 29·46 38

No. 1 (to the north of No. 12) did not get the shift to N.W. so early as No. 12. This indicates a northerly tendency in the track of the weather. Notice how the temperature of the sea fell 14° in nine hours. In the case of No. 1 the gradient for an easterly wind seems to have been steeper than that for a westerly, judging by the relative forces of those winds.

Note.—From this time more positions and instrumental readings will be given, in case the reader may wish to trace the progress of any change. The 8 a.m. position of the given day is entered in the margin, so will not be repeated with the extract for that hour.

No. 22.
S.S. "Pennsylvania."
In { 43° 0' N.
    59° 11' W.
    8 a.m. G.T. 1st.
Bound W. by Sly.
To { 42 31' N.
    61 42' W.
    8 a.m. G.T. 2nd.

	Air.	Bar.	Sea.

8 a.m. Wind N.E. Freshening breeze with heavy rain - - - - - - - 46° 29·58 52°

Noon. E.S.E. Strong wind and dirty appearances 52 29·31 52

4 p.m. E.S.E. Fresh gale and rain, high sea (42° 50' N. 60° 49' W.) - - - - 53 29·17 52

9 p.m. W. by S. Strong gale and terrific hail squalls - - - - - - - 50 29·17 53   at 8 p.m.

Midnight. W. by N. Ditto Ditto - - 49 29·27 51

4 a.m., 2nd. N. by W. Gale began to moderate - 46 29·47 50

No. 22 was to the westward of No. 1 and going west, whilst the latter ship was going east. She had the changes of barometer and wind before that ship.

No. 13.
S.S. "India."
In { 42° 0' N.
    59° 55' W.
    8 a.m. G.T. 1st.
Bound E.N.Ely.
To { 43° 55' N.
    54° 47' W.
    8 a.m. G.T. 2nd.

8 a.m. E.N.E. Fresh breeze and gloomy with drizzle, barometer ? 29·94.

Noon. E.N.E. Strong breeze, squally with rain; barometer ? 29·56.

5 p.m. E. by S. Strong breeze, dark and hazy, 42° 33' N., 58° 10' W., barometer ? 29·41 at 4 p.m.

8 p.m. S.E. Strong breeze; barometer ? 29·21.

10 p.m. S.S.E. Set close-reefed topsails. At 10.50 p.m. barometer ? 29·11.

1 a.m., 2nd. S.W. Barometer rising.

5 a.m. West. Moderate gale, squally and gloomy; barometer rising.

No. 13 commenced to the westward and ended to the eastward of No. 22, and it will be seen that she kept the south-easterly wind longer, and got the shift to the westward and lowest barometer later, indicating that she travelled with the area of low pressure.

	Air.	Bar.	Sea.		No. 21. S.S. "Denmark."
8 a.m. East. Fresh breeze, rain and cloudy, heavy easterly sea - - - - - - -	40°	? 29·93	42°	In	42° 34′ N. 61° 14′ W. 8 a.m. G.T. 1st. Bound E. by Nly.
11 a.m. East. Fresh gale with rain and high head sea - - - - - - -	41	? 29·73 at noon.	42		
4 p.m. E.S.E. In 43° 0′ N. 59° 54′ W. - -	43	? 29·47	42	To	43° 54′ N. 56° 6′ W. 8 a.m. G.T. 2nd.
5.30 p.m. Wind veering south-westerly.		at 8 p.m.			
7 p.m. S.S.W. Fresh gale, high easterly sea	? 56	? 29·33	44		
10 p.m. S.W.					
4 a.m., 2nd. West. Fresh gale and clear, very heavy easterly sea; in 43° 27′ N. 58° 0′ W. - -	39	? 29·53	40		

At 10 p.m. No. 21 had the wind S.W., whilst No. 13 had it south-south-easterly, and 21 was a little to the westward, indicating the curvature of the wind round the area of lowest pressure.

	Air.	Bar.	Sea.		No. 37. S.S. "Austrian."
8 a.m. East, 6; showers of hail and sleet - -	33°	29·88	38°	In	43° 10′ N. 63° 26′ W. 8 a.m. G.T. 1st. Bound West.
Noon. E. by S., 7; moderate and fine, but hazy -	37	29·52	38		
4.20 p.m. N.E. by N., 5; thick rainy weather 43° 3′ N. 65° 35′ W. - - - - -	37	29·22	38	To	43° 27′ N. 69° 4′ W. 8 a.m. G.T. 2nd.
8.20 p.m. N.N.W., 7; strong breeze and cloudy -	30	29·40	38		
0.20 a.m., 2nd. N.W. by W., 7; strong breeze and squally, with short head sea - - - -	33	29·67	40		
4.20 a.m. N.W. by W., 7; strong breeze and clear, with short chopping sea, 43° 21′ N. 68° 23′ W. -	22	29·98	38		

No. 37 had the wind back from E. through N.E. and N. to N.W., indicating that the lowest pressure passed to the south of her, whilst it seems to have passed to the north of all the other ships which experienced it.

Mr. Allison, at Halifax, says, "February 1st. Heavy snowstorm, "with high wind, backing from S.E. to N.N.W. Faint aurora. Fall "of barometer from 8 p.m. (local time), 31st January to 4 p.m. (local "time) 1st of February 1·103 in."

It seems, then, that Halifax, like No. 37, had the wind back from S.E. to E., N.E. and N.W., indicating that a wave of low pressure passed to the north-eastward along the land, and that its point of lowest pressure passed to the southward of Halifax and No. 37.

See Diagram 1 for a continuous record of this ship's observations and for a section of the northern part of the area of low pressure. It will be noticed how much sharper the change of pressure was with No. 37 going west than with No. 53 going east. (See Diagram 2.)

No. 52.
S.S. "Delta."
In { 34° 1′ N.
      64° 36′ W.
      8 a.m. G.T. 1st.
Bound South.
To { 32° 29′ N.
     64° 50′ W.
     8 a.m. G.T. 2nd.

	Air.	Bar.	Sea.
8 a.m. S., 8; heavy south-east sea and rain	67°	29·71	67°
Noon. S.W., 8. Rain	68	29·61	67
4.20 p.m. S.W., 8; rain, in 33° 15′ N. 64° 40′ W.	65	29·81	67
8.20 p.m. W.N.W., 7. Fine	63	29·81	63
4.20 a.m., 2nd. W.N.W., 5. Fine	63	30·06	65

Here (at 8.20 p.m.) we have No. 52 to the southward of the area of low pressure, which she entered on the 31st.

In the remarks on No. 38 for January 31st allusion was made to her having a west-north-westerly gale at about 5 a.m. this day, when No. 52 was experiencing one from S.E. Now (at 8 a.m.) it will be seen that the one has a S. gale whilst the other has one from W.N.W. It seems quite clear that the area of low pressure to which these winds were related travelled to the north-eastward, and crossed rapidly over several ships in that direction before 24 hours had elapsed, causing a snowstorm at Halifax.

The following Bermuda observation has been received from General Lefroy. 4.20 p.m. G.T., bar. 29·86, wind S.W., 7. It agrees well with the observation of No. 52, taken at the same time. We are not sure that the barometer reading was corrected for temperature.

No. 16.
S.S. "City of London."
In { 40° 13′ N.
      70° 22′ W.
      8 a.m. G.T. 1st.
Bound West.
To { 40° 40′ N.
     74° 2′ W.
     8 a.m. G.T. 2nd.

	Air.	Bar.	Sea.
8 a.m. Light westerly wind, with mist and drizzle	47°	29·64	39°
8.40 a.m. W.N.W. Light, ditto	—	29·58	40
0.40 p.m. N.W. by N. Fresh breeze	—	29·58	42
4.50 p.m. N.W. by N. Strong breeze, in 40° 28′ N. 72° 45′ W.	40	29·71	42

8.50 p.m. Off Sandy Hook light, moderate north-westerly wind and clear.

The remarks on the 31st show that No. 16 had passed through a light southerly wind, changing to the westward. She does not seem to have had any bad weather from the area of low pressure to the southward of her at 8 a.m. of the 1st (see Chart), which indicates that it was *not* moving to the *north-westward*.

No. 3.
S.S. "Etna."
In { 42° 21′ N.
      71° 4′ W. (Boston).
      8 a.m. G.T. 1st.
Bound South.
To { 40° 34′ N.
     70° 50′ W.
     8 a.m. G.T. 2nd.

	Air.	Bar.	Sea.
8 a.m. N. by E. Fresh breeze. Heavy snow fell an hour previous	—	? 29·65	—
5.45 p.m. N.W. Strong breeze and clear, with a cross sea	—	fallen	—
5.45 a.m., 2nd. W. by N. Strong breeze and cloudy	30°	29·90	34°

No. 9.
S.S. "Colorado."
In New York 1st.

A light south-easterly wind, and hazy weather.

53

Fresh gale from N.W., and occasional showers of snow.   No. 18.
S.S. " Virginia.'
Nos. 9 and 18 were both in New York, and give diametrically opposite   In New York 1st.
winds, and very different weather! The remarks are very general, so
probably one gave the early and the other the latter part of the day.

8 a.m. Wind N.N.W., *11 miles per hour*.   New York Observatory.
8 a.m. G.T. 1st
Barometer 29·69, air 30°. The barometer gradually rose throughout   To 8 a.m. G.T. 2nd.
the 24 hours.

The thermometer rose to 36° at 8 p.m.; then gradually decreased to
23° at 5 a.m.

The wind continued north-westerly throughout, oscillating considerably.
Its velocity amounted to *27 miles per hour* from 6 to 9 p.m., after which
it decreased.

					Air.	Bar.	Sea.	
8 a.m.	W.N.W., 10	-	-	-	61°	29·64	62°	No. 38. Ship " Nicoline."
Noon.	W.N.W., 10.							In ⎰ 34° 13' N. ⎱ 74° 36' W.
5 p.m.	N.W., 8 to 7, in 34° 11' N. 74° 38' W.	-	53	29·95	66			8 a.m. G.T. 1st. Bound to New York.
9 p.m.	N.N.W., 6, 3. Cyclonic wind, with a clear sky	-	-	-	-	-	54	—	70	To ⎰ 34° 13' N. ⎱ 74° 54' W.
1 a.m., 2nd. Variable, 3. Wind and sea decreasing rapidly	-	-	-	-	-	53	30·18	69	8 a.m. G.T. 2nd.

This north-westerly wind did not reach No. 52 (a ship 10° to the
eastward) until between 4.20 and 8.20 p.m. At 8 a.m. she was
experiencing a southerly gale, giving good evidence that an area of low
pressure existed between her and No. 38.

The remark, "Cyclonic wind," at 9 p.m., shows that the captain
understood how the north-westerly wind he was then experiencing was
related to the same area of low pressure which had given him a southerly
wind some hours previous.

GENERAL REMARKS ON CHART FOR 8 A.M., GREENWICH TIME,
FEBRUARY 1ST, 1870.

The logs of 34 ships have been consulted.

The same order has been followed, commencing with the most easterly
ship.

The wind is still southerly in the British Isles, and south-easterly in
Norway and Iceland.

It is calm in Cumberland Sound, fresh northerly in Newfoundland at
0.30 p.m., westerly at Terceira, with a light west-south-westerly air at
Madeira. We have already given the remarks on the weather at Halifax
and Bermuda after the extracts from logs Nos. 37 and 52.

There is a great difference between the barometer readings at Heart's Content and St. John's, Newfoundland, at 0.30 p.m of this day. In some cases it seems quite impossible to believe that both are right.

The Chart for 8 a.m., Greenwich time, of the 31st January, shows a ridge of higher pressure to the westward of Ireland between 15° and 25° W. By referring to Plate VII., in the Quarterly Weather Report, it will be seen that this ridge passed Valencia about midnight 31st; Armagh about 3 a.m., 1st February; Glasgow about 9 a.m.; and Aberdeen about 10 a.m of the 1st. It reached Falmouth about 6 a.m, Stonyhurst at 10 a.m., and Kew at 11 a.m. of the 1st. In all cases, excepting Kew, the rising barometer was accompanied by a veering of the wind to the westward. The greatest extent of veer was at Valencia and Falmouth, but in all cases, except Kew, the wind backed again as the barometer fell. Diagram 3 shows two other slight ridges to the west of Ireland on the 3rd and 4th. Plate VII., Quarterly Weather Report, indicates that they were felt at the observatories. These facts point to an easterly or north-easterly movement in the weather changes.

It is interesting to notice how these undulations seem to sweep by, causing slight wind changes, but leaving the prevailing wind southerly over these islands, which seems to be related to a more permanent atmospherical depression in the centre of the Atlantic.

This day's Chart seems to show that the area of low pressure, which was south of Newfoundland on the 30th, had expanded or merged into the more permanent low pressure over the central part of the Atlantic, giving rise to one system of wind. At the same time there seems to have been a local eddy just to the west of Ireland, which, so far as the changes of wind indicated, was travelling to the north-eastward, and another wave coming forward in about 70° W., between New York and No. 52.*

On the coast of Portugal and near Madeira the wind is light northerly, and the barometer is higher at Madeira than at Gibraltar. This splitting, as it were, of the air on the coast of Portugal, part going to the north and part south, is not uncommon.

Between 20° and 40° W. all the ships seem to have experienced a strong westerly gale, gradually changing to N.W. and N. with most of them, the more westerly ships getting the changes first. The ships to the north

---

* Three or four isobars might have been drawn on the north-eastern side of this wave, using the barometers of Nos. 1 and 16 to the northward, and Nos. 26 and 52 to the southward. The isobars would run in a north-westerly and south-easterly direction. It would assist the reader if he were to pencil them on the Chart, for they show how the winds of Nos. 18 and 38 were blowing into the wave of low pressure on one side, whilst those of No. 52 and the ships to the N.N.E. of her were blowing into it on the other side.

of 50° N. do not seem to have had so much wind as those to the south. This westerly gale seems to have existed over 10° of latitude at the same time.

Between 40° and 50° W. the ships have a decreasing north-westerly wind with a rising barometer, excepting No. 26, which vessel has a light south-easterly wind. Between 8 a.m. of the 1st and 2nd all the others got a change to S.E., with a falling barometer, the change taking the south-westerly ships first.

Between 50° and 65° W., all the vessels excepting No. 37 had a change of wind from S.E. to S., and S.W., and some to N.W., indicating that a lower pressure than that experienced by each ship passed to the north of her. No. 37 had the change from E. to N.E., N., and N.W., indicating that a lower pressure passed to the south of her, and she was the most north-western ship. The figures already alluded to illustrate these changes.

Extracts and Remarks to accompany the Chart for February 2nd, 1870.

A fresh southerly wind, amounting to a gale at Holyhead, is still blowing over the British Isles and Western Europe, although, as we have already remarked, a ridge of higher pressure crossed over our self-registering observatories yesterday, causing a partial veering and backing in the wind. This merging of a transitory disturbance into the normal state of pressure and wind does not seem uncommon.

		Standard Instruments.		No. 50.
		Air.	Bar.	S.S. "Hotspur."
8 a.m.	W.S.W., 3. High westerly sea	51°	29·76	In { 44° 8′ N. / 9° 6′ W. / 8 a.m. G.T. 2nd.
Noon.	W., 3. Squally; high westerly sea. In 44° 3′ N., 9° 6′ W.	51	29·78	Bound South.
8 p.m.	S.W. by S., 2. Moderate breeze and passing squalls. High westerly sea	51·5	29·67	To { 42° 26′ N. / 9° 49′ W. / 8 a.m. G.T. 3rd.

		Air.	Bar.	Sea.	No. 54.
					S.S. "Bremen."
8 a.m.	South, 2.	48°	29·41	52°	In { 49° 42′ N. / 10° 28′ W. / 8 a.m. G.T. 2nd.
Midnight.	South, 2. Off Lizard	48	29·63	51	Bound East.
4 a.m., 3rd.	South, 2. Off Eddystone	48	29·68	50	To { 50° 10′ N. / 3° 40′ W. / 8 a.m. G.T. 3rd.

No. 54. Causes the barometer to rise with a south wind by steaming to the eastward, but she does not get the baffling wind experienced by No. 14 to the westward of Ireland. See the next extract.

No. 14.
S.S. "Europa."
In { 54° 57' N.
12° 40' W.
8 a.m. G.T. 2nd.
Bound E.N.Ely.
To Rathlin Light 3rd.

8 a.m. Southerly, 4. A heavy westerly swell.
9 a.m. Light baffling south-easterly winds; barometer rising.
Midnight. Ditto.
No. 14 experienced the usual unsettled wind which seems to exist to the westward of Ireland. It will be noticed that her barometer was also rising with a southerly wind, and she was bound to the eastward.

No. 2.
S.S. "City of Cork."
In { 51° 30' N.
17° 8' W.
8 a.m. G.T. 2nd.
Bound West.
To { 51° 15' N.
22° 2' W.
8 a.m. G.T. 3rd.

	Air.	Bar.	Sea.
8 a.m. S. by W. Moderate breeze, decreasing	49°	29·10	48°
9 a.m. N.W. by N. Light airs.			
11 a.m. N. by W. Light breeze	48	rising	47
3.15 p.m. N. by W. Fresh steady breeze and cloudy, with showers. In 51° 28' N., 18° 32' W.	49	29·30	48
1.15 a.m., 3rd. W. by S. Light wind, strong westerly swell	50	29·56	50
4.15 a.m. S.W. by S. Light breeze and overcast	50	falling	51

The changes in the wind indicate that No. 2 passed through a wave of low pressure, having its lowest pressure to the north of her, and at 4 a.m., 3rd., the wind was backing as another approached her. It will be seen how Nos. 2 and 14, as well as Valencia, seem to have felt the heavy westerly swell of the wind blowing at No. 39.

No. 29.
Ship "Chatillon."
In { 32° 7' N.
18° 36' W.
8 a.m. 2nd.
Bound S.S.Wly.
To { 31° 5' N.
19° 13' W.
8 a.m. 3rd.

The only entry is "Calm."

No. 29 is near Madeira, where it is also calm.

No. 39.
S.S. "Westphalia."
In { 49° 3' N.
25° 11' W.
8 a.m. G.T. 2nd.
Bound West.
To { 48° 58' N.
29° 52' W.
8 a.m. G.T. 3rd.

	Air.	Bar.	Sea.
8 a.m. W.N.W., 10	50°	29·32	50°
1.45 p.m. N.W., 10 to 9. In 49° 3' N. and 26° 5' W.	53	29·68	51
5.45 p.m. N.W., 6 to 2	53	29·70	52
9.45 p.m. S.W., 5	52	29·58	53
1.45 a.m., 3rd. S.W., 9. In 49° 0' N., 28° 37' W.	54	29·29	53
5.45 a.m. W., 9	53	29·39	50

No. 39 seems to have experienced the changes of wind and barometer belonging to the western side of one wave of low pressure and the eastern side of another, as they passed over her to the eastward, or she through them to the westward. The Chart shows that the area of low pressure alluded to was to the W. of 35° W. at 8 a.m. See Diagram 4 for sections of these waves.

	Air.	Bar.	Sea.	
8 a.m. N.W. by W. Fresh gale and heavy squalls	49°	29·42	54°	No. 48. S.S. "Calabria." In { 49° 14' N. 25° 54' W. 8 a.m. G.T. 2nd. Bound Easterly. To { 50° 15' N. 17° 4' W. 8 a.m. G.T. 3rd.
1.30 p.m. Fresh N.W. by W. gale and squally, sea going down. 49° 12' N., 23° 37' W.	50	29·85	53	
2.30 p.m. W. by S. Ditto weather.	—	falling	—	
5.30 p.m. W. by S. Fresh breeze.	51	29·55	52	
9.30 p.m. N.W. by N. Moderate and fine.	50	29·85	52	
2.30 a.m., 3rd. South-westerly; light wind and cloudy.				

No. 48 passed about 1½ degree south of No. 2 about 3 a.m. of the 3rd, when they experienced similar weather. It will be noticed (p. 67) that at 10.12 a.m. *of the* 3*rd* No. 2 had a sudden shift to N.W. with rain, freshening into a strong gale and high sea, now it will be seen (p. 56) that she felt the sea of this gale at 1.15 a.m. of the 3rd. This north-west gale seems to have been the same as that out of which No. 48 had steamed on her eastern route. No. 39 seems to have steamed out of the same gale on her westerly route, but only to go into another wave of low pressure, with the wind backing to the southward.

	Air.	Bar.	Sea.	
8 a.m. N.W. by W. Strong gale and heavy cross sea.	52°	29·57	56°	No. 17. S.S. "Helvetia." In { 49° 16' N. 30° 4' W. 8 a.m. G.T. 2nd. Bound West. To { 48° 51' N. 33° 0' W. 8 a.m. G.T. 3rd.
10 a.m. N. by W. Strong breeze.	52	29·65	56	
2 p.m. South-westerly. Light, with cross sea. 49° 8' N., 30° 30' W.	51	29·79	56	
6 p.m. S. by W. Strong breeze and thick weather.	51	29·45	55	
11 p.m. W. by S. Fresh gale and fine.	—	about 29·30	—	
2 a.m., 3rd. W. by N. Strong head gale with heavy squalls and sea.	—	rising	—	

No. 17 seems to have got the changes of wind before No. 39, a vessel about 5° to the eastward, and steaming after her.

	Air.	Bar.	Sea.	
8 a.m. N.W. by N., 7. Heavy westerly and cross sea, heavy squalls and hail showers.	—	29·08	—	No. 4. S.S. "Prussian." In { 51° 30' N. 32° 5' W. 8 a.m. G.T. 2nd. Bound West. To { 50° 28' N. 36° 12' W. 8 a.m. G.T. 3rd.
Noon. Variable, 5.				
2.15 p.m. S.E. by S., 5. In 51° 8' N., 33° 12' W.	51°	29·76	50°	
10.15 p.m. S.W. by W., 7. Heavy squalls with rain.	—	lowest 29·25	—	

		Air.	Bar.	Sea.

1.15 a.m., 3rd. W. by S., 7. Heavy squalls with hail showers. - - - - - - 51° 29·32 —

3.15 a.m. W. by S., 9 to 10. Heavy squalls and showers of hail. Heavy westerly sea.

No. 4 was 2° north of No. 17, and No. 17 does not seem to have had a south-east wind at all, for with her it only backed to S. by W. The lowest pressure seems to have passed north of each ship, but nearest to No. 4.

By considering the 8 a.m. Chart, it will be seen that the south-east wind was then S.W. of No. 4, indicating the north-easterly route of the area of low pressure.

No. 10.
S.S. "Manhattan."
In { 48° 7' N.
     32° 22' W.
     8 a.m. G.T. 2nd.
Bound W.S.Wly.
To { 47° 20' N.
     34° 20' W.
     8 a.m. G.T. 3rd.

8 a.m. W. by N., 9. More moderate gale and cloudy.
2.10 p.m. Light S. by E. breeze. In 47° 53' N., 32° 31' W.
7.10 p.m. Strong S. by W. wind, veering to the westward.
10.10 p.m. W. by N. Unsteady, with rising westerly sea.
2.10 a.m., 3rd. Strong west gale, with heavy westerly sea.
6.10 a.m. Blowing harder, with heavy head sea.

At 3 a.m. of the 3rd, Nos. 17, 4, and 10, after having had a shift of wind to south, seem to have been experiencing parts of the same westerly gale, which indicates that the area of low pressure, which was east of Newfoundland at 8 a.m. of the 2nd, had swept over them by 3 a.m. of the 3rd.

No. 45.
"Carl Georg."
In { 43° 9' N.
     32° 36' W.
     8 a.m. G.T. 2nd.
Bound E.N.Ely.
To { 44° 32' N.
     29° 6' W.
     8 a.m. G.T. 3rd.

	Air.	Bar.	Sea.

8 a.m. N.W., 10. Heavy north-west gale; barometer oscillating. - - - - - — 30·12 —

2 p.m. N.W., 10. Kept before the wind; barometer oscillating. In 43° 36' N., 31° 34' W. - - 59° 30·07 —

6 p.m., N.W., 9. Kept before the wind. - - 58 30·22 —

6 a.m., 3rd. N. W., 9.

No. 45 seems to have kept company with the north-west gale as it travelled to the eastward, and not to have got the shift to S., which Nos. 17, 4, and 10 had. The high barometer of No. 45 is worthy of notice, whilst she had the hardest gale of the four ships in nearly the same longitude. It is clear that their winds are all related to the same barometrical gradient, and she, being the most southern ship, has the highest barometer, where the gradient is probably in this case a little steeper than with the more northern ships.

59

	Air.	Bar.	Sea.	
8 a.m. Wind *had been* N.W. by W., moderate, but gloomy and threatening. *Now* variable.	48°	—	54°	No. 11. S.S. "Iowa." In { 48° 58′ N. 37° 45′ W. 8 a.m. G.T. 2nd.
10.30 a.m. S.E. by S. Weather looking very threatening.	48	—	54	Bound S.Wly. slow. To { 48° 4′ N. 38° 29′ W. 8 a.m. G.T. 3rd.
0.30 p.m. S.E. by S. Fresh gale and hazy with rain.				
2.30 p.m. S. by W. Double-reefed fore-and-afters set. In 48° 50′ N., 38° 15′ W.	50	—	54	
3.30 p.m. W. by S. Clearing up.				
9.30 p.m. West. Wind increasing, sea rising.				
0.30 a.m., 3rd. West. Strong gale with severe showers.	41	—	56	
6.30 a.m. W. by S. Strong gale and heavy showers.				

At 8 a.m., 2nd. No. 11 seems to have been on the verge of the shift to the south-eastward, which came to No. 4, a ship to the N.E. of her, about noon. The Chart shows No. 11 in the variables, between a N.W. and a S.E. gale, which were blowing very near each other.

	Air.	Aneroid Bar.	Sea.	
8 a.m. S.E. by S., 6. Overcast, squally with thunder.	50°	29·81	52°	No. 30. H.M.S. "Orontes." In { 45° 39′ N. 39° 32′ W. 8 a.m. G.T. 2nd.
1.50 p.m. S. by W. 5. Overcast, misty.	61	29·52	57	Bound E.N.Ely. To { 47° 23′ N. 33° 58′ W. 8 a.m. G.T. 3rd.
2.30 p.m. S. by W. 4 to 5. Overcast, misty. In 46° 14′ N. 38° 19′ W.	61	29·48	57	
4.30 p.m. S.W. by W., 4. Overcast, squally with rain.	58	29·47	64	
8.30 p.m. West, 5 to 6. Overcast.	60	29·50	59	
6.30 a.m., 3rd. West, 6 to 9. Squally, heavy west-north-west sea.	49	29·54	54	

No. 30 had the southerly wind before No. 11, indicating that the area of low pressure to which it was related was travelling to the northward.

	Air.	Bar.	Sea.	
8 a.m. S.S.W. Blowing strong.	?60°	30·13	—	No. 25. S.S. "Cuban." In { 41° 21′ N. 39° 39′ W. 8 a.m. G.T. 2nd.
2.30 p.m. South-westerly. Moderate gale. In 41° 41′ N., 38° 22′ W.	?60	30·17	—	Bound E. by Nly. To { 42° 26′ N. 34° 52′ W. 8 a.m G.T. 3rd.
0.30 a.m., 3rd. W.N.W. Weather clearing.				
6.30 a.m., W.N.W. gale. Hard squalls with rain, high sea.	?45	30·16	—	

No. 25 seems to have been on the south-eastern side of the area of low pressure, which caused No. 30 (on its north-eastern side) to have a south-easterly wind, whilst she had it south-westerly.

H 2

		Air.	Bar.	Sea.
No. 20. S.S. "The Queen." In { 47° 9' N. 41° 8' W. 8 a.m. G.T. 2nd. Bound E. by Nly. To { 48° 35' N. 35° 11' W. 8 a.m. G.T. 3rd.	8 a.m. Wind S.E. by E. Fresh gale. Split several sails. - - - - - - -	45°	29·74	45°
	1.30 p.m. S. by W. Strong wind and dark cloudy weather.			
	2.40 p.m. South-westerly. Strong wind. In 47° 34' N., 39° 47' W. - - - -	50	29·24	54
	3.40 p.m. S.W. by W. Strong wind and dark cloudy weather. - - - - -	—	rising	54
	3.40 a.m., 3rd. West by N. Strong gale with heavy hail squalls and high sea. - - - -	47	29·39	53

No. 20 was bound to the eastward, still the area of low pressure shown to the westward of her on the 8 a.m. Chart, swept over her in the course of the day, as proved by the changes of wind. This indicates that it went very quickly to the eastward.

		Air.	Bar.	Sea.
No. 49. S.S. "Marathon." In { 46° 19' N. 44° 55' W. 8 a.m. G.T. 2nd. Bound E.N.Ely. To { 48° 3' N. 38° 21' W. 8 a.m. G.T. 3rd.	8 a.m. Wind S.W. by W. Strong gale with heavy rain. - - - - - -	40°	29·18	47°
	3 p.m. Ditto. Fresh breeze, gloomy and overcast. In 46° 40' N., 43° 33' W. - - -	40	?29·21	41
	4 p.m. Ditto Strong gale, heavy westerly sea.			
	3 a.m., 3rd. Ditto, ditto Very high sea. -	41	29·27	43

The wind is dittoed S.W. by W. for 36 hours from 3 a.m. of the 2nd, and then W.S.W. for another 24 hours. It will be noticed that she was bound eastward with the weather changes.

No. 49 seems to have had the south-easterly wind which Nos. 20 and 30 were experiencing at 8 a.m. of the 2nd, between 9 and 11 p.m. of the 1st, and she was the most western ship.

		Air.	Bar.	Sea.
No. 26. S.S. "Venezuelan." In { 38° 35' N. 45° 32' W. 8 a.m. G.T. 2nd. Bound E.N.Ely. To { 41° 12' N. 41° 34' W. 8 a.m. G.T. 3rd.	8 a.m. Wind S.W. Moderate gale and cloudy. -	64°	30·00	—
	3 p.m. W.S.W. Brisk gale, thick and rainy. (Lat. 39° 32' N., long. 44° 18' W.) - - -	67	29·97	—
	11 p.m. N.W. Strong breeze. - - -	—	30·10	—
	7 a.m., 3rd. N.W. Strong breeze. - -	58	30·10	—

No. 26 like Nos. 25 and 45, being well to the south, has a comparatively high barometer, though she seems to be experiencing a gale.

The wave of low pressure which at 8 a.m. of 2nd had Nos. 20 and 30 on its eastern side had already partially swept over Nos. 49 and 26.

At 8 a.m. these ships were nearly 8° of latitude apart, but they were experiencing a similar gale.

61

		Air.	Bar.	Sea.	No. 55.
8 a.m.	Wind W., 5 to 7. Unsettled, stormy. -	44°	?29·31	46°	S.S. "Rhein."
3.15 p.m.	West, 7. Stormy. In 45°34′ N., 48°42′ W.	33	29·62	40	In { 45° 53′ N. / 46° 55′ W. / 8 a.m. G.T. 2nd.
7.15 p.m.	West, 7 to 8. High wild sea. - -	34	29·77	39	Bound W. by Sly.
3.15 a.m., 3rd.	West, 7. Ditto. - - -	34	30·03	43	To { 44° 38′ N. / 51° 28′ W. / 8 a.m. G.T. 3rd.

It will be remembered that No. 55 got the south-easterly wind (which at 8 a.m. was to the eastward of her) at about 3 a.m. Her winds do not seem to have been so strong as those experienced by other ships.

		Air.	Bar.	Sea.	No. 53.
8 a.m.	Wind W., 8. Sea decreasing. - -	40°	29·45	40°	S.S. "Weser."
3.20 p.m.	Wind W., 8. High west sea. In 44°56′ N., 50°1′ W. - - - -	36	29·68	36	In { 44° 13′ N. / 51° 56′ W. / 8 a.m. G.T. 2nd.
7.20 a.m., 3rd.	Wind W., 8. High south-west sea.	34	29·97	42	Bound E.N.Ely.
					To { 46° 15′ N. / 44° 36′ W. / 8 a.m. G.T. 3rd.

See Diagram 2 for the continuous record of the instruments, &c., on board No. 53. She seems to have had a westerly wind until the morning of the 5th, when it died away, with a falling barometer, just as she entered the area of extremely low pressure accompanying the gale of that day.

		Air.	Bar.	Sea.	No. 1.
8 a.m.	Wind W. by S. Fresh breeze, *easterly* sea going down. - - - - -	42°	29·48	38°	S.S. "City of Antwerp."
					In { 43° 49′ N. / 53° 4′ W. / 8 a.m. G.T. 2nd.
3.25 p.m.	Wind W.N.W. Strong gale and high westerly sea. In 44° 28′ N., 51° 8′ W. -	34	29·66	38	Bound E.N.Ely.
7.25 a.m., 3rd.	Wind W. Strong breeze and westerly sea. - - - - - -	33	30·04	35	To { 45° 56′ N. / 46° 8′ W. / 8 a.m. G.T. 3rd.

No. 1 remarks on the easterly sea, no doubt the effect of the easterly gale which had passed over her on the 1st.

					No. 12.
8 a.m.	Wind N.W., 8. Moderate gale and very high sea.				S.S. "Dacian."
3.30 p.m.	Wind N.W., 7. Moderate gale. In 41° 55′ N., 52° 17′ W.				In { 41° 43′ N. / 53° 51′ W. / 8 a.m. G.T. 2nd.
6.30 p.m.	Wind N.N.W., 6. More moderate.				Bound E. by Nly.
4.30 a.m., 3rd.	Wind N.N.W., 6. Strong wind and clear weather.				To { 42° 41′ N. / 49° 21′ W. / 8 a.m. G.T. 3rd.

It may be that the variation was not applied to the direction of this ship's wind, as stated to have been in her log. It certainly seems to be more northerly than might be expected.

62

		Bar.
No. 13. S.S. "India." In { 43° 55' N. 54° 47' W. 8 a.m. G.T. 2nd. Bound E.N.Ely. To { 46° 20' N. 48° 51' W. 8 a.m. G.T. 3rd.	8 a.m. Wind W. Moderate gale and squally gloomy weather. - - - - - - - 3.30 p.m. Wind W. Hard gale, squally, and high sea. In 44° 35' N., 53° 4' W. - - - - - 1.30 a.m., 3rd. Wind W.N.W. Strong breeze and high sea. - - - - - - - 5.30 a.m. Wind W.N.W. Fresh breeze and very cloudy. - - - - - - -	? 29·58 ? 29·82 Rising fast. ? 30·05

		Air.	Bar.	Sea.
No. 21. S.S. "Denmark." In { 43° 54' N. 56° 6' W. 8 a.m. G.T. 2nd. Bound E. by Nly. To { 45° 22' N. 50° 23' W. 8 a.m. G.T. 3rd.	8 a.m. Wind W., 8. Fresh gale and high sea. - 11.30 a.m. Wind W., 8. Tremendous high sea, immense seas breaking on board. 3.30 p.m. Wind W., 8. Fresh gale, very high sea. In 44° 20' N., 54° 10' W. - - - - - 11.30 p.m. Wind W.N.W. Strong breeze, with cloudy weather. 3.30 a.m., 3rd. Wind W.N.W. Fresh breeze and cloudy, all possible sail set. - - - - -	36° 32 31	? 29·81 ? 30·08 ? 30·20	39° 33 37

		Bar.
No. 46. S.S. "Nemesis." In { 43° 7' N. 57° 24' W. 8 a.m. G.T. 2nd. Bound W. by Sly. To { 41° 46' N. 62° 1' W. 8 a.m. G.T. 3rd.	8 a.m. Wind W., 8 to 9. Strong gale, squally, heavy confused sea. - - - - - - - 4 p.m. Wind W., 7. Heavy sea. In 42° 35' N., 58° 30' W. 5 p.m. Wind W.N.W. Moderate gale, heavy sea. 8 p.m. Wind W.N.W., 6. Strong wind, sea going down. - - - - - - - 4 a.m., 3rd. Wind W. Moderate breeze. - -	? 29·72 ? 29·95 — ? 30·05 ? 30·03

		Air.	Bar.	Sea.
No. 22. S.S. "Pennsylvania." In { 42° 31' N. 61° 42' W. 8 a.m. G.T. 2nd. Bound W. by Sly. To { 41° 42' N. 64° 52' W. 8 a.m. G.T. 3rd.	8 a.m. Wind W. by N., 6. Had been strong, now more moderate, with hail squalls. - - - 4 p.m. Wind W. by N., 6. Fresh breeze and clear. In 42° 22' N., 62° 9' W. - - - - 8 p.m. Wind W. by N., 6. Fresh breeze. - 3 a.m., 3rd. Wind S.W. by S. Gentle breeze and hazy. - - - - - - - 4 a.m. Wind S. by W. Same weather. -	40° 38 36 — 34	29·68 30·28 30·45 falling 30·40	49° 45 50 50 50

			Standard Instruments.				No. 52. S.S. "Delta."
			Air.	Bar.	Sea.		
8 a.m.	Wind N.W. by N., 5. Turbulent sea.	-	60°	30·12	68°	In	{ 32° 29' N. 64° 50' W. 8 a.m. G.T. 2nd. Bound South.
11.20 a.m.	Arrived at Bermuda. 32° 19' N., 64° 52' W.					To Bermuda.	

The following observations at Bermuda were sent by General Lefroy:
10 a.m., local time (2.18 p.m. G. T.) Bar. 30·16. Wind "generally"
N.E. 4.

		Standard Instruments.				No. 37. S.S. "Austrian."
		Air.	Bar.	Sea.		
8 a.m.	Wind N.W. by W., 7. Clouds rising in south; a short, chopping sea. - -	18°	30·02	30°	In	{ 43° 27' N. 69° 4' W. 8 a.m. G.T. 2nd. Bound Westerly.
0.36 p.m.	Arrived at Portland in 43° 39' N., 70° 15' W.				To Portland, Maine.	

See Diagram 1 for a continuous record of this ship's data. Considering Nos. 52 and 37, there seems to have been a north-westerly wind from Portland to Bermuda, in the rear of the area of low pressure which had gone to the north-eastward.

		Air.	Bar.	Sea.		No. 3. S.S. "Etna."
8 a.m.	Wind W. by N., 6. Strong breeze. -	29° ?	29·93	32°	In	{ 40° 34' N. 70° 50' W. 8 a.m. G.T. 2nd. Bound West.
4.45 p.m.	S.W. by W., 5. Moderate and fine.					
In 40° 33' N., 70° 42' W. - - -		34 ?	30·15	36		
5.45 p.m.	S.S.W., 5. Moderate breeze and fine.	36 ?	30·13	36	To	{ 40° 27' N. 73° 51' W. 8 a.m. G.T. 3rd.
8 a.m.	Wind doubtful, light cloudy weather. -	—	—			No. 9. S.S. "Colorado."
4 p.m.	S.E. by S. Fresh breeze and cloudy, Sandy Hook Lightship abeam. - - -				In	{ New York. 8 a.m. G.T. 2nd. Bound East.
4.45 a.m., 3rd.	S.W. by S., Light breeze and fine clear weather. - -	46°	—	42°	To	{ 40° 36' N. 70° 4' W. 8 a.m. G.T. 3rd.
8 a.m.	Wind north-westerly, light; weather clear.	—	—	—		No. 16. S.S. "City of London." At { Quarantine Ground, New York. 8 a.m. G.T. 2nd.

8 a.m. Wind N.W. ¼ N., *6 miles per hour.* New York Observatory.
Barometer 30·22, air 26°. The barometer was steady until 2 p.m., 8 a.m. G.T. 2nd.
then pressure decreased until 9 p.m., when it was 30·01; then rose To 8 a.m. G.T. 3rd.
gradually until 5 a.m. 3rd, when it was steady at 30·16 until 8 a.m.

The thermometer oscillated between 23° and 30° during the forenoon, then steadily rose to 43° at 9.30 p.m., nearly the hour of minimum pressure. At 10.30 p.m. it was 35°, and afterwards oscillated between 35° and 30°.

At 11 a.m. the wind shifted suddenly to E. by N., afterwards gradually veering to S.E. at 6 p.m.

At 10 p.m. it suddenly shifted from S. by E. through W. to N. by W., its force was *very* light.

From these data we may suppose that the slight area of low pressure between New York and Halifax on the 8 a.m. Chart of the 3rd, had passed over New York between 2 and 9 p.m. of the 2nd. The changes of wind experienced by No. 9 indicate that it also passed over her.

		Air.	Bar.	Sea.
No. 38. Ship " Nicoline." In { 34° 13' N. / 74° 54' W. / 8 a.m. G.T. 2nd. Bound North. To { 36° 8' N. / 74° 7' W. / 8 a.m. G.T. 3rd.	8 a.m. Wind variable, 1; followed by light southerly breeze and fine weather. -	54°	30·18	70°
	5 p.m. S.S.W., 3. - - -	61	30·20	72
	9 p.m. South, 5; fine weather and smooth sea. -	62	30·16	73
	5 a.m., 3rd. S. by E. 4, then light and variable from S. to N.N.W. and afterwards very light from east. -	63	—	72

GENERAL REMARKS ON CHART FOR 8 A.M., GREENWICH TIME, FEBRUARY 2ND, 1870.

The logs of 34 ships have been consulted.

The southerly wind, amounting to a gale at Holyhead, still holds over the British Islands and Western Europe. There seems to be a ridge of high pressure over the cold high land from the South of Spain to Lyons, having a south-west wind on its north-western, and a north-east wind on its south-eastern side.

Norway has still a strong south-east wind, whilst it is easterly in Iceland.

In Cumberland Sound it is calm.

In Belleisle there was a north-west gale at 4 p.m., whilst at the same time it was N.N.E. at Forteau.

In Newfoundland a very heavy westerly gale was blowing throughout the afternoon.

The following telegram was received from Heart's Content this day.

"A fresh southerly breeze with snow from 6 to 11 p.m., (9.30 p.m. 1st., to 2.30 a.m. 2nd, Greenwich time,) the wind then went to west and increased to a heavy gale at 4 a.m., 2nd, (7.30 a.m. Greenwich time), still continuing strong at 9 a.m. 2nd, (0.30 p.m. Greenwich time), barometer fell from 29·81 to 28·50 between 6 p.m. and 1 a.m. (9.30 p.m. 1st, and 4.30 a.m., 2nd, Greenwich time.)"

At Terceira the wind was light N.W., whilst at Madeira it was calm.

The changes of wind and action of the barometer experienced by each ship between 8 a.m. of the 2nd, and 8 a.m. of the 3rd indicate that they were affected by certain areas or waves of low pressure which seem to move in a north-easterly direction, as the more southerly or westerly ships got the changes first.

There seems to have been the same tendency to an eddy, round an area of low pressure off the west coast of Ireland, as on former days.

This day's Chart shows two systems of wind with an area of high pressure between them.

The high south-east wind spoken of at Halifax, on the 1st, has now extended to nearly 40° W., and Halifax, we are told, has a north-north-westerly wind. The hours of the changes are not given.

The telegram from Heart's Content seems clearly to show that the southerly wind which is between 40° and 45° W. on the 8 a.m. Chart of the 2nd, commenced at Heart's Content about 9.30 p.m. of the 1st, giving a speed to the eastward of nearly 40 miles an hour to the area of low pressure to which it was related.

This easterly progress of the change of wind is very clearly perceived by comparing this day's Chart with that of the 1st inst.

The area of low pressure which Diagram 1 shows to have passed over No. 37 in 65° 35' W., on the 1st, has now passed on to the eastward of Newfoundland, indicating a speed of about 40 miles an hour.

The variable wind experienced by No. 11 in about 38° W., just on the ridge between a north-west and south-east wind, is worthy of remark. The barometer curves on the Diagrams give sections of several of these ridges.

It will be remembered that on the 1st, between 20° and 40° W., there were strong westerly winds. North-westerly winds have now taken their place; indicating the easterly progress of a ridge of high pressure.

Then again on the 1st the ships between 40° and 50° W., had the wind N.W., decreasing, with a rising barometer, now they have it S.E. to S.W. with a falling barometer. This looks as if the weather experienced between 40° and 50° W. on the 1st, had shifted on the 2nd to the eastward of 37° W.

The extremely hard westerly gale at St. John's, Newfoundland, indicates that there was a very low pressure to the north of that station.

The general prevalence of an area of low pressure to the north and high to the south is as marked on this as on the preceding Charts.

Extracts and Remarks to accompany the Chart for February 3rd, 1870.

A southerly wind still prevails over the British Isles and Western Europe, being now light or moderate.

		Air.	Bar.	Sea.
No. 24. S.S. "Nile." In? { 49° 52' N. 4° 22' W. 8 a.m. G.T. 3rd. Bound W. S. Wly. To { 48° 9' N. 8° 5' W. 8 a.m. G.T. 4th.	8 a.m. S.W., 4. Moderate and fine, heavy westerly sea.	—	29·61	—
	0.20 p.m. S.S.W. Light breeze and fine, heavy westerly sea. In 49° 33' N., 5° 11' W.	—	29·04	—
	4.20 a.m., 4th. S. Strong breeze, heavy hail squalls, and head sea.	—	29·41	—
	5.20 a.m. West. Shift of wind to west. In 48° 20' N., 7° 42' W.	—	29·40	—

Plate VII. of the Quarterly Weather Report shows that the shift to West came to Valencia about 5 a.m., 4th, and to Falmouth between noon and 3 p.m. of the same day.

		Air.	Bar.	Sea.
No. 19. S.S. "England." In { 51° 55' N. 7° 4' W. 8 a.m. G.T. 3rd. Bound West. To { 51° 24' N. 12° 20' W. 8 a.m. G.T. 4th.	8 a.m. S.S.W. 3. Light breeze.	49°	29·52	49°
	0.30 p.m. S.S.W. Light breeze and clear, high south-west swell. In 51° 40' N., 8° 20' W.	49	29·58	47
	0.30 a.m., 4th. S.S.E., 7. Strong breeze, high south-south-east sea rising.	51	29·28	50
	2.50 a.m. Wind hauling to the Westward in all sails. In 51° 21' N., 11° 14' W.	—	—	—
	3.30 a.m. West, 7. Strong breeze and cloudy, high westerly sea.	—	Inclined to rise.	52

No. 7. S.S. "Minnesota." In { 51° 48' N. 7° 51' W. 8 a.m. G.T. 3rd. Bound West. To { 51° 21' N. 13° 17' W. 8 a.m. G.T. 4th.	8 a.m. S., 2. Light wind, fine and clear. 0.30 p.m. S.S.W. Light wind, fine and clear. In 51° 40' N., 8° 20' W. 11.30 p.m. S.E. Strong wind and cloudy. 2.30 a.m., 4th. West. Blowing hard; a sudden shift of wind and heavy rain. In 51° 21' N., 11° 57' W.

Nos. 24, 19, and 7 remark on the sudden shift of wind to W. The various hours at which it took place with the different ships indicate that it moved quickly to the Eastward.

67

		Standard Instruments.			No. 50.
		Air.	Bar.	Sea.	S.S. "Hotspur."
8 a.m.	W.N.W., 3. Cloudy and squally.	53°	29·82	—	In { 42° 26′ N. / 9° 49′ W. / 8 a.m. G.T. 3rd.
0.40 p.m.	W.N.W., 3. Fine. In 42° 7′ N., 9° 58′ W.	54	29·87	—	Bound South.
4.40 p.m.	S.S.W., 2. Overcast, squally.	55	—	—	To { 39° 47′ N. / 10° 12′ W. / 8 a.m. G.T. 4th.
8.40 p.m.	S., 2. Heavy rain and squally.	54	29·85	—	

The rain continued all night.

No further observations until 8 a.m. of the 4th, when the wind had gone to W. and barometer risen to 30·39.

		Standard instruments.			No. 35.
		Air.	Bar.	Sea.	S.S. "Tarifa."
8 a.m.	Wind W.S.W., 3. Fine weather.	49°	29·53	51°	In { 51° 37′ N. / 12° 13′ W. / 8 a.m. G.T. 3rd.
1 p.m.	S.S.W., 4. In 51° 33′ N., 13° 24′ W.	50	29·47	51	Bound West.
5 p.m.	S., 5. Gloomy (in 51° 34′ N., 14° 2′ W.)	50	29·29	51	
9 p.m.	Wind, W.S.W., 5, Rain, westerly swell.	49	29·15	51	To { 51° 39′ N. / 17° 22′ W. / 8 a.m. G.T. 4th.
1 a.m., 4th.	W. by N., 5. Cloudy, squally.	49	29·23	52	

No. 35 gets the change of wind to west before No. 7, and she is from 4° to 5° west of her. Diagram 3 is a continuous record of the data observed on board No. 35. It shows a section of the small depression of the barometer accompanying the shift of wind from S. to W., which was experienced by so many ships as well as at Valencia and Falmouth.

		Air.	Bar.	Sea.	No. 48.
					S.S. "Calabria."
8 a.m.	Wind south-westerly. Gentle breeze, direction doubtful.	50°	29·47	51°	In { 50° 15′ N. / 17° 4′ W. / 8 a.m. G.T. 3rd.
1 p.m.	S. by W. Moderate breeze and cloudy.	51	29·45	52	Bound Eastward.
9 p.m.	S. Fresh gale, hazy, with rain.	48	?29·17	50	To Queenstown.

No. 29.
"Chatillon."
In { 31° 5′ N. / 19° 13′ W. / 8 a.m. G.T. 3rd.
Bound S.S.Wly.
To { 29° 50′ N. / 20° 15′ W. / 8 a.m. G.T. 4th.

8 a.m. W.S.W., 4. Overcast with considerable swell. The Chatillon is very far south.

		Air.	Bar.	Sea.	No. 2.
					S.S. "City of Cork."
8 a.m.	S. by W., force not given, but it was light, with dull weather at 5.20 a.m.	49°	29·42	51°	In { 51° 15′ N. / 22° 2′ W. / 8 a.m. G.T. 3rd.
10.12 a.m.	W. by N. No force given. Sudden shift with rain.	—	—	—	Bound West.
1.30 p.m.	W. by N. Strong increasing breeze. In 51° 11′ N., 23° 10′ W.	48	?29·30	50	To { 50° 41′ N. / 24° 54′ W. / 8 a.m. G.T. 4th.

		Air.	Bar.	Sea.

9.30 p.m. W. by S. Strong gale, high sea, heavy squalls with hail and rain. - - - - 48° ? 29·34 49°

Both Nos. 2 and 7 remark on the sudden shift to W., the former in about 22° 40′ W. at 10.12 a.m. of the 3rd., the latter in about 11° 57′ W. at 2.30 a.m. of the 4th, which gives a speed of about 26 miles per hour to the westerly shift of wind travelling to the eastward. By a similar comparison between Nos. 24 and 2 the amount of easting per hour was somewhat more than the above.

No. 45.
Ship "Carl Georg."
In { 44° 32′ N.
     29° 6′ W.
     8 a.m. G.T. 3rd.
Bound E.N.Ely.
To { 45° 50′ N.
    25° 47′ W.
    8 a.m. G.T. 4th.

	Wind.	Air.	Bar.	Sea.
8 a.m.	? N.W., 9. Still blowing hard. -	57°	30·21	58°
1.50 p.m.	? N.W., 6. In 44° 50′ N., 28° 17′ W.	57	30·08	58
9.50 p.m.	South, 6; thick, with heavy rain. -	57	29·82	57
			rising.	
5.50 a.m., 4th.	N.W., 6. - - - -	59	29·72	55

The position of No. 45 in relation to the area of lowest pressure leads to the supposition that the wind was south-westerly at 8 a.m. and 1.50 p.m. instead of being N.W.

No. 39.
S.S. "Westphalia."
In { 48° 58′ N.
     29° 52′ W.
     8 a.m. G.T. 3rd.
Bound Westerly.
To { 48° 34′ N.
    33° 21′ W.
    8 a.m. G.T. 4th.

	Wind.	Air.	Bar.	Sea.
8 a.m.	West, 10. Violent rain squalls. -	50°	29·46	49°
2 p.m.	West, 10. In 48° 56′ N., 31° 8′ W.	49	29·49	50
6 a.m., 4th.	W. by N., 10. Sky looking threatening.	43	29·76	50

See Diagram 4 for a continuous record of this ship's data.

No. 17.
S.S. "Helvetia."
In { 48° 51′ N.
     33° 0′ W.
     8 a.m. G.T. 3rd.
Bound W.S. Wly. (very slowly.)
To { 48° 28′ N.
    34° 41′ W.
    8 a.m. G.T. 4th.

	Wind.	Air.	Bar.	Sea.
8 a.m. heavy sea.	West, 9. Strong gale; hard squalls; - - - -	49°	29·44	55°
2.15 p.m.	West, 9. Strong gale; hard squalls.			
	In 48° 45′ N., 33° 34′ W. - - -	47	29·54	54
2.15 a.m. 4th.	West. Gale slightly moderating;			
high topping sea.	- - - -	45	29·72	51

No. 30.
H.M.S. "Orontes."
In { 47° 23′ N.
     33° 58′ W.
     8 a.m. G.T. 3rd.
Bound E. by Nly.
To { 49° 4′ N.
    28° 14′ W.
    8 a.m. G.T. 4th.

	Wind.	Aneroid Bar.		Sea.
8 a.m.	West, 6 to 9. Squally. -	47°	29·59	52°
2 p.m.	W. by N., 6 to 9. Squally. In 47° 50′ N.,			
32° 18′ W.	- - - - - -	48	29·57	53
	2 a.m., 4th. West, 5 to 8. Hail squalls. In 48°40′ N.,			
29° 37′ W.	- - - - - -	45	29·59	48

No. 30 seems to have travelled East with the depression, whilst No. 17 had a rising barometer as she went to the West.

	Wind.	Air.	Bar.	Sea.	No. 10. S.S. "Manhattan."
8 a.m.	W. by N. Constant heavy gale and sea.	—	—	—	In { 47° 20′ N. / 34° 20′ W. / 8 a.m. G.T. 3rd.
2.20 p.m.	W. by N. Terrific gale and heavy dangerous sea. In 47° 2′ N., 34° 40′ W. Ship labouring fearfully; shipping heavy seas.	—	—	—	Bound W.S.Wly. slowly. To { 46° 24′ N. / 36° 14′ W. / 8 a.m. G.T. 4th.
2.20 a.m., 4th.	W. by N. Heavy gale and hard squalls. In 46° 33′ N., 35° 53′ W.	—	—	—	

No. 10 was very near No. 30 at 8 a.m., but seems to have experienced much worse weather going West than No. 30 going East. It must, however, be remembered that the wind was fair for No. 30.

	Wind.	Air.	Bar.	Sea.	No. 25. S.S. "Cuban."
8 a.m.	W.N.W., 7 to 8. Moderate gale; high sea; labouring heavily and shipping heavy seas.	45°	30·16	—	In { 42° 26′ N. / 34° 52′ W. / 8 a.m. G.T. 3rd.
2.15 p.m.	W.N.W., 7 to 8. Moderate gale. In 42° 43′ N., 33° 37′ W.	45	30·16	—	Bound E. by Nly. To { 43° 37′ N. / 29° 50′ W. / 8 a.m. G.T. 4th.
2.15 a.m., 4th.	W.N.W., 9 to 10. Blowing very hard, heavy beam sea. In 43° 19′ N., 31° 6′ W.	—	—	—	

No. 25 is further south and has a much higher barometer than Nos. 10 and 30, but she seems to have nearly as much wind as No. 10, and more than No. 30.

	Wind.	Air.	Bar.	Sea.	No. 20. S.S. "The Queen."
8 a.m.	W. by N., 9. Strong gale; heavy hail squalls and high sea.	46°	29·45	53°	In { 48° 35′ N. / 35° 11′ W. / 8 a.m. G.T. 3rd.
2.10 p.m.	W. by N., 9. Strong gale. In 48° 57′ N., 33° 32′ W.	44	29·55	50	Bound Easterly. To { 49° 37′ N. / 28° 33′ W. / 8 a.m. G.T. 4th.
6.10 p.m.	W. by N., 9. Strong gale.	44	29·57	50	
6.10 a.m., 4th.	W. by N., 8. Fresh gale; hard squalls; hail and snow.	40	29·59	52	

	Wind.	Air.	Bar.	Sea.	No. 4. S.S. "Prussian."
8 a.m.	W. by S., 9 to 10. Very heavy sea, and hail squalls.	52°	29·25	54°	In { 50° 28′ N. / 36° 12′ W. / 8 a.m. G.T. 3rd.
2.30 p.m.	W. by S., 9 to 10. Very heavy sea. In 50° 13′ N., 37° 16′ W.	—	29·43	—	Bound W.S.Wly. To { 49° 45′ N. / 38° 1′ W. / 8 a.m. G.T. 4th.
	The same wind and weather held throughout.	—	rising	—	

No. 49. S.S. "Marathon." In $\begin{cases} 48° 3' N. \\ 36° 21' W. \\ 8\text{ a.m. G.T. 3rd.} \end{cases}$ Bound Easterly. To $\begin{cases} 49° 15' N. \\ 31° 18' W. \\ 8\text{ a.m. G.T. 4th.} \end{cases}$	8 a.m.	Wind. S.W., 9 to 10.	Heavy westerly gale; very high sea.	Air.	Bar. 29·35	Sea.
	2.30 p.m.	S.W., 9.	Heavy westerly gale. In 48° 30' N., 36° 25' W.	42°	29·42	47°
	2.30 a.m., 4th.	S.W. by W., 9.	Strong gale; heavy hail squalls; heavy sea. In 49° N., 32° 54' W.	37	29·48	48

No. 11. S.S. "Iowa." In $\begin{cases} 48° 4' N. \\ 38° 29' W. \\ 8\text{ a.m. G.T. 3rd.} \end{cases}$ Bound S.Wly. slow. To $\begin{cases} 47° 6' N. \\ 40° 3' W. \\ 8\text{ a.m. G.T. 4th.} \end{cases}$	8 a.m.	Wind. W. by S., 9 to 10.	Strong gale; hard squalls; heavy sea.	—	—	—
	2.35 p.m.	W. by S., 9.	Strong gale; hard squalls; heavy sea. In 47° 47' N., 38° 34' W.	—	—	—
	2.35 a.m., 4th.	W.N.W., 8.	Moderating; sea falling. In 47° 19' N., 39° 35' W.	—	—	—

No. 11, going West, got the wind more northerly and moderating. This does not seem to have come to No. 49 going East, although they were very near each other at 8 a.m. of the 3rd. It will be seen that on the 4th No. 49 steamed into a more *southerly* wind.

No. 26. S.S. "Venezuelan." In $\begin{cases} 41° 12' N. \\ 41° 34' W. \\ 8\text{ a.m. G.T. 3rd.} \end{cases}$ Bound E.N.Ely. To $\begin{cases} 43° 18' N. \\ 37° 14' W. \\ 8\text{ a.m. G.T. 4th.} \end{cases}$	8 a.m.	Wind. N.W. ½ W., 6.	Strong breeze and cloudy.	Air. 59°	Bar. 30·13	Sea. —
	2.40 p.m.	W.N.W., 5.	Steady breeze and fine. In 41° 50' N., 40° 31' W.	65	30·28	—
	2.40 a.m., 4th.	W.N.W., 5.	Steady breeze, swell from W.N.W. In 42° 50' N., 38° 17' W.	—	30·10	—
	3.40 a.m.	W. by S.	Steady breeze.	—	—	—

No. 26, going to the eastward, had the wind backing to the southward, whilst it veered to the northward with No. 11 going to the westward. It must be remembered that No. 26 was nearly 5° further south.

No. 53. S.S. "Weser." In $\begin{cases} 46° 15' N. \\ 44° 36' W. \\ 8\text{ a.m. G.T. 3rd.} \end{cases}$ Bound E. by Nly. To $\begin{cases} 47° 52' N. \\ 36° 33' W. \\ 8\text{ a.m. G.T. 4th.} \end{cases}$	8 a.m.	Wind. West, 8.	High south-westerly sea.	Air. 34°	Bar. 29·96	Sea. 42°
	2.50 p.m.	West, 8.	In 46° 46' N., 43° 22' W.	35	30·00	41
	2.50 a.m., 4th.	W.S.W., 8.	In 47° 30' N., 38° 25' W.	37	29·91	41

No. 53, like 26, is bound to the eastward, and has also a backing wind, though by referring to Diagram 2 it will be seen that it soon veered to West again.

71

	Wind.		Air.	Bar.	Sea.		No. 1.

8 a.m.	W. by S., 6 to 7.	Strong breeze, with westerly sea.	34°	30·05	35°	In	S.S. "Antwerp."
							{ 45° 56′ N.
							  46° 8′ W.
							  8 a.m. G.T. 3rd.

9 a.m.	W. by N., 6 to 7.	Ditto.	33	30·06	35		Bound E.N.Ely.

3 p.m.	W. by N., 6.	Ditto. In 46° 32′ N., 44° 5′ W.	32	30·13	37	To	{ 48° 0′ N.
							  38° 47′ W.
							  8 a.m. G.T. 4th.

3 a.m., 4th.	W. by S.	Strong breeze. In 47° 32′ N., 40° 27′ W.	31	30·02	42		

Here again the wind backs slightly, with the ship going to the eastward.

	Wind.		Air.	Bar.	Sea.		No. 13.

8 a.m.	W. by N., 5.	Fresh breeze and cloudy.	—	?30·16	—	In	S.S. "India."
							{ 46° 20′ N.
							  48° 51′ W.
							  8 a.m. G.T. 3rd.

3 p.m.	N.W. by W., 6 to 7.	Strong breeze. In 47° 6′ N., 47° 0′ W.	—	?30·15	—		Bound E.N.Ely.

3 a.m., 4th.	W. by N., 6 to 7.	Strong increasing breeze. In 48° 22′ N., 44° 0′ W.	—	?30·01	—	To	{ 48° 53′ N.
							  42° 43′ W.
							  8 a.m. G.T. 4th.

	Wind.		Air.	Bar.	Sea.		No. 12.
8 a.m.	N.N.W., 6.	Still very heavy sea.	—	—	—		S.S. "Dacian."

3 p.m.	N.N.W., 5.	In 43° 1′ N., 48° 4′ W.	—	—	—	In	{ 42° 41′ N.
							  49° 21′ W.
							  8 a.m. G.T. 3rd.

8 p.m.	W., 6.	In 43° 26′ N., 47° 14′ W.	—	—	—		Bound E.N.Ely.

4 a.m., 4th.	W.S.W., 6.	Still heavy sea.	—	—	—	To	{ 44° 11′ N.
							  45° 6′ W.
							  8 a.m. G.T. 4th.

It is probable that this wind should be corrected for variation, which would make it less northerly.

	Wind.		Air.	Bar.	Sea.		No. 21.
8 a.m.	W. by N., 5.	Fresh breeze.	30°	?30·24	37°		S.S. "Denmark."

3 p.m.	W. by N., 4.	Moderate breeze. In 45° 50′ N., 48° 44′ W.	31	?30·22	34	In	{ 45° 22′ N.
							  50° 23′ W.
							  8 a.m. G.T. 3rd.

3 a.m., 4th.	W. by N., 4.	Moderated breeze; heavy northerly swell. In 46° 23′ N., 46° 2′ W.	32	?30·14	37	To	Bound Easterly.
							{ 46° 37′ N.
							  44° 55′ W.
							  8 a.m. G.T. 4th.

No. 21 only gives the wind loosely as "north-westerly" for 36 hours.

	Wind.		Air.	Bar.	Sea.		No. 55.
8 a.m.	West, 5.	Wind and sea decreasing.	32°	30·19	40°		S.S. "Rhein."

3.30 p.m.	West, 5.	In 44° 13′ N., 52° 37′ W.	35	30·27	39	In	{ 44° 38′ N.
							  51° 28′ W.
							  8 a.m. G.T. 3rd.

7.30 p.m.	Calm		35	30·25	44		Bound W. by Sly.

3.30 a.m., 4th.	N.E., 5.	Calm sea. In 43° 25′ N., 55° 48′ W.	35	30·12	39	To	{ 43° 8′ N.
							  56° 56′ W.
							  8 a.m. G.T. 4th.

			Air.	Bar.	Sea.

No. 46.
S.S. "Nemesis."
In { 41° 46' N.
     62° 1' W.
     8 a.m. G.T. 3rd.
Bound W. by Sly.
To { 40° 48' N.
     67° 49' W.
     8 a.m. G.T. 4th.

Wind.
8 a.m.   S.W. by S. Moderate breeze and clear. — ? 29·94 —
4.15 p.m. W. by S.   Do.   do.   In
41° 22' N., 63° 46' W., followed by calms and light
airs. -   -   -   -   -   -   — ? 29·90 —
4.15 a.m., 4th. N. by W. Light breeze with rain.
In 40° 56' N., 66° 54' W. -   -   -   -   — ? 29·91 —

It seems probable that the southerly wind experienced by No. 46 at 8 a.m. was the same as that experienced by various ships to the eastward of her later in the day on the 3rd, and by New York in the evening of the 2nd.

The following observations, taken at Bermuda, were sent by General Lefroy :—

10 a.m. local time (2.18 p.m. G. T.). Bar. 30·10; wind "generally" S.E., 5.

The barometer was falling, as it was 30·04 five hours later. This direction of wind and falling barometer indicate that the north-eastern edge of the area of low pressure, which was to the northward of Bermuda on the 4th, was passing over that island on the 3rd. (See the 8 a.m. Chart of the 4th.)

No. 22.
S.S. "Pennsylvania."
In { 41° 42' N.
     64° 52' W.
     8 a.m. G.T. 3rd.
Bound W. by Sly.
To { 40° 58' N.
     69° 56' W.
     8 a.m. G.T. 4th.

Wind.   Air.   Bar.   Sea.
8 a.m.   S. by E., 5. Moderate breeze, gradu-
ally freshening with rain.   -   -   -   -   40°   30·27   53°
11.20 a.m. S.W. by S., 5. Ditto.   -   -   -   —   —   —
4.25 p.m. S.W. by W., 3. In 41° 20' N., 66° 18' W. 47 30·16 50
6.25 p.m. N. by W., 3.   Light wind and cloudy.   —   —   —
9.25 p.m. N. by E., 4.   Moderate wind, light rain. In 41° 13' N., 67° 30' W.

The north-easterly wind continued until she reached New York.

No. 9.
S.S. "Colorado."
In { 40° 36' N.
     70° 4' W.
     8 a.m. G.T. 3rd.
Bound Easterly.
To { 41° 19' N.
     64° 24' W.
     8 a.m. G.T. 4th.

Wind.   Air.   Bar.   Sea.
8 a.m.   S.S.W. ½ W., 2. Light breeze and
fine. -   -   -   -   -   -   -   -   —   —   —
4.30 p.m. N.E. ½ E., 2. Overcast and
foggy. In 40° 40' N., 68° 0' W.   -   -   —   —   —
4.30 a.m., 4th. E.N.E., 6. Strong breeze;
easterly sea. In 41° 0' N., 65° 20' W.   -   —   —   —

No. 3.
S.S. "Etna."
In { 40° 27' N.
     73° 51' W.
     8 a.m. G.T. 3rd.
To { New York.
     8 a.m. G.T. 4th.

                                                    Air.   Bar.   Sea.
8 a.m. Wind W. by N. ½ N. Light breeze and
misty. -   -   -   -   -   -   -   -   — ?30·05 —
The wind remained moderate, but no other direction was given throughout the day. The weather was fine and clear.

A.M. Wind north-north-westerly, moderate. Frosty weather.   No. 18.
S.S. "Virginia."
In New York.

A.M. North-westerly, moderate. Fine clear weather.   No. 16.
S.S. "City of London."
In New York.

8 a.m. Wind N. by W., *two miles per hour*. Barometer 30·16, air 33.   New York Observatory.
Barometer kept pretty steady till 8 p.m., then gradually rose about   8 a.m. 3rd. to 8a.m. 4th.
·25 in. in the next 12 hours.
Temperature 31° at 2 p.m., it then rose to 37° by 7 p.m., from which time it gradually decreased to 20° by 8 a.m., 4th.
The wind veered through N. to E.N.E. by 4 p.m., then backed to N. by E. by 7 p.m., veering again to E.N.E. by 8 p.m., and to N. again by 9 p.m., where it continued steady till 8 a.m., 4th. Force light.

	Air.	Bar.	Sea.
8 a.m. Wind S. by W., 3 -	61°	30·13	72°
1 p.m. North-north-easterly, and variable, 2. Rippling on the edge of the Gulf Stream. Sea temperature fallen 19°.	56	30·14	53
5 p.m. E.N.E., 2. In 36° 45′ N. 73° 33′ W.	56	30·08	53
5 a.m., 4th. N.E., 6. Sea unusually phosphorescent	48	—	50

No. 38.
Ship "Nicoline."
In { 36° 8′ N.
     74° 7′ W.
     8 a.m. G.T. 3rd.
Bound North.
To { 37° 2′ N.
     73° 52′ W.
     8 a.m. G.T. 4th.

The change of wind from S. by W. to north-easterly as the ship passed from the hot to the cold water is worthy of remark.

General Remarks on Chart for 8 a.m., Greenwich Time, February 3rd, 1871.

The logs of 33 ships have been consulted.
The southerly wind still prevails over the British Islands, drawing westerly in Spain and more easterly in Norway.
In Iceland the wind was strong north-easterly, whilst it was north-westerly in Cumberland Sound. In the Straits of Belle Isle, and Newfoundland it was westerly, blowing hard from W. in Belle Isle at 4 p.m.
The remark from Halifax on the 3rd is "Cold, level snow fall from N.E., with slowly rising barometer."
At Terceira and Madeira the wind was light westerly.
On referring to Plate VII. of the Quarterly Weather Report for this date it will be seen that a slight rise of the barometer took place at the

self-registering observatories, accompanied by a decrease in force, a corresponding slight veering of the wind, and fall in the temperature.

At Armagh and Falmouth there was a more sudden dip in the temperature; at the former station the wind was very light and backed round through E., N.E., and N.W. to S., where it freshened, and the thermometer rose. A similar action of the thermometers took place with the barometer rise alluded to on the 31st and 1st.

On comparing this day's Chart with that of the 2nd it will be seen that on the 2nd the first southerly wind on the eastern side of an area of low pressure was in about 38° W., whilst to-day it seems to have extended to 22° W., where the wind is south-westerly, indicating that the area of lowest pressure had moved to the N.E. since the 2nd at a rate of from 20 to 30 miles an hour. It will also be noticed that the westerly gale which was south of Newfoundland yesterday is now in about 35° W.

Unfortunately we have no ships between 55° and 60° N., for their logs would have shown if the strong S.E. gale experienced by No. 20 on the 2nd were now blowing between those parallels in about 25° W.

The tracks of some of these areas of low pressure seem to run N.E. on a line which takes them to the westward of the British Isles, and they seem curiously to merge into the prevailing area of low pressure which exists in the central part of the Atlantic.

Extracts and Remarks to accompany the Chart for February 4th, 1870.

The southerly wind has again freshened over the British Isles, amounting to a gale at Cork.

The similarity of directions at most land stations to those experienced on the 3rd is very remarkable.

			Wind.		Air.	Bar.	Sea.
No. 6. S.S. "Nestorian."		8 a.m.	S.E., 6. Passing showers	-	44°	29·49	—
In	⎧ 54° 42′ N. 5° 27′ W. 8 a.m. G.T. 4th. Bound Wly.	0.30 p.m. 6° 8′ W.)	S.E., 6. Off Fair Head (55° 14′ N., · · · · ·	-	48	29·46	—
		4.30 p.m.	S.S.E., 4. At anchor at Moville	-	45	29·34	—
To	⎧ 55° 18′ N. 11° 4′ W. 8 a.m. G.T. 5th.	8.30 p.m.	S.S.W., 4 · · ·	-	44	29·34	47°
		4.40 a.m., 5th.	S.W. by W., 4 · ·	-	43	29·44	48

It will be noticed that No. 6 steamed to the westward, north of Ireland, and the wind drew more westerly as she increased her distance from the land, just as we see it was to the south of Ireland at 8 a.m. This persistent southerly wind on our coasts, whilst it is westerly a few degrees to the westward, is a remarkable feature in these Charts.

	Wind.	Standard Instruments.			No. 24.
		Air.	Bar.	Sea.	S.S. "Nile."
8 a.m.	W. Moderate breeze, squally and showery.	—	29·38	—	⎧ 48° 9' N.
0.40 p.m.	W., 6 to 7. Strong breeze, heavy south-westerly sea and squalls. In 47° 50′ N., 8° 44′ W.	—	29·36	—	In ⎨ 8° 5' W. ⎩ 8 a.m. G.T. 4th. Bound S.Wly.
6.40 p.m.	S.W. by W. ½ W. Fresh gale, heavy west sea, heavy squalls, rain and hail	—	—	—	⎧ 45° 42' N. To ⎨ 11° 41' W. ⎩ 8 a.m. G.T. 5th.
1.40 a.m., 5th.	W. Strong gale, heavy west sea	—	—	—	

	Wind.				No. 50.
					S.S. "Hotspur."
8 a.m.	W., 3. Moderate and fine, north-westerly sea.	57°	30·01	—	⎧ 39° 47' N.
0.40 p.m.	W., 3. Moderate and fine. In 39° 19′ N., 10° 15′ W.	57	30·05	—	In ⎨ 10° 12' W. ⎩ 8 a.m. G.T. 4th. Bound S.S.Ely.
This wind remained steady until 8.30 p.m.					⎧ 37° 9' N. To ⎨ 8° 48' W. ⎩ 8 a.m. G.T. 5th.

	Wind.				No. 19.
					S.S. "England."
8 a.m.	W., 6 to 7. Strong breeze, high westerly sea.	49°	29·30	51°	⎧ 51° 24' N.
1 p.m.	W., 6 to 7. Ditto; in 51° 21′ N., 13° 24′ W.	50	29·30	50	In ⎨ 12° 20' W. ⎩ 8 a.m. G.T. 4th. Bound West.
1 a.m., 5th.	W. by N. ¼ N. Moderate gale, high west-north-westerly sea; threatening appearances followed.	49	29·48	51	⎧ 51° 4' N. To ⎨ 17° 5' W. ⎩ 8 a.m. G.T. 5th.
6 a.m.	S. Fresh gale at 0 a.m.	50	29·35	52	

This south gale is the commencement of the very heavy gale experienced on the 5th. It is curious that this day's Chart does not show that any of the more western ships were experiencing this south wind at 8 a.m. Still it may have existed where we have no observations, in about 50° W. to the northward of No. 23, which ship had a light south-easterly wind at 8 a.m. of the 4th, and we know that Bermuda had a fresh S.E. breeze on the 3rd.

	Wind.		No. 7.
			S.S. Minnesota."
8 a.m.	W. by S., 8. Fresh gale, high sea.		⎧ 51° 21' N.
1 p.m.	W. by N., 7. Strong breeze and squally. In 51° 15′ N., 14° 37′ W.	In ⎨ 13° 17' W. ⎩ 8 a.m. G.T. 4th. Bound West.
Midnight.	S.W. by W. Moderate gale.		⎧ 51° 15' N. To ⎨ 18° 49' W. ⎩ 8 a.m. G.T. 5th.
5 a.m., 5th.	S.W. by S. Strong wind and squally with rain.		

				Standard Instruments.		
		Wind.		Air.	Bar.	Sea.

No. 35.
S.S. "Tarifa."
In { 51° 39′ N.
      17° 22′ W.
      8 a.m. G.T. 4th.
Bound West.
To { 51° 20′ N.
      22° 2′ W.
      8 a.m. G.T. 5th.

8 a.m.   W. by N., 5. Heavy cum. round horizon - - - - - - 46°   29·30   51°
                                                                                                                               steady.
1.15 p.m.   W. by S., 6. Squally with rain. In 51° 43′ N., 18° 47′ W. Current N. 11 miles -   44   29·29   50
                                                                                                                                   rising.
5.30 a.m., 5th.   S.W. by W., 5. Squally. In 51°22′N., 21° 26′ W. - - - - - - 45   29·34   50
                                                                                                                                   falling.

In the remarks No. 35 says, northerly set, owing to strong southerly wind. It will be seen, by referring back, that the wind had been southerly on our coasts for several days.

Twelve hours after the last entry above, No. 35 steamed into a wind of hurricane force, commencing at S. and veering to W., with the barometer down to 27·33!! See Diagram 3 for a continuous record of this ship's observations.

No. 2.
S.S. "City of Cork."
In { 50° 41′ N.
      24° 54′ W.
      8 a.m. G.T. 4th.
Bound W.
To { 50° 24′ N.
      28° 39′ W.
      8 a.m. G.T. 5th.

8 a.m.   W. Fresh gale, frequent squalls - 40°   29·45   44°
                                                                                                                  rising.
1.40 p.m.   W. More moderate. In 50° 31′ N., 25° 26′ W. - - - - - - 38   29·46   44
                                                                                                                  falling.
3.40 a.m., 5th.   S.W. by W. Moderate breeze, west sea, overcast - - - - - - 49   29·26   46
5.50 a.m.   S.E. by S. Light airs. In about 50° 24′ N., and 28° 20′ W. - - - - 49   29·05   46
6.50 a.m.   E. by S. Light breeze - - 49   28·95   46

At 3.30 p.m. of the 5th, No. 2 steamed into a gale of hurricane force. The barometer was 27·75, and the wind had gone from E. by N. to N.W. by N. This was the lowest barometer she experienced, and it is evident by the way the wind changed that she passed to the northward of a lower pressure.

No. 45.
Ship "Carl Georg."
In { 45° 50′ N.
      25° 47′ W.
      8 a.m. G.T. 4th.
Bound E.N.Ely.
To { 47° 3′ N.
      21° 58′ W.
      8 a.m. G.T. 5th.

8 a.m.   N.W., 7 - - - - - - 59°   29·78   55°
1.40 p.m.   N.W., 7. In 46° 9′ N., 25° 1′ W.   57   29·87   55
5.30 a.m., 5th.   N.W., 8. Violent hail and rain squalls. In about 47° N., 22° W. - - - 54   29·72   55

No. 45 seems to have had a steady north-west wind for a day and a half, whilst the ships going to the westward had it veering to the southward. Her barometer was unsteady, but not falling like those of ships going to the westward. These facts indicate that she was travelling in front of the bad gale to the westward of her.

NOTE.—The German logs are said to give the *true* direction of the wind. If the "Carl Georg's" wind were given magnetic by mistake, then the variation would make it agree better in direction with the ships near her. It will be seen that a similar difference exists between her wind and that of ships near her on the 3rd.

	Wind.	Air.	Bar.	Sea.	
8 a.m.	W. by N., 5 to 7. Squally, with passing showers.	41°	29·64	48°	No. 30. H.M.S. "Orontes." In { 49° 4′ N. 28° 14′ W. 8 a.m. G.T. 4th. Bound E. by Nly.
1.45 p.m.	W., 5 to 7. In 49° 29′ N., 20° 55′ W.	45	29·60	48	
5.45 a.m., 5th.	S. by W. to S.W. by W., 2. In 50° 28′ N., 23° 0′ W.	53	29·35	53	To { 50° 38′ N. 22° 21′ W. 8 a.m. G.T. 5th.

The positions of Nos. 2 and 30 are given at about 5.30 a.m. of the 5th, and it is interesting to notice that No. 2 was in the same latitude as No. 30, but 5° to the west of her, where she was experiencing a light south-easterly wind, whilst No. 30 had it south-westerly. At the same time No. 49 was but 2° west of No. 30, and had a light south-easterly wind.

	Wind.	Air.	Bar.	Sea.	
8 a.m.	W. by N., 8. Fresh gale, heavy snow squalls.	40°	29·62	50°	No. 20. S.S. "The Queen." In { 49° 37′ N. 28° 33′ W. 8 a.m. G.T. 4th. Bound Ely.
1.45 p.m.	W. by N., 7 to 8. Moderate gale and gloomy. In 49° 50′ N., 26° 53′ W.	40	29·62	52	
2.45 a.m., 5th.	W. by N. Moderate wind and drizzle.	—	—	—	To { 50° 23′ N. 22° 11′ W. 8 a.m. G.T. 5th.
5.45 a.m.	W. by N. Ditto. In about 50° 20′ N., 22° 49′ W.	47	29·50	52	
7.45 a.m.	S. by W. Increasing wind with drizzle.				

It will be seen that at 5.50 a.m. of the 5th, No. 2 (bound W.) was very near the spot where No. 20 was at 8 a.m. of the 4th, and she (No. 2) had the wind S.E. by S., light airs; whereas No. 20 (bound E.) kept the westerly wind until 7.45 a.m. of the 5th, when it drew to S. by W., with a fast falling barometer, even though she was on the starboard tack, showing that the low pressure was catching her up.

	Wind.	Air.	Bar.	Sea.	
8 a.m.	S.W. by W., 7. Gale moderating, wind drawing more southerly.	45°	30·08	—	No. 25. S.S. "Cuban." In { 43° 37′ N. 29° 50′ W. 8 a.m. G.T 4th. Bound E.N.Ely.
9 a.m.	S.W. by S.				
2 p.m.	S.W. by W., 6. Strong breeze, and cloudy. In 43° 53′ N. 28° 34′ W.	45	29·95	—	To { 45° 11′ N. 24° 53′ W. 8 a.m. G.T. 5th.

		Wind.				Air.	Bar.	Sea.
	11 p.m.	S. by W., 7. Freshening	-	-	-	45°	falling	—
	6 a.m., 5th. S. by W., 8. Fresh increasing gale, and very high sea. About 45° 0′ N. and 25° 20′ W.				-	—	—	—

It will be seen that No. 25 got the southerly gale before the ships to the northward and eastward of her.

		Wind.				Air.	Bar.	Sea.
No. 49. S.S. "Marathon." In { 49° 15′ N. 31° 8′ W. 8 a.m. G.T. 4th. Bound E. by Nly. To { 50° 7′ N. 24° 38′ W. 8 a.m. G.T. 5th.	8 a.m.	S.W. by W., 9. Strong gale, heavy squalls of hail, and heavy sea.	-	-	-	36°?	29.46	49°
	2 p.m.	S.S.W., 8. Fresh gale; heavy sea. In 49° 30′ N., 29° 23′ W.	-	-	-	40?	29·38	49
	3 a.m., 5th.	South-easterly, 3. Light wind, and gloomy.	-	-	-	—	falling	—
	6 a.m.	South-easterly, 3. With heavy rain. In about 50° 5′ N., 25° 10′ W.	-	-	-	44?	28·76	54

It seems worthy of notice that at about 6 a.m. of the 5th, No. 2, in the same latitude as, but about 3° W. of, No. 49, had a similar light south-easterly wind, whilst No. 25 in the same longitude as No. 49, but 5° south of her, had a fresh increasing gale from S. by W. It will be found that 10 hours later No. 2 steamed into a northerly gale of hurricane force, hence we may conclude that an area of low pressure passed between her and No. 25, having little or no gradient on its north-eastern side, but a steep one on its western and south-eastern sides.

		Wind.				Air.	Bar.	Sea.
No. 39. S.S. "Westphalia." In { 48° 34′ N. 33° 21′ W. 8 a.m. G.T. 4th. Bound W.S.Wly. To { 47° 33′ N. 37° 34′ W. 8 a.m. G.T. 5th.	8 a.m.	W. by N., 10. Sky looking threatening.	-	-	-	44°	29·75	51°
	2.16 p.m.	W. by N., 10. In 48° 27′ N., 34° 7′ W.				46	29·72	50
	2.16 a.m., 5th.	N., 7. In 47° 50′ N., 36° 30′ W.	-			44	29·08	52
	6.16 a.m.	N., 7. In 47° 35′ N., 37° 12′ W.	-			41	28·95	52

This falling barometer, with the wind drawing north, as the ship went to the west, looks as if the area of low pressure was intensifying at the positions she was passing through. For a continuous record of this ship's observations see Diagram 4.

This seems to be a case in which an area of low pressure going to the north-eastward caused the barometer to fall, and wind to back from N. to N.W. on board a ship on its western edge. Diagram 4 shows that in a few hours after our last extract the wind was north-westerly, with nearly hurricane force.

	Wind.				Air	Bar.	Sea.	No. 17.
8 a.m.	W. by N., 8. Fresh gale, and heavy							S.S. "Helvetia."
cross sea	-	-	-	-	45°	29·73	52°	In { 48° 28' N. / 34° 41' W.
2.20 p.m.	W. by N., 6 to 7. Strong wind.							8 a.m. G.T. 4th.
In 48° 23' N., 35° 5' W.		-	-	-	45	29·65	54	Bound W. by Sly. slowly
0.20 a.m., 5th.	N.W. by N., 6 to 7. Strong wind;							To { 47° 38' N. / 37° 36' W.
heavy beam sea.	-	-	-	-	—	falling		8 a.m. G.T. 5th.
2.20 a.m.	N. by W., 6. Freshening breeze,							
with constant rain.	In 47° 52' N. and 36° 48' W.			-	40	29·31	50	
6.20 a.m.	N. by W., 7. Strong breeze,-with							
constant rain.	In 47° 40' N., 37° 18' W.			-	39	28·95	48	

No. 17, like No. 39, had a falling barometer, with the wind drawing north, even though she was steaming to the westward. This also looks as if the area of low pressure was in the act of forming, or, at any rate, closing with her.

	Wind.		No. 10.
8 a.m.	W.N.W., 8. Gale more moderate.		S.S. "Manhattan."
11.30 a.m.	W. ½ S.		In { 46° 24' N. / 36° 14' W.
2.30 p.m.	N.W. by N. Decreasing wind, unsettled weather, and		8 a.m. G.T. 4th.
heavy swell.	In 46° 4' N., 37° 5' W.		Bound W. by Sly.
11.30 p.m.	N. by W. Increasing wind, and threatening appearances.		To { 45° 14' N. / 39° 40' W.
6.30 a.m, 5th.	N. to W.N.W. Strong gale, veering to the westward		8 a.m. G.T. 5th.
in the squalls.	In 45° 18' N., 39° 26' W.		

No. 10 gives no barometer readings. She has the wind veering from W. to N., with an increasing force. In the latter part her wind is inclined to back to the westward.

	Wind.			Air.	Bar.	Sea.	
8 a.m.	W. by S., 8. Constant rain		-	40°	29·91	51°	No. 53.
2.18 p.m.	W., 5. Ditto. In 48°15' N., 34° 28' W.			41	29·71	51	S.S. "Weser."
2.18 a.m., 5th.	West, 1. Ditto. In 48° 45' N.,						In { 47° 52' N. / 36° 33' W.
30° 33' W.	-	-	-	44	29·35	51	8 a.m. G.T. 4th.
6.18 a.m.	South, 7. Ditto, sea nearly calm.						Bound E. by Nly.
In 48° 55' N., 29° 15' W.	-	-	-	44	28·87	50	To { 49° 0' N. / 28° 40' W.
							8 a.m. G.T. 5th.

At 8 a.m. of the 4th No. 53 was about 1¼° N. of No. 10. They were experiencing a similar wind, but No. 10 going west got a strong gale from N. to W.N.W., whilst No. 53 going E. got it fresh from S., which afterwards increased to a hurricane from S.W.

See Diagram 2 for a continuous record of this ship's data. It shows how soon she experienced a hurricane.

80

		Wind.		Air.	Bar.	Sea.
No. 26. S.S. "Venezuelan." In {43° 18' N. 37° 14' W. 8 a.m. G.T. 4th. Bound E.N.Ely. To {45° 11' N. 32° 10' W. 8 a.m. G.T. 5th.	8 a.m. and cloudy. 10.30 a.m. and gloomy. 2.24 p.m. cloudy. In 43° 51' N., 36° 2' W. 3.24 p.m. rainy weather. 8.24 p.m. 10.24 p.m. gloomy and threatening. 3.24 a.m., 5th. sea. In 44° 43' N., 33° 9' W. 6.24 a.m. 32° 33' W.	W. by S., 6. Increasing breeze W. by S., 6 to 7. Strong breeze S.W. by S., 6 to 7. Ditto and W. by S., 6 to 7. Ditto, thick S.W. by S. In 44° 15' N., 35° 12' W. S.W. by S., 7. Moderate gale, S. by W., 8. Hard gale, heavy S. by W., 9. Heavy gale. In 45° N.,		51° — 60 — — — 50	30·11 30·08 30·00 — — 29·60 — 29·00	— — — — — — — —

No. 26 was running to the eastward in the same latitude, but about 7° to the westward of No. 25. They seem to have had somewhat similar wind and weather, though the most western ship had the strongest wind.

		Wind.		Air.	Bar.	Sea.
No. 4. S.S "Prussian." In {49° 45' N. 38° 1' W. 8 a.m. G.T. 4th. Bound W.S. Wly. slow. To {48° 41' N. 40° 14' W. 8 a.m. G.T. 5th.	8 a.m. heavy sea. 2.33 p.m. ing. In 40° 35' N., 38° 17' W. 2.33 a.m., 5th. 48° 58' N., 39° 39' W. 6.33 a.m. In 48° 43' N., 39° 58' W.	W. by S., 10. Hail squalls, very W. by S., 9. Gale and sea moderat- W. by S., 7 Snow showers. In W. by S., 7. Snow and head sea.		47° 44 44 40	29·72 29·50 29·26 29·22	51° 54 52 54

		Wind.		Air.	Bar.	Sea.
No. 1. S.S. "City of Antwerp." In {48° 0' N. 38° 47' W. 8 a.m. G.T. 4th. Bound E. by Nly. To {49° 25' N. 32° 8' W. 8 a.m. G.T. 5th.	8 a.m. 9.30 a.m. 2.30 p.m. showers. In 48° 32' N., 36° 49' W. 6.30 p.m. 2.30 a.m., 5th. with rain. 40° 7' N., 33° 42' W. 6.30 a.m. rain. 40° 21' N., 32° 38' W.	W. by S., 5. Fresh breeze. W. by N., 6. Fresh breeze. W. by N., 6. Fresh breeze, passing N.W., 5. Moderate breeze, cloudy. N.E. by E., 4. Light breeze, E.N.E., 6 to 7. Strong breeze and		34° 35 38 38 38 37	29·91 29·89 29·74 29·59 29·33 28·93	50° 50 50 50 48 45

Here is a fast falling barometer with the wind veering from N.W. to E.N.E.

81

	Wind.		Air.	Sea.	No. 11.
8 a.m.	W.N.W.	Moderate but variable in force, changeable appearances. - - - -	45°	56°	S.S. "Iowa." In { 47° 6′ N. / 40° 3′ W. / 8 a.m. G.T. 4th. Bound S.Wly.
2.45 p.m.	W. by N.	Variable in force. In 46° 51′ N., 40° 36′ W. - - - - - -		48 59	To { 45° 39′ N. / 42° 28′ W. / 8 a.m. G.T. 5th.
4.45 p.m.	N.W. by N.	Moderate, but variable in force.			
8.45 p.m.	N. by E.				
11.45 p.m.	N.E. by E., to N. by E.	Increasing rapidly.			
6.45 a.m., 5th.	N.W., 8.	Fresh gale, heavy snow showers. In 45° 41′ N., 42° 19′ W. - - - - -		32 48	

	Wind.		Air.	Bar.	Sea.	No. 13.
8 a.m.	W. by N., 7.	Strong increasing breeze, and cloudy. - - - - -	—	?29·83	—	S.S. "India." In { 48° 53′ N. / 42° 43′ W. / 8 a.m. G.T. 4th. Bound E.N.E.
2.45 p.m.	W. by S., 6.	Strong breeze. In 49° 37′ N., 40° 57′ W. - - -	—	?29·51	—	To { 51° 11′ N. / 36° 29′ W. / 8 a.m. G.T. 5th.
2.45 a.m., 5th.	N.E. by N., 2.	Light variable airs, dull and cloudy. - - - -	—	?29·12	—	
6.45 a.m.	N.E. by N., 2.	Ditto, ditto. In 51° 5′ N., 36° 51′ W. - - - - -	—	?28·93	—	

	Wind.		Air.	Bar.	Sea.	No. 21.
8 a.m.	W. by N.	Moderate breeze, with snow; heavy N.Wly. swell. - -	30°	?30·12	37°	S.S. "Denmark." In { 46° 37′ N. / 44° 55′ W. / 8 a.m. G.T. 4th. Bound E. by Nly.
2.50 p.m.	W. by N. to N.W. by N.	Ditto, ditto. In 46° 56′ N., 43° 20′ W. -	31	?29·96	41	To { 47° 58′ N. / 39° 9′ W. / 8 a.m. G.T. 5th.
6.50 a.m., 5th.	W. by N. to N.W. by N.	Fresh increasing breeze, heavy snow and high sea. In 47° 54′ N. and 39° 23′ W. - - - -	33	?29·43	44	

	Wind.			No. 12.
8 a.m.	W.S.W., 6.	Clear weather, heavy sea.		S.S. "Dacian." In { 44° 11′ N. / 45° 6′ W. / 8 a.m. G.T. 4th. Bound E. by Nly.
2.50 p.m.	E.	Heavy clouds with rain. In 44° 39′ N., 43° 52′ W.		
9.50 p.m.	N.E., 7.	Moderate gales, high sea.		To { 45° 36′ N. / 42° 24′ W. / 8 a.m. G.T. 5th.
3.50 a.m., 5th.	North, 8.	Very high cross sea.		
6.50 a.m.	North, 8.	Ditto. Slowed engines. In 45° 33′ N., 42° 31′ W.		

At 6.50 a.m. Nos. 12 and 11 were in nearly the same position with the wind differing four points; this may arise from No. 12 not having applied the variation as she is reported to have done. No barometer observations are given.

29539.   L

		Wind.		Air.	Bar.	Sea.
No. 23. S.S. "Atrato." In { 32° 6′ N. / 51° 42′ W. / 8 a.m. G.T. 4th. Bound N.Ely. To { 34° 47′ N. / 47° 58′ W. / 8 a.m. G.T. 5th.	8 a.m. 3.20 p.m. 4.50 p.m. 7.20 a.m., 5th.	South-south-easterly, 4. Moderate breeze and fine, considerable swell. - Southerly, 5 to 6. Moderate to fresh breeze and fine. In 32° 56′ N., 50° 38′ W. South-westerly, 6. Just veered to S.W., a fresh breeze; squally and rainy. - N. by W., 6 to 7. Strong breeze, squally and overcast. - - -		— — — —	30·31 30·25 30·23 30·22	— — — —

About 4 p.m. of the 4th No. 23 was experiencing a strong S.W. wind, whilst ships to the N.W. of her had a N.Ely. gale. Buys Ballot's law tells us that there must have been an area of low pressure between them. Most probably this was an early stage of the gale, which blew with such intensity in the middle of the Atlantic on the 5th. The N.E. wind may have been of great extent, as it was also blowing in Iceland.

		Wind.		Air.	Bar.	Sea.
No. 55. S.S. "Rhein." In { 43° 8′ N. / 56° 56′ W. / 8 a.m. G.T. 4th. Bound W. by Sly. To { 41° 27′ N. / 63° 16′ W. / 8 a.m. G.T. 5th.	8 a.m. 4 p.m. 4 a.m., 5th.	N.N.E, 6. Smooth sea; overcast with snow. - - - - - N.N.E., 6. Wind decreasing. In 42° 37′ N., 59° 0′ W. - - - - N.N.W., 5. Clearing. In 41° 44′ N., 62° 15′ W. - - - - -		35° 29 29	30·11 30·07 30·39	39° 37 51

		Wind.		Air.	Bar.	Sea.
No. 9. S.S. "Colorado." In { 41° 19′ N. / 64° 24′ W. / 8 a.m. G.T. 4th. Bound E.N.Ely. To { 42° 53′ N. / 59° 14′ W. / 8 a.m. G.T. 5th.	8 a.m. Noon. 4 p.m. 5 a.m., 5th.	N.E., 7. Strong breeze and easterly sea rising. - - - - - N.N.E., 8. Fresh gale; heavy sea; hard frost. - - - - - N.N.E., 7. Moderate gale; heavy easterly sea. - - - - - N.N.W., 5. Fresh breeze; freezing hard. - - - - -		32° 32 30 23	— — — —	37° 37 38 36

The following observations, taken at Bermuda, were sent by General Lefroy:—

2.18 p.m. G. T., 4th. Barometer 30·011. Wind generally variable, force 3.

At 4.18 p.m., ditto. The wind was N.W. 2.

It will be remembered that on the 3rd Bermuda had a fresh S.E. breeze; this, taken together with the above N.W. wind, looks as if an area of low pressure had passed this island on its route to the N.Ed.

	Wind.		Air.	Bar.	Sea.	No. 46.
8 a.m.	N. by W.	Increasing wind; thick cloudy weather. - - - - -	—	? 29·98	—	S.S. "Nemesis." In { 40° 48′ N. 67° 49′ W. 8 a.m. G.T. 4th.
4.40 p.m.	N. by E., 5.	Cloudy. In 40° 31′ N., 70° 2′ W. - - - -	—	? 30·13	—	Bound Westerly. To New York.

The wind was moderate from N.E., then calm, followed by north-westerly wind, which changed to N.E. near Fire Island.

	Wind.		Air.	Bar.	Sea.	No. 22.
8 a.m.	N.E. by N., 6 to 7.	Strong freshening wind, with sleet. - - - -	39°	30·36	40°	S.S. "Pennsylvania." In { 40° 58′ N. 69° 56′ W. 8 a.m G.T. 4th.
4.48 p.m.	N.E. by N., 6.	Thick. In 40° 45′ N., 72° 0′ W. - - - - -	36	30·58	39	Bound Westerly. To { 40° 40′ N. 74° 2′ W.
4.48 a.m., 5th.	N. by E., 6.	Fresh breeze, and cloudy. - - - -	33	30·58	36	8 a.m. G.T. 5th.

	Wind.		Standard Instruments.			No. 36.
			Air.	Bar.	Sea.	S.S. "Palmyra."
8 a.m.	N.E. by N., 6.	Passing snow showers.	33°	30·28	42°	In { 40° 21′ N. 71° 27′ W. 8 a.m. G.T. 4th.
4.40 p.m.	N.N.E., 6.	Fine, but cloudy. In 40° 7′ N., 69° 47′ W. - - -	34	30·39	45	Bound East.
4.40 a.m., 5th.	E.N.E., 5.	Fine. In 40° 0′ N., 67° 30′ W. - - - - -	34	30·42	45	To { 40° 2′ N. 66° 58′ W. 8 a.m. G.T. 5th.

See Diagram 5 for a continuous record of this ship's observations. It is copied from Capt. Watson's very neat Diagrams sent in with his log. He is a regular observer for this office.

	Wind.		Air.	Bar.	Sea.	No. 3.
a.m.	N.E.	Moderate and clear. - - -	—	? 30·16	—	S.S. "Etna." In New York, 4th.
p.m.	North-westerly.	Moderate and clear, with hard frost.				

	Wind.					No. 16.
7 a.m.	North-westerly.	Light breeze, and fine clear weather throughout.				S.S. "City of London." In New York, 4th.
p.m.	Easterly.					

	Wind.					No. 18.
	North-westerly.	Moderate north-westerly winds, fine weather and hard frost. The only entry for the day, hour not given.				S.S. "Virginia." In New York, 4th.
6 a.m., 5th.	N.E.	Strong breeze and hard frost.				

8 a.m. Wind N. ½ E., *15 miles per hour;* barometer 30·46; air 20°. The gradual rise in barometer continued till 2 p.m., when it was 30·58. After this, a gradual fall set in, amounting to ·22 by 8 a.m. 5th.

New York Observatory.
 8 a.m. 4th.
 To 8 a.m. 5th.

Temperature decreased to 18° by 2 p.m. (lowest temperature being coincident with maximum barometer reading), after which there was a slight rise.

The wind kept pretty steady at N. till about 4 p.m., but subsequently drew more to the eastward. Force light.

		Wind.					Air.	Bar.	Sea.
No. 38. Ship "Nicoline." In { 37° 2' N. 73° 52' W. 8 a.m. G.T. 4th. Nearly stationary. To { 36° 40' N. 73° 58' W. 8 a.m. G.T. 5th.		8 a.m. N.N.E., 8. Sea unusually phosphorescent.	-	-	-	-	47°	30·09	50°
		5 p.m. N.E., 9. In 37° 2' N., 73° 59' W.				-	47	30·15	49
		5 a.m., 5th. N.E. by E., 9. Heavy rain. Wind and sea increasing.	-	-	-	-	51	29·91	52

GENERAL REMARKS ON CHART FOR 8 A.M., GREENWICH TIME, FEBRUARY 4TH, 1870.

The logs of 34 ships have been consulted and the same system followed.

The southerly wind still prevails over the British Islands and Western Europe, and has freshened into a gale at some places, being more southwesterly in the south, and south-easterly in Norway.

In Iceland it is strong from N.E., whilst it is N.W. in Cumberland Sound.

In New York, and with ships in that neighbourhood, the wind is N.W. to north-easterly. It is blowing a gale from the latter quarter with No. 38 at sea.

At Terceira, at 11 a.m., the wind is light north-westerly, whilst there is a light air from S.E. at Madeira, at 10 a.m.

At Belle Isle, at 4 *p.m.*, there is a strong westerly gale.

The hardest gale still lies between 45° to 50° N. and 30° to 40° W., where the wind is westerly.

There is the same general tendency in the air to blow round an area of low pressure in the central part of the Atlantic. There are also indications of a depression coming from the westward. For by roughly sketching a Chart for 6 a.m. of the 5th, we find that Nos. 1, 10, 13, 17, 26, 39, and 53 seem to have winds governed by an area of low pressure, having a central position with regard to them.

It is probable that the area had a N.Ely. course, for No. 2, bound W., had the wind change from E. to N.E. and N.W., whilst No. 35, 7° further east, but also bound west, had the wind change to S., S.W., and W., leading to the supposition that the area of lowest pressure passed between them.

It may be well to mention that the lowest barometer reading known in these latitudes was experienced on the 5th, and to consider whether any signs of its coming are shown on this Chart.

The extracts from logs show that a strong S.Wly. wind prevailed in about 33° N. and 50° W., whilst a N.Ely. gale was blowing in about 42° N. and 62° W. These winds show themselves further to the N.Ed. at 8. a.m., 5th (see the Chart for that date), when they are blowing with greater intensity. Hence we may conclude that the area of low pressure between them had advanced to the N.Ed., and become deeper as it progressed. We have also the very rare case of several ships having falling barometers as they steamed to the westward in a northerly wind. This fact supports the idea that the depression was becoming deeper as it advanced.

It may be worth noticing in connection with the coming gale, that there is a strong N.E. wind in Iceland, a strong N.W. wind in Cumberland Sound, which has generally very little wind, and a N.E. gale near New York, showing that the northerly current on the western side of the Atlantic has intensified, whilst we have strong southerly winds on its eastern side.

Extracts and Remarks to accompany the Chart for 8 a.m., February 5th, 1870.

The wind is generally southerly in Western Europe and Great Britain, blowing a fresh gale in Norway, Shetland, and the Hebrides; but in the Bay of Biscay it is chiefly W., whilst in the south of Ireland it is light from the north-westward, showing that a higher pressure exists over the sea to the westward of Ireland; but it can only be of slight extent, as a fresh southerly wind exists 7° W. of Valencia. We propose to say more on this subject in the general remarks, after comparing this day's Chart with the plates in the Quarterly Weather Report.

	Wind.	Standard Instruments.			
		Air.	Bar.	Sea.	
8 a.m.	N.N.E., 2. Fine, sea smooth. -	57°	30·39	—	No. 50. S.S. "Hotspur."
0.30 p.m.	Calm, fine. - - -	61	30·35	—	⎰ 37° 9′ N.
8.30 p.m.	Calm. In 36° 30′ N., 7° 13′ W.	55	30·36	—	In ⎱ 8° 48′ W. 8 a.m. G.T. 5th.

It will be noticed that No. 50 is far south, also that her wind is northerly, as it is in the south of Spain, where the isobars take a peculiar trend in accordance with the direction.

To ⎰ 36° 0′ N.
⎱ 5° 15′ W.
8 a.m. G.T. 6th.
Bound E. by Sly.

		Wind.		Air.	Bar.	Sea.
No. 6 S.S. "Nestorian." In {55° 18' N., 11° 4' W., 8 a.m. G.T. 5th. Bound West. To {55° 6' N., 17° 46' W., 8 a.m. G.T. 6th.	8 a.m. 1 p.m. and 12° 30' W. 3 p.m. 4 p.m. 8 p.m. drizzling rain. 5 a.m., 6th. squalls. 6 a.m. 7 a.m.	W. by N. ¼ N., 4. Heavy westerly swell. S. by W. ½ W., 7. Ditto. In 55° 16' N., - - - - - S.S.E., 7. In 55° 15' N., 12° 58' W. - S.S.E. ¼ E. 8 - - - - S.S.E. ½ E. 9. Hard gale, heavy sea, In 55° 13' N., 14° 7' W. - - S. ¼ E., 10. Whole gale, terrific - - - - - - S. by W. ¼ W., 11. In 55° 6' N., 17° 20' W. S. by W. ¼ W. 11. Perfect hurricane,		44° 43 46 48 49 45	29·52 29·48 29·36 At 5 p.m. 29·23 28·93 28·24	47° 48 49 50 50 50

with terrific squalls; shipping large quantities of water which stove in the smoking room.

It will be seen that No. 6, like Valencia, had a north-westerly wind of short duration; but it soon backed to the southward, with a fast falling barometer. By referring to Plate VIII. in the Quarterly Weather Report, it will be seen that Valencia had similar changes to those of No. 6, but not so intense.

		Wind.		Air.	Bar.	Sea.
No. 24. S.S. "Nile." In {45° 42' N., 11° 41' W., 8 a.m. G.T. 5th. Bound S.Wly. To {43° 55' N., 14° 38' W., 8 a.m. G.T. 6th.	8 a.m. sea. - 1 p.m. In 45° 12' N., 12° 33' W. 3 p.m. 8 p.m. In 44° 44' N., 13° 11' W. 2 a.m., 6th. sea, both increasing. - 5 a.m. sea. -	S.W. by W., 6. Strong breeze, heavy - - - - - - S.W., 5. Fresh breeze, heavy sea. - - - - S.W., 5. Ditto. In 45° 4' N., 12° 37' W. S.W., 7. Wind and sea increasing. S.W. by S., 8. Fresh gale and high - - - - - S.W. by S., 9. Hard gale, very high - - - - - -		— — — — — —	29·77 29·88 29·90 29·94 — 29·79	— — — — — —

		Wind.		Air.	Bar.	Sea.
No. 19. S.S. "England." In {51° 4' N., 17° 5' W., 8 a.m. G.T. 5th. Bound Wly. To {51° 16' N., 21° 20' W., 8 a.m. G.T. 6th.	8 a.m. 1.15 p.m. 50° 59' N., 18° 2' W. - 3.15 p.m. 8.15 p.m. hard squalls.	S. by E., 8. Fresh gale, high sea. - S. by W. ¼ W., 10. Strong gale. In - - - - - S.S.E., 9. In 51° 1' N., 18° 20' W. - S. by W. ¼ W., 10. Strong gale and In 51° 5' N., 19° 6' W. - -		50°? 48 48 48	29·33 29·10 29·04 28·65	52° 51 51 52

Wind.	Air.	Bar.	Sea.

0.15 a.m., 6th. S.W. by S., 10.   Tremendous squall; a heavy sea washed away bridge boat and stove in the front of poop.

2.15 a.m.   S.W. ¼ S., 10. Tremendous squall. In 51° 10′ N., 20° 13′ W. A heavy sea washed away standard compass, poop ventilator, front and side of wheelhouse, gutted captain's cabin, and injured fourth officer and several seamen.   -   -   -   47°   28·29   50°

3.15 a.m.   S.W. ¼ S., 10. Tremendous squall; another sea washed main boom adrift, smashed engine-room skylight, bridge ventilators, rails, and funnel stays.

4.35 a.m.   S.W. ¼ S., 10. Wind and weather the same; sea washed away galley skylight.

6.15 a.m.   S.W. by W. ½ W., 10. No change given as to force of wind and weather. In 51° 15′ N., 21° 19′ W.   -   -   -   -   -   -   49   28·47   51

It will be noticed that at 6.15 a.m. of the 6th, when No. 19 is experiencing a shift of wind to the westward, with a rising barometer, No. 6 bears N. 32° E., 272 miles from her, and has the wind S. by W., 11, with a falling barometer; blowing a perfect hurricane with terrific squalls. This indicates northing in the route of the gale.

Wind.		Bar.	No. 7. S.S. "Minnesota."

8 a.m.   S.W. by S., 6.   Strong wind and squally, with rain.

In ⎰ 51° 15′ N
   ⎱ 18° 49′ W.
   8 a.m. G.T. 5th.
   Bound West.

9 a.m.   S.E. by S., 6.   Strong breeze and gloomy. Set square sail.

To ⎰ 51° 7′ N.
   ⎱ 22° 6′ W.
   8 a.m. G.T. 6th.

11 a.m.   S.E. by E.

1.20 p.m. S.E. by E., 9.   In 51° 15′ N., 19° 59′ W., strong gale, constant rain; took in square sail.   -   ???   28·85

2.20 p.m. S. by E., 8.   Fresh gale, and thick with constant rain. Split main stay sail.

3.20 p.m. S. by E., 8.   In 51° 14′ N., 20° 12′ W.   falling.

4.20 p.m. Passed No. 20, "The Queen."

8.20 p.m. S. by W., 9.   Strong gale, with constant rain. In 51° 12′ N., 20° 45′ W.

11.20 p.m. S. by W., 11. Blowing with hurricane violence; sea making a clean breach over the ship; coals shifted, and hove ship down to starboard; broke

88

No. 7.
S.S. "Minnesota"
—continued.

in port iron cabin doors ; smashed the starboard bridge boat ; stove in after hatches, and washed tarpaulin off main hatch, &c., &c. - - -   ? ? ? 28·25 —

Bar.
lowest

Wind.
0.20 a.m., 6th. S.W. by W., 11. In 51° 10′ N., 21° 12′ W.
1.20 a.m. S.W. by W., 10. Moderating, but blowing very hard.
2.20 a.m. W. by S., 9 to 10. Moderating, but blowing very hard, with violent squalls. In 51° 10′ N., 21° 25′ W.
7.20 a.m. West, 9. Strong gale, with high sea. In 51° 8′ N., 22° 0′ W.

No. 7 was about a degree west of No. 19, and experienced similar weather, but seems to have got the changes of wind first; both ships suffered much damage from the sea.

The barometer readings are rather loosely entered at noon each day.

No. 45.
Ship "Carl Georg."
In { 47° 3′ N.
    21° 58′ W.
    8 a.m. G.T. 5th.
Bound Easterly.
To { 47° 42′ N.
    17° 51′ W.
    8 a.m. G.T. 6th.

Wind.   Air.   Bar.   Sea.
8 a.m. N.W., 8. Violent wind, with hail and rain squalls ; high wild sea. - - - -   53° 29·83   55°
1.20 p.m. N.W., 8. High wild sea ; barometer unsteady. In 47° 20′ N., 21° 4′ W. - - -   52 29·94   55
3 p.m. N.W., 8. Barometer unsteady. In 47° 22′ N., 20° 45′ W. - - - -   — 29·94   —
5.20 p.m. N.W., 7.
9.20 p.m. W., 7. Heavy hail squalls from W. and S.W. In 47° 29′ N., 19° 47′ W. - -   51 29·81   55
5.20 a.m. 6th. S.W., 6. Wind increasing from S.W., heavy rain ; barometer constantly falling. In 47° 39′ N., 18° 15′ W. - - - -   53 29·69   54

It will be noticed that No. 45 has had the wind almost constant at N.W. for three days, and that this direction does not seem to agree well with that given by other ships near her. The log seems carefully kept, but her barometer seems too high.

No. 35.
S.S. "Tarifa."
In { 51° 20′ N.
    22° 2′ W.
    8 a.m. G.T. 5th.
Bound West.
To { 51 4′ N.
    24° 58′ W.
    8 a.m. G.T. 6th.

                                                                    Standard Instruments.
Wind.   Air.   Bar.   Sea.
8 a.m. S.W. by S., 4. - - - - -   46° 29·26   51°
9.16 a.m. S. by W., 4. - - - - -   46 29·20   52
11.16 a.m. - - - - - - -   — 28·85   —
1.35 p.m. S. by E., 7; squally, with rain. In 51° 10′ N., 23° 44′ W. - - - -   52 28·42   52

	Wind.	Standard Instruments.		
		Air.	Bar.	Sea.
3.35 p.m.	South, 8. In 51° 8′ N., 23° 49′ W.	—	27·95	—
5.35 p.m.	S. by W., 9. Squally, with rain	52°	27·76	51°
7.35 p.m.	S. by W., 10. Ditto. In 51° 3′ N., 23° 50′ W. Barometer at its lowest.	—	27·33	—
9.35 p.m.	S.W. by S., 11. Ditto.	54	27·61	52
11.35 p.m.	S.W. by W., 12. From 8.35 p.m., 5th, to 0.35 a.m., 6th, blew a hurricane; sea not so high as might be expected.	—	27·61	—
1.35 a.m., 6th.	S.W. by W., 11. Squally. In 50° 56′ N., 24° 13′ W.	55	27·62	52
5.35 a.m.	S.W. by W., 10. Hail squalls. In 51° 2′ N., 24° 47′ W.	44	27·72	51

See Diagram 3 for a continuous record of these observations.

The remarkably low barometer experienced by No. 35 at 7.35 p.m. is borne out by the observations of Nos. 2 and 53. A Chart is given for *3 p.m.* of the 5th: there it will be seen that No. 2 had a gale of hurricane force from N.W. by N., the wind having shifted since 2 p.m. from N.E. by N., proving that she passed to the N. of the lowest pressure, or rather that it passed to the south of her. At the same time her barometer was 27·75! and as the wind was northerly, according to Buys Ballot's law the barometer must have been lower still to the eastward of her.

Then, again, at 3 p.m. of the 5th No. 53 gives the barometer 28·02! wind S.W., force 11. With the wind S.W. we may infer that there was a lower pressure to the N.W. of her. Judging from the positions of the area of lowest pressure at 8 a.m., 3 p.m., and 8 p.m. of the 5th, and again at 8 a.m. of the 6th, it seems probable that it was moving to the N.E. at the rate of about 30 miles per hour, so that No. 53 was, to a certain extent, going with it; but of course it passed her, and at 5.40 p.m. she records the wind S.W. by W., 12; barometer at its lowest, 27·73! At 9.40 p.m. her wind drew to W.N.W., 12; the barometer having risen ·88 in four hours.

At 3 p.m. of 5th, No. 35 had the wind S., 8; barometer 28·07; but she was steering to the westward, and Nos. 2 and 53 show that there was a very low pressure to the S.W. of her, which was travelling to the N.E.; hence, from her position on the Chart, it will be seen that she was likely to meet it. This she did at 7.35 p.m., when her barometer was 27·33; and it was followed by a shift of wind to S.W.; blowing with hurricane force for four hours. It will be seen that her barometer did not rise quickly immediately after the passage of the lowest pressure, as if a long strip of low pressure had passed over her. Between 9.40 a.m. and 1.40 p.m. of the 6th, however, when the wind shifted to W.N.W., it (like that of No. 53) rose · 8 in four hours.

No. 7 is the only ship near No. 35 which was also bound to the westward (see the 3 p.m. Chart) and she was nearly 4° further E., whilst the lowest pressure was west of No. 35; she logs the wind of hurricane force, with the sea making a clean breach over her; her coals shifted, and she suffered much damage. Her barometer was not very trustworthy.

No. 19, also bound to the westward, was two degrees to the eastward of No. 7, and therefore nearly 6° E. of No. 35, so that she did not pass so near the lowest pressure; still she suffered much damage from the sea, and had several of her crew injured. Her barometer fell to 28·29.

		Wind.	Air.	Bar.	Sea.
No. 20. S.S. "The Queen." In { 50° 23′ N. 22° 11′ W. 8 a.m. G.T. 5th. Bound E. by Nly. To { 51° 23′ N. 15° 56′ W. 8 a.m. G.T. 6th.	8 a.m.	S. by W., 5. Increasing and backing to the southward.	47°	? 29·50	57°
	1.20 p.m.	S. by W., 8. Increasing gale, thick and rainy (in 50° 33′ N., 20° 46′ W.)	51	? 29·20	52
	3.20 p.m.	S. by W., 9. (In 50° 38′ N., 20° 16′ W.)	—	? 29·45	—
	3.50 p.m.	Passed No. 7, (the " Minnesota ")	—	—	—
	5.20 p.m.	S.W. by S., 9. Heavy gale and sea	52	29·10	54
	1·20 a.m., 6th.	S.W. by W., 9. Strong gale. 10 p.m. to midnight, furious squalls, with lightning at 11 p.m. In 51° 4′ N., 17° 54′ W.	52	? 28·60	53
	2.20 a.m.	S by W., 10. Strong gale; terrific squalls; heavy cross sea; and heavy lightning at times.	—	—	—
	5.20 a.m.	S. by W., 10. Strong gale and heavy sea. In 51° 16′ N., 16° 44′ W.	46	? 28·64	52

No, 20 only gives the wind south-westerly, westerly &c. As she closed with the land the wind moderated.

		Wind.	Air.	Aneroid.	Sea.
No. 30. H.M.S. "Orontes." In { 50° 38′ N. 22° 21′ W. 8 a.m. G.T. 5th. Bound Easterly. To { 50° 25′ N. 20° 16′ W. 8 a.m. G.T. 6th.	8 a.m.	S. by E., 3. Squally, with drizzle.	53°	29·19	52°
	1.20 p.m.	S. by E., 7 to 9. Squally with rain, went easy, 24 revolutions; and rounded-to on the starboard tack. In 50° 59′ N. 20° 59′ W.	53	28·71	52
	2.20 p.m.	S.E. by S., 9. Squally, with rain.	53	28·62	53
	3.20 p.m.	South 9; Ditto. In 50° 50′ N., 20° 55′ W.	53	28·59	55

91

	Wind.		Air.	Aneroid.	Sea.
5.20 p.m.	South, 9.	Squally, with rain.	55°	28·45	54°
6.20 p.m.	S.W., 10.	Squally; overcast.	55	28·42	54
8.20 p.m.	S.W. by W., 9 to 10.	Blue sky; clouds and squalls	52	28·38	52
9.20 p.m.	Ditto, ditto, ditto.		50	28·38	52
10.20 p.m.	A sea smashed the foremost boat on port bow.		—	—	—
1.20 a.m., 6th.	W. by S., 9 to 10. Lightning and passing showers. (In 50° 35′ N., 20° 59′ W.)		48	28·47	52
5.20 a.m.	W.S.W., 8 to 9. Detached clouds, squally with lightning, still hove to. (In about 50° 27′ N., 20° 50′ W.)		47	28·67	—

Nos. 30 and 20 were very near each other at 8 a.m. of the 5th, and both bound to the eastward.

It will be seen that at 1.20 p.m., No. 30 hove-to, whilst No. 20 continued her course.

At about 2 a.m. of the 6th, the wind backed to S. by W. with No. 20, whilst it veered to W. by S. with No. 30. With No. 20 the barometer was inclining to rise very slightly in spite of the backing wind, showing the effect of steaming fast to the eastward, whilst with No. 30 it rose briskly as she lay hove-to, with the wind veering to the westward, the area of lowest pressure having swept past her.

	Wind.		Air.	Bar.	Sea.	
8 a.m.	S.E.	Light wind; gloomy and heavy rain.	43°?	28·63	52°	No. 49.
10 a.m.	S.E.	Continual gale and rain. In 50° 10′ N., 24° 10′ W.	42	?28·51	51	S.S. "Marathon."
1.30 p.m.	S.E.	Ditto, gale and sea. In 50° 18′ N., 23° 11′ W.	43	?28·47	52	In { 50° 7′ N. / 24° 38′ W. / 8 a.m. G.T. 5th.
2.30 p.m.	S. by W.	Ditto, weather. In 50° 22′ N., 22° 55′ W.				Bound E. by Nly.
3.30 p.m.	S. ¼ W.	In 50° 26′ N., 22° 40′ W.,				To { 51° 42′ N. / 18° 4′ W. / 8 a.m. G.T. 6th.
5.30 p.m.	S. by W.	Ditto weather. In 50° 36′ N., 22° 6′ W.	52	?28·28	52	
7.30 p.m.	S. by W.	In 50° 45′ N., 21° 34′ W.				
9.30 p.m.	S. by W.	At 11.30 p.m. sea damaged starboard side of saloon. In 50° 54′ N., 21° 1′ W.	55	?28·28	57	

	Wind.	Air.	Bar.	Sea.

1.30 a.m., 6th. S. by W., 11.* Hard gale; high sea; lightning in all quarters. In 51° 12′ N., 19° 55′ W. - - - - - 49°? 28·28 57°
2.30 a.m. S.W. by S. Hard gale, heavy sea, breaking on board at times. In 51° 16′ N., 19° 38′ W.
5.30 a.m. S.W. by W. Ditto, ditto. In 51° 30′ N., 18° 49′ W. - - .. - 42 ? 28·46 56

The entries in No. 49 are sometimes "southerly," "westerly," &c.

At 1.30 p.m. of the 5th No. 49 was about S.S.E. 56 miles from No. 35, their winds and barometers agreeing very fairly, No. 49 going east seems to have had a slightly falling barometer down to 28·28, where it remained steady for eight hours, whilst No. 35 going west had a fall of more than one inch in six hours, when the wind drew more westerly and blew with hurricane force.

No. 25.
S.S. "Cuban."
In { 45° 11′ N.
24° 53′ W.
8 a.m. G.T. 5th.
Bound E.N.Ely.
To { 46° 50′ N.
19° 30′ W.
8 a.m. G.T. 6th.

	Wind.	Air.	Bar.	Sea.

8 a.m. S. by W., 9. At 9.40 a.m., blowing very hard, heavy squalls and rain. - - - ? 45°? 29·10 —
1.30 p.m. S. by W., 9. Hard gale; tremendous sea. In 45° 33′ N., 23° 48′ W. - - — ? 29·10 —
9.30 p.m. W. by N. Heavy rain. In 46° 6′ N., 21° 57′ W. - - - - - ? 45 — —
2.30 a.m., 6th. W. by N. Hard squalls. In 46° 27′ N., 20° 48′ W. - - - — ? 29·22 —
5.30 a.m. W.S.W. Daylight, much vivid lightning in S.W. and N.W. In 46° 40′ N., 20° 7′ W. — — —

No. 25 was well to the southward and seems to have got a very hard gale.

No. 2.
S.S. "City of Cork."
In { 50° 24′ N.
28° 39′ W.
8 a.m. G.T. 5th.
Bound West slowly.
To { 50° 5′ N.
31° 26′ W.
8 a.m. G.T. 6th.

	Wind.	Air.	Bar.	Sea.

8 a.m. E. by S., 4. - - - - 49° 28·82 47°
10 a.m. N.E. by E., 5. Fresh increasing breeze with rain. In 50° 23′ N., 29° 0′ W. - - 49 28·67 49
Noon. N.E. by N., 6, 7. Strong increasing breeze; heavy rain. In 50° 23′ N., 29° 21′ W. - 48 28·55 49
2 p.m. N.E. by N., 8. Fresh gale; mist with rain. In 50° 22′ N., 29° 43′ W. - - - 49 28·42 48

---

* From a remark in the captain's letter 25th October 1870, the gale was force 11.

	Wind.	Air.	Bar.	Sea.
3 p.m.	N.W. by N., 11 to 12. Gale increasing to a hurricane; sea running very high. In 50° 21′ N., 29° 49′ W.	—	27·75	—
4 p.m.	N.W. by N., 11 to 12. Ditto. In 50° 20′ N., 29° 55′ W.	47°	27·97	48°
5 p.m.	-	—	28·09	—
6 p.m.	N.W. by N., 9. Strong gale. In 50° 18′ N., 30° 7′ W.	42	28·20	47
8 p.m.	N.W. by N., 9. Ditto. In 50° 16′ N., 30° 18′ W.	38	28·47	47
10 p.m.	N.W. by N., 8. Moderating, but very squally. In 50° 14′ N., 30° 30′ W.	36	28·65	47
Midnight.	N.W. by N., 8. In 50° 12′ N., 30° 42′ W.	34	28·85	46
1 a.m., 6th.	W. by N., 8.			
2 a.m.	W. by N., 8. Heavy sea; hard hail squalls. In 50° 11′ N., 30° 52′ W.	34	28·97	46
7. a.m.	W. by N., 7. Sea abating. In 50° 7′ N., 31° 14′ W.	38	29·00	46

This easterly wind from 8 a.m. to 2 p.m. considered in connection with the northerly and southerly winds near her, is very interesting. It seems to have been merely a back drift or eddy caused by the collision of those two main currents of air.

See remark to No. 35 for further allusions to No. 2. Also the Charts for 3 p.m. and 8 p.m. of the 5th.

	Wind.	Air.	Bar.	Sea.
8 a.m.	S.S.W., 8.	49°	28·65	51°
10 a.m.	S.W., 9. In 49° 5′ N., 28° 2′ W.	55	28·43	51
1.40 p.m.	S.W., 10. Very high S.W. sea. In 49° 15′ N., 26° 44′ W.	55	28·16	56
3.40 p.m.	S.W., 11. In 49° 19′ N., 26° 11′ W.	51	27·94	55
5.40 p.m.	S.W. by W., 12. In 49° 22′ N., 25° 38′ W.	47	27·73	54
9.40 p.m.	W.N.W., 12. High S.W. and N.W. sea. In 49° 28′ N., 24° 39′ W.	50	28·61	53
1.40 a.m., 6th.	W.N.W., 9. In 49° 34′ N., 23° 37′ W.	43	28·73	50
5.40 a.m.	W.N.W., 8. In 49° 41′ N., 22° 34′ W.	42	28·86	50

No. 53.
S.S. "Weser."
In { 49° 0′ N.
28° 40′ W.
8 a.m. G.T. 5th.
Bound Easterly.
To { 49° 47′ N.
21° 57′ W.
8 a.m. G.T. 6th.

See remark to No. 35 (p. 89) and the Charts for 3 p.m. and 8 p.m. of the 5th.

See Diagram 2 for a continuous record of this ship's observations; the quick movement of both barometer and thermometer is well shown there.

94

The 8 a.m. Chart of to-day shows how very near together were a N.E. and S.W. wind. (See Nos. 53 and 1.)

		Wind.		Air.	Bar.	Sea.
No. 1. S.S. " City of Antwerp." In { 49° 25′ N. 32° 8′ W. 8 a.m. G.T. 5th. Bound Easterly. To { 49° 52′ N. 25° 4′ W. 8 a.m. G.T. 6th.	8 a.m.	E.N.E., 8.	Rain; wind increasing.	-	37°	28·73	48°
	10 a.m.	E.N.E., 9.	Rain. In 49° 31′ N., 31° 37′ W.	37	28·61	48
	11 a.m.	N.E. by N., 9.	Rain.			
	Noon.	N.E. by N.	Rain. In 49° 37′ N., 31° 6′ W.	42	28·51	48
	2 p.m.	N.N.W., 10.	Rain. In 49° 42′ N., 30° 35′ W.	44	28·48	50
	3 p.m.	N.W. by N., 10.	High sea. In 49° 43′ N., 30° 17′ W. - - - -		3.30 p.m. 28·41	—
	4 p.m.	N.W. by N., 10.	High sea. In 49° 43′ N., 29° 59′ W. - - - - -	49	28·48	49
	5 p.m.	N.W. by W., 10.				
	6 p.m.	N.W. by W., 10.	In 49°44′ N., 29°23′ W.	48	28·58	48
	8 p.m.	N.W. by W., 10.	In 49°45′ N., 28°47′ W.	50	28·63	50
	10 p.m.	N.W. by W., 9.	In 49°46′ N., 28°10′ W.	50	28·76	50
	2 a.m.	N.W by W., 7.	In 49°48′ N., 26°56′ W.	50	28·87	50
	6 a.m.	N.W. by W., 6.	Sea going down, in 49° 50′ N., 25° 44′ W. - - - -	45	28·96	49

It will be seen that No. 1, being to the S.W. of the lowest pressure at 3 p.m., does not get a lower barometer, for although she is standing towards the lowest pressure it is going to the N.E. faster than she is. The direction and changes of her wind show that she was first on the north-western and then on the south-western side of an area of low pressure. Its speed to the north-eastward, and the E.N.E. wind being dead against her, prevented her steaming into the area of lowest pressure. This is another case of the barometer falling as the wind drew more northerly, strongly indicating that an area of low pressure coming from the south-westward passed to the eastward of No. 1, and that she, steaming to the eastward, closed with the lowest pressure until the wind shifted to the W. of N.

		Wind.			Air.	Bar.	Sea.
No. 26. S.S. " Venezuelan." In { 45° 11′ N. 32° 10′ W. 8 a.m. G.T. 5th. Bound E.N.Ely. To { 47° 0′ N. 26° 59′ W. 8 a.m. G.T. 6th.	8 a.m.	S. by W., 10.	Heavy gale and sea.	-	52°	28·97	—
	10 a.m.	W. ½ S., 10 to 11.	Terrific gale.	In 45° 20′ N., 31° 44′ W. -	—	28·93	—
	2 p.m.	W. by N., 10 to 11.	Ditto.	In 45° 38′ N., 30° 53′ W. - - -	60	28·99	—
	3 p.m.	W. by N., 10 to 11.	Ditto.	In 45° 43′ N., 30° 40′ W. - - -	—	29·02	—
	6 p.m.	W. by N., 9.	Strong gale.	In 45° 56′ N., 30° 2′ W. - - -	—	29·10	—

95

	Wind.		Air.	Bar.	Sea.
10 p.m.	W. by N., 9. Hard gale; very heavy squalls; thunder and lightning. In 46° 14′ N., 29° 11′ W. - - - - -		46°	29·09	—
2 a.m., 6th.	W. by S., 9. Ditto. In 46° 32′ N., 28° 19′ W. - - - - -		—	29·12	—
6 a.m.	W. by N., 9. Strong gale, heavy squalls. In 46° 50′ N., 27° 28′ W. - - -		—	29·08	—

It will be seen that at 8 a.m. of the 5th Nos. 1 and 26 were in the same longitude, but 4° of latitude apart, and that whilst No. 1 had the wind E.N.E., 8, No. 26 had it S. by W., 10; so that the area of lowest pressure must have been between them.

	Wind.	Air.	Bar.	Sea.	
8 a.m.	N. ½ E., 1. Very cloudy. - -	—	? 28·96	—	No. 13. S.S. "India."
10.24 a.m.	N. ½ E., 3. Gloomy; passing snow showers. In 51° 25′ N., 35° 51′ W. - - -		falling.		In { 51° 11′ N. 36° 29′ W. 8 a.m. G.T. 5th.
0.20 p.m.	N. ½ E., 3 to 4 - - -	—	? 28·80	—	Bound E. by Nly.
2.20 p.m.	N. ½ E., 5. Fresh breeze and cloudy. In 51° 46′ N., 34° 51′ W. - - -		falling.		To { 52° 37′ N. 30° 26′ W. 8 a.m. G.T. 6th.
3.20 p.m.	N.N.W., 6. In 51° 49′ N., 34° 36′ W.	—	? 28·83	—	
6.20 p.m.	N.N.W., 6 to 7. Strong breeze; cloudy. In 51° 58′ N., 33° 52′ W. - - -				
		—	? 28·68	—	
8.20 p.m.	N.W., 6. In 52° 3′ N., 33° 22′ W.				
10.20 p.m.	N.W., 6. In 52° 9′ N., 32° 53′ W.				
Midnight.	W.N.W.				
2.20 a.m., 6th.	W.N.W., 5. In 52° 20′ N., 31° 54′ W.	—	? 28·73	—	
3.20 a.m.	W., 5.				
4.20 a.m.	W., 5. Heavy easterly swell; very cloudy and squally. - - - -				
		—	? 28·75	—	

The northerly wind of this ship at 8 a.m., with a falling barometer, indicates that a lower pressure was passing to the eastward of her.

It is plain that she crossed the wake of the great gale several hours after it had swept to the north-eastward. At 4 a.m. of the 6th she was experiencing a heavy easterly swell whilst the wind was westerly. This shows how long a swell lasts after its wind has passed on. As she was steaming to the eastward she was more likely to notice a swell from that quarter than from any other.

She seems to have had much less wind than ships further south.

		Wind.	Air.	Bar.	Sea.
No. 17. S.S. "Helvetia." In { 47° 38′ N. 37° 36′ W. 8 a.m. G.T. 5th. Bound W.S.Wly. To { 46° 47′ N. 39° 46′ W. 8 a.m. G.T. 6th.	8 a.m. 8.30 a.m. 11.30 a.m. 2.34 p.m. 3.34 p.m. 10.34 p.m. 2.34 a.m., 6th. 6.34 a.m.	N. by W., 8. Very squally, with sleet. - N.W. by N., 8. Ditto weather. In 47° 37′ N., 37° 40′ W. N.W. by W., 9. Very heavy squalls, with hail. In 47° 29′ N., 38° 6′ W. N.W. by W., 9. Ditto weather. In 47° 22′ N., 38° 32′ W. W. by N., 9. Ditto weather, and snow. In 47° 20′ N., 38° 36′ W. W. by N., 10 to 11. Terrific gale. In 47° 6′ N., 39° 6′ W. N.W. by W., 9. Slightly moderating. In 46° 58′ N., 39° 23′ W. N.W. by W., 9. Heavy hail squalls. In 46° 50′ N., 39° 40′ W. -	38° 35 37 39 37	28·98 29·13 29·14 29·18 29·64	48° 50 52 53 52

It will be remembered that on the 4th, No. 17 had a falling barometer with a northerly wind, and never got any part of the southerly wind belonging to this gale, though she got a terrific gale from W. by N. This looks as if the area of lowest pressure was always to the eastward of her.

		Wind.	Air.	Bar.	Sea.
No. 39. S.S. "Westphalia." In { 47° 33′ N. 37° 34′ W. 8 a.m. G.T. 5th. Bound W. by Sly. To { 46° 42′ N. 41° 4′ W. 8 a.m. G.T. 6th.	8 a.m. 10.16 a.m. 2.35 p.m. 6.35 p.m. 10.35 p.m. 2.35 a.m., 6th. 6.35 a.m.	N.N.W., 8. Constant rain. - N.W., 10. Constant snow, hail or rain. In 47° 26′ N., 37° 4′ W. - W. by N., 10 to 11. Snow and hail. In 47° 14′ N., 38° 51′ W. - W.S.W., 10. In 47° 7′ N., 39° 22′ W. West, 8. In 47° 0′ N., 39° 53′ W. W. by N., 10 to 12. Squalls with hurricane force. In 46° 53′ N., 40° 24′ W. - W. by N., 10. In 46° 46′ N., 40° 55′ W.	40° 39 35 34 39 44 43	28·98 29·03 29·16 29·18 29·08 29·39 29·71	51° 50 47 47 50 57 55

No. 39 had the hardest blow in the warmest water. It will be seen by referring to the extracts for the 6th, that the wind lulled as she got into cooler water. See Diagram 4 for her continuous record, which shows the very rare case of a quickly falling barometer, with a northerly wind, even though the ship was bound to the westward.

'97

	Wind.	Air.	Bar.	Sea.	
8 a.m.	N.W. by W., 6 to 7. Snow.	—	? 29·43	—	No. 21. S.S. "Denmark."
10.52 a.m.	Ditto ditto. Snow and hail. In				In { 47° 58′ N. 39° 9′ W.
48° 9′ N., 38° 37′ W. - - - -		36°	? 29·39	54°	8 a.m. G.T. 5th.
2.30 p.m.	Ditto, 7 to 9. Heavy snow and hail				Bound E. by Nly. 49° 18′ N.
squalls. In 48° 21′ N., 37° 32′ W. - - -		33	? 29·35	56	To { 32° 44′ W.
3.30. p.m.	West by northerly.				8 a.m. G.T. 6th.
6.30 p.m.	West by northerly, 7 to 8. Squally.				
In 48° 34′ N., 36° 27′ W. - - - -		33	? 29·45	51	
10.30 p.m.	West by northerly, 5 to 6. Moderate				
breeze. In 48° 47′ N., 35° 22′ W. - -		34	? 29·31	51	
2.30 a.m., 6th. West by northerly, 6. Fresh breeze.					
In 49° 0′ N., 34° 17′ W. - - - -		34	? 29·38	50	
6.30 a.m.	West by northerly, 6. Squally. In				
49° 12′ N., 33° 13′ W. - - - -		41	? 29·44	51	

No. 21, bound E., had much less wind than the ships near her, which were bound W.

	Wind.				
8 a.m.	N.W. by W., 9. Hard snow squalls, gale just set in				No. 10. S.S. "Manhattan."
after an unsteady northerly wind.					In { 45° 14′ N. 39° 40′ W.
2.40 p.m.	W. by N., 10. Fearful gale, tremendous sea, washed				8 a.m. G.T. 5th. Bound W.S.Wly.
away topgallant bulwarks, and broke skylights, &c. In 44° 55′ N.,					To { 43° 56′ N. 42° 10′ W.
40° 39′ W.					8 a.m. G.T 6th.
6.40 p.m.	W. by N., 10. Snow squalls; fearfully high and				
broken sea. 44° 41′ N., 41° 0′ W.					
6.40 a.m., 6th. W. by N., 8. More moderate, and less sea. In					
44° 1′ N., 42° 4′ W.					

	Wind.	Air.	Bar.	Sea.	
8. a.m.	W. by S., 7. Overcast and misty,				No. 4. S.S. "Prussian."
with passing showers of snow, and a westerly sea. -		38°	29·22	54°	In { 48° 41′ N. 40° 14′ W.
10.33 a.m.	W. by S., 8. Ditto with squalls.				8 a.m. G.T. 5th. Bound W.S.Wly.
In 48° 33′ N., 40° 33′ W. - - - -		34	—	—	To { 47° 48′ N. 42° 49′ W.
2.44 p.m.	W. by S., 8. Ditto weather and sea.				8 a.m. G.T. 6th.
In 48° 20′ N., 41° W. - - - -		33	—	—	
6.44 p.m.	W. by S., 7. Ditto. In 48° 13′ N.,				
41° 25′ W. - - - - -		—	29·23	—	
10.44 p.m.	N.W. by W., 10. Heavy squalls,				
very heavy confused sea. In 48° 5′ N., 41° 51′ W. -		—	29·34	—	
2.44 a.m., 6th. N.W. by W., 10. Ditto weather and					
sea. In 47° 58′ N., 42° 16′ W. - - -		—	29·55	—	
6.44 a.m.	N.W. by W., 9. Wind unsteady. Ditto				
weather and sea. In 47° 50′ N., 42° 42′ W. -		—	29·75	—	

98

No. 4 gave the wind W. by S. for nearly three days. The ships near her about 8 a.m. of the 5th had the wind much more northerly.

No. 12.
S.S. "Dacian."
In { 45° 36' N.
    42° 24' W.
    8 a.m. G.T. 5th.
Bound Ely. very slow.
To { 45° 44' N.
    41° 21' W.
    8 a.m. G.T. 6th.

	Wind.
8 am.	N. 8. Very high cross sea.
11 a.m.	N.W., 8. In 45° 41' N., 42° 16' W.
2.50 p.m.	N.W., 8. In 45° 58' N., 41° 51' W.
3.50 p.m.	N.N.E., 9. Very heavy seas, carried away part of wheel-house and stove starboard quarter-boat, hove ship to. In 45° 57' N., 41° 49' W.
8.50 p.m.	N.N.E., 10. Squalls. Close-reefed mainsail, and main-topsail blown away. Got out a floating anchor. Shipping large quantities of water over all, disabling two officers and two seamen. In 45° 54' N., 41° 43' W.
2.50 a.m., 6th.	N.N.E., 10. Hard squalls and rain; lost bulwarks and stove starboard lifeboat. In 45° 48' N., 41° 31' W.

The change to N.N.E. experienced by No. 12 at 4 p.m. does not seem to have come to ships near her. No. 12 had the wind from this direction for two days and a half, according to her log. The variation is said to have been applied to the direction of the wind; if it were not, then the wind was three points more westerly, which would agree better with that of her neighbours.

No. 11.
S.S. "Iowa."
In { 45° 39' N.
    42° 28' W.
    8 a.m. G.T. 5th.
Bound S.Wly. very slowly.
To { 44° 49' N.
    43° 55' W.
    8 a.m. G.T. 6th.

	Wind.	Air.	Bar.	Sea.
8 a.m.	N.W., 8. Severe snow squalls; heavy northerly sea.	31°	—	49°
2.53 p.m.	N.W., 9. Showers of snow and sleet. In 45° 11' N., 43° 11' W. Sea struck the mainsail; carried away No. 1 boat, rails, &c. &c.	31	—	49
2.53 a.m., 6th.	W. by N., 8. Inclining to moderate, sea still very high. In 44° 56' N., 43° 42' W.	40	—	50

No. 23.
S.S. "Atrato."
In { 34° 47' N.
    47° 58' W.
    8 a.m. G.T. 5th.
Bound N.Ely.
To { 37° 15' N.
    43° 55' W.
    8 a.m. G.T. 6th.

	Wind.			
8 a.m.	N. by W., 6. Strong breeze; overcast and squally.	—	?30·25	—
4 p.m.	North, 5. Fresh to moderate breeze, confused sea. In 35° 40' N., 46° 39' W.	—	?30·31	—

The wind decreased and was light northerly until 8 a.m. of the 6th, when it was light and variable from the northward, with a heavy confused sea.

No. 23 seems to have followed in the rear of the area of low pressure and its accompanying gale, getting only the sea which it left behind it.

	Wind.		Air.	Bar.	Sea.	No. 9.
8 a.m.	N.N.W., 5.	Fresh breeze; freezing hard. - - - - - - -	23°	—	36°	S.S. "Colorado." In {42° 53' N. / 59° 14' W. / 8 a.m. G.T. 5th.
4 p.m.	North, 5.	Ditto, ditto. Fine and clear; with a heavy N.E. sea rising. In 43° 31' N., 57° 30' W. - - - - - -	28	—	41	Bound E. by Nly. To {44° 43' N. / 53° 27' W. / 8 a.m. G.T. 6th.
8 p.m.	N. ¼ W., 5.	Ditto. In 43° 50' N., 56° 26' W. - - - - - -	27	—	36	

8 a.m., 6th. North-westerly light.

The north-easterly swell, or probably northerly, after applying the variation, seems to have come from a distant stronger wind. It will be seen that a heavy northerly gale was blowing in about 40° W. and a heavy north-easterly gale in Iceland.

	Wind.		Air.	Bar.	Sea.	No. 55.
8 a.m.	N.E., 5.	Surface temperature suddenly decreasing. - - - - -	30°	30·42	40°	S.S. "Rhein." In {41° 27' N. / 63° 16' W. / 8 a.m. G.T. 5th.
4.22 p.m.	N.E., 4.	Cloudy. In 40° 50' N., 65° 30' W. - - - - - -	26	30·41	43	Bound W. by Sly. To {40° 33' N. / 71° 52' W. / 8 a.m. G.T. 6th.
0.22 a.m., 6th.	N.E., 5.	Heavy rain. In 40° 40' N., 69° 25' W. - -	35	30·13	39	
4.22 a.m.	N.E., 5.	In 40° 37' N., 70° 38' W.	38	30·08	43	

The following Bermuda observations and extract from a local paper were sent by General Lefroy:

2.18 p.m. G. T. Bar. 29·911 (falling). Wind generally S., 6.

"A whirl of wind of great force, but fortunately very limited in its circumference, and of only a few seconds duration in its intensity, coming from about S. by W., passed over the western portion of the harbour and town of Hamilton about one o'clock on Saturday last. (5.18 p.m. G. T., February 5th, 1870.) It first struck the dismantled barque "Mary and Louisa" and the brigantine "T. A. Darrell," lying moored together, bows on to the eastern portion of Washington's point. The shore fasts of both vessels instantly snapped, but fortunately the stern moorings held, and both vessels swung round to the wind. The "T. A. Darrell" having a swept hold, was nearly thrown on her beam ends. The whirl, in its course over the town, did some damage to several houses, but nothing very serious."

Here we have a strong southerly breeze to the eastward (at Bermuda), and a heavy N.E. gale to the westward, experienced by No. 38. Buys Ballot's law tells us that there must have been a low pressure between them. These are the very elements for a revolving gale. More observations would probably have shown it on the Chart. The whirl experienced at Bermuda may have been caused by the near contact of these opposite currents.

		Wind.		Standard Instruments.		
				Air.	Bar.	Sea.
No. 36. S.S. "Palmyra."	8 a.m.	N.E., 6.	Fine.	35°	30·32	40°
In { 40° 2' N. 66° 58' W. 8 a.m. G.T. 5th.	4.22 p.m. 65° 40' W.	East, 6.	Overcast. In 40° 7' N.,	47	30·16	61
Bound Easterly. To { 40° 19' N. 62° 51' W. 8 a.m. G.T. 6th.	4.22 a.m., 6th. In 40° 15' N., 63° 31' W.	East, 5.	Passing showers of rain.	55	29·97	59

See Diagram 5 for a continuous record of this ship's observations.

		Wind.		Air.	Bar.	Sea.
No. 38. Ship "Nicoline."	8 a.m.	N.E. by E., 10.	Sea increasing,			
In { 36° 40' N. 73° 58' W. 8 a.m. G.T. 5th.	and phosphorescent. 4.56 p.m.	N.E. by N., 9.	Ship working fright-	52°	29·87	51°
Bound E. by Sly. To { 36° 34' N. 72° 51' W. 8 a.m. G.T. 6th.	fully. In 36° 33' N., 74° 5' W. 4.56 a.m., 6th.	N.N.E., 10.		56 52	29·78 29·88	66 71

Since the 4th the "Nicoline" experienced a change in the surface temperature of the water from 49° to 71°, and she is now experiencing a heavy N.E. gale along the edge where these waters meet. The current is drifting her to the N.E. against the wind, making it appear stronger.

		Wind.		Air.	Bar.	Sea.
No. 3. S.S. "Etna." In New York.	A.M.	N. Moderate; overcast.		—	30·18	—
No. 16. S.S. "City of London." In New York. Bound Easterly. To { 40° 36' N. 70° 47' W. 8 a.m. G.T. 6th.	P.M. A.M. 8 p.m.	N.E. Moderate; cloudy. South-easterly. Moderate. N.E. by N., 5. Fresh breeze and overcast.				
No. 18. S.S. "Virginia." In New York. Bound Easterly. To { 40° 34' N. 71° 13' W. 8 a.m. G.T. 6th.	6 a.m. 8 p.m.	N.E. N.E.	Strong breeze; hard frost. Ditto. In 40° 30' N. 73° 21 W.	34°	30·48	40°
No. 22. S.S. "Pennsylvania." In { 40° 40' N. 74° 2' W. 8 a.m. G.T. 5th. To New York.	8 a.m. 10 a.m.	N. by E., 5. N.E. by N.	Fresh breeze.			
New York Observatory. 8 a.m. G.T. 5th. To 8 a.m. G.T. 6th.	8 a.m.	N.E. ½ N.	*16 miles per hour*	—	30·36	22°

The barometer continued remarkably steady until 3 p.m., after which it fell slightly until 8 a.m., 6th.

The temperature gradually rose to 34° at 3 a.m., 6th, after which it fell slightly.

The light north-easterly wind continued throughout the day till 9 a.m., when the force decreased to a very light air, and by 1 a.m., 6th, it had backed to north.

GENERAL REMARKS ON THE CHART FOR 8 A.M. GREENWICH TIME, FEBRUARY 5TH, 1870.

The logs of 34 ships have been consulted, and the same system followed.

The southerly wind still prevails over Great Britain and the western coasts of Europe, but it is light north-westerly in the south of Ireland, and with No. 6 to the N.W. of Ireland, indicating a slightly higher pressure over the sea to the westward.

Plate VIII. in the Quarterly Weather Report shows that Valencia had a light N.W. wind until about 9 a.m., and that a ridge of highest pressure passed that place about 11 a.m., accompanied by a veering of the wind from N.W. to S.E., it having fallen very light for three hours near the time that the highest pressure was passing. The S.E. wind freshened into a strong gale.

The 8 a.m. Chart of this day shows that a south-easterly wind was then blowing with No. 19 in 17° W. This seems to prove that the crest of highest pressure was between Valencia and No. 19 at 8 a.m. No. 6 seems to have had the highest pressure a few minutes after 8 a.m. as her wind soon backed more southerly with a falling barometer. Plate VIII. shows that this crest of highest pressure passed all the self-registering observatories, causing a corresponding veering and backing in all their winds, excepting that of Valencia, where it seemed to veer round by N. and N.E. to S.E. The *direction* of wind at Valencia and Falmouth was most affected by it, but in all cases it blew from S.E. to S. after the passage of the highest pressure. At Valencia and Aberdeen its force exceeded 50 miles an hour.

In the remarks on No. 50 we have called attention to the peculiar trend which the isobars take in Spain, accompanied by a corresponding wind.

It seems worthy of notice how the lowest pressure was over the Atlantic, and the highest pressure over Europe during the passage of this wave which disturbed the wind at all our observatories, and as might be expected it was preceded and followed by a southerly wind. This is just as if a ridge of higher pressure had travelled to the north-eastward, up the inclined plane of pressure from the centre of the Atlantic to Europe, carrying with it a system of wind, northerly on its eastern, and southerly on its western side. Diagram 3 gives a section of it in about 21° W. on the 4th, and we have marked its position on the 8 a.m. Chart of the 5th as an area of " higher pressure." This ridge evidently had a north-easterly route, which is proved by the times at which Plate VIII. shows it to have passed the different observatories.

These waves of varying pressure have been shown to be very common. It is worthy of notice that their crests are generally accompanied by a decrease of temperature and less wind : this will be seen by consulting any of the Plates in the Quarterly Weather Report.

In Iceland a strong N.E. gale is blowing whilst it is light N.W. in Cumberland Sound.

In New York, and with ships in that neighbourhood, the wind is fresh northerly, whilst No. 38 in 74° W. has a very heavy N.E. gale. At the same time there is a strong southerly wind at Bermuda.

At Terceira at *11 a.m.* a S.W. gale is blowing.

At Belle Isle at *4 p.m.* there is a westerly gale.

This day is remarkable for having, so far as I can learn, the lowest barometer ever recorded in this part of the Atlantic,* and between the 8 a.m. Chart of the 5th, and that of the 6th two intervening Charts have been drawn, one for 3 p.m., the other for 8 p.m.

It will be seen from the remarks on p. 10 of the Quarterly Weather Report for 1870, that simultaneously with this low reading of 27·33 ins., the barometer at St. Petersburg was above 30·99 ins.!!!

It may be well to remark with respect to this very low pressure, that it took place in the central part of the Atlantic, where we have reason to suppose that the barometer is usually much lower at this season of the year than on either side, the prevailing wind being northerly or north-westerly to the west of it, and southerly or south-westerly to the eastward of it. If, then, the pressure be normally lower here, we should expect that (as wind force depends on difference of pressure) with the same amount of wind, the pressure would be lower in this place than in positions nearer to the land.

The 8 a.m. Chart of the 5th gives a decided indication of an area of low pressure in about 48° N., and 30° to 35° W., where are ships with S.W., S.E., N.E., N.W., and W.N.W. winds blowing spirally into it. It

---

* In the 5th No. of Meteorological Papers published by Admiral FitzRoy, Dr. Clouston says of his station in the Orkney Islands, " On the 24th January, 1840, the mercury was " as low as 27·69 inches." In the 10th No. 27·45 ins. is said to have been observed there.

will be seen that to the eastward of this area southerly gales extend from 50° N. to the southward as far as Terceira, whilst to the westward of it northerly gales extend down to latitude 35° N.

There can be little doubt but that more ships would have modified the isobars drawn by joining Nos. 23, 26, and 39 ; and that the intervening isobars would have been curved to the south-westward instead of being straight lines. Still, considering the limited number of observations, it does not seem fair to modify them. As they are, they give the idea of a trough of low pressure gradually getting deeper in a north-easterly direction.

The 3 p.m. Chart shows that the area of lowest pressure had travelled to the north-eastward between 30 and 40 miles an hour, having a wind of hurricane force from N.W. on its western side, and from S.W. on its southern side. The remarks following the extract from log No. 35 show that as both the ships experiencing these winds had the barometer down to 27·75., No. 35, steering to meet the lower pressure, which, according to Buys Ballot's law, must have existed between these ships, might well have her barometer down to 27·33, which is the reading given at 7.35 p.m.; although at 3 p.m. her barometer was only down to 28·07, and the wind S., 8. I may here remark that the log of the "Tarifa" was very carefully kept, giving readings of the barometer every two hours; also that she had standard instruments supplied by this office. Captain Murphy had taken the trouble to paste a piece on to the barometer diagram as it only extended to 28 ins. He gives six readings below 28 inches, which, being confirmed by those of Nos. 2 and 53, seem to prove that his entries are quite correct. The isobars on this Chart give a gradient of nearly ·8 of an inch to 50 miles, but the barometers were not standards, though, by comparison with others near them they seem good.

It will be seen that the hardest gale came to most ships after the wind shifted from S. to S.W. and N.W.

The way in which at 8 a.m. the S. of Ireland, and No. 6 to the N.W. of Ireland, had northerly winds in the midst of a general southerly wind, shows how impossible it is always to judge of the weather to the west of Ireland by the telegrams from Valencia, for here we have a case of a small ridge of higher pressure to the westward, causing a northerly wind, which is usually a sign of finer weather, but which was followed quickly by a heavy southerly gale.

The 8 p.m. Chart for the 5th has been drawn because, about this hour, No. 35 experienced the lowest pressure, viz., 27·33 ; her strongest wind followed about four hours later, when the wind shifted to the S.W. The isobars on this Chart show a gradient of about ·4 of an inch to

50 miles. The position of lowest pressure shows a progress of about 35 miles an hour to the north-eastward since 3 p.m.

The 3 p.m. and 8 p.m. Greenwich time Charts for this day speak for themselves. Any land observations taken near these hours have been entered on them.

If the reader wishes to know the weather experienced by any ship between or after these hours it will be found by referring to the extracts from the logs of all important changes between 8 a.m., 5th, Greenwich time, and 8 a.m., 6th, Greenwich time, which have already been given.

Extracts and Remarks to accompany the Chart for 8 a.m., Greenwich Time, February 6th, 1870.

The higher pressure which existed to the West of Ireland yesterday morning has swept by, causing a slight veering and backing in the wind as already remarked, and now the wind is again southerly over the British Islands and Western Europe, amounting to a hard gale at Cork and in the north.

		Standard Instruments.		
		Air.	Bar.	Sea.
No. 50. S.S. "Hotspur." In { 36° 0' N., 5° 15' W., 8 a.m. G.T. 6th. Bound East. To { 36° 42' N., 1° 23' W., 8 a.m. G.T. 7th.	8 a.m. Calm and fine (near Gibraltar)	58°·5	30·32	—
	Noon, ditto. In 36° 4' N., 4° 36' W.	62	30·29	—
	It remained nearly calm and fine until 8 p.m., and apparently until 8 a.m of the 7th.			
	Wind.	Air.	Bar.	Sea.
No. 41. S.S. "Hammonia." In { 49° 28' N., 5° 44' W., 8 a.m. G.T. 6th. Bound West. To { 49° 54' N., 12° 26' W., 8 a.m. G.T. 7th.	8 a.m. S.S.W., 6. Sea increasing from S.W.	46°	29·93	44°
	0.30 p.m. S.S.W., 8. Sea from W.S.W. and W. In 49° 34' N. 7° 8' W.	50	29·89	44
	8.30 p.m. W.S.W., 8. 49° 42' N., 0° 20' W.	48	29·68	50
	4.30 a.m., 7th. S., 7. 49° 51' N., 11° 32' W.	48	29·36	52
	No. 41 felt the sea of the distant westerly gale. The S. wind which she experienced at 4.30 a.m. of the 7th, with a falling barometer, was soon followed by a W. gale, veering to N., and a rising barometer. See the Chart for 8 a.m. of the 7th, showing a small eddy to the S.W. of Ireland.			
	Wind.	Air.	Bar.	Sea.
No. 28. S.S. "West Indian." In { 52° 47' N., 5° 56' W., 8 a.m. G.T. 6th. Bound S.S.Wly. To { 51° 48' N., 6° 31' W., 8 a.m. G.T. 7th.	8 a.m. S.S.W., 9. Strong gale and heavy rain.	50°	29·48	—
	0.20 p.m. S., 9. Ditto. In 52° 57' N., 5° 39' W.	51	29·38	—
	7.20 p.m. S.W., 7. Decreasing gale, and thick.	—	rising	—
	6.20 a.m., 7th. Variable; moderate breeze; heavy S.W. sea. In 52° 4' N., 6° 12' W.	—	20·47	—

105

No. 28, like Valencia (see Plate VIII., Quarterly Weather Report), had a strong southerly gale, which lulled in the latter part of the day. It will be seen that it began to decrease at Valencia at about 7 a.m., whilst it lasted till noon with No. 28, a ship East of Valencia.

	Wind.	Air.	Bar.	Sea.	
8 a.m.	S.W., 9. Very high sea. - -	—	29·74	—	No. 24. S.S. "Nile."
1 p.m.	S.W., 5 to 6. Fine weather. Heavy sea. 43° 35′ N., 15° 7′ W. - - - - -	—	29·60	—	In { 43° 55′ N. 14° 33′ W. 8 a.m. G.T. 6th.
2 p.m.	S.W. by W., 9. Heavy sea, doing damage. - - - - -	—	—	—	Bound S.S.Wly. To { 42° 5′ N. 16° 10′ W. 8 a.m. G.T. 7th.
1 a.m., 7th.	W. by S. ½ S., 9. Ditto. 42° 38′ N., 15° 47′ W. - - - - -	—	29·70	—	
5 a.m.	S.W. by W. ½ W., 9. Heavy squalls, and sea with rain. 42° 19′ N., 16° 0′ W. -	—	29·85	—	

	Wind.	Air.	Bar.	Sea.	
8 a.m.	S. ¼ W., 7. Moderating; sea going down.	45°	28·66	51°	No. 20. "The Queen."
1 p.m.	S., 5. Moderate breeze. In 51° 36′ N., 14° 40′ W. - - - - -	49	28·80	50	In { 51° 23′ N. 15° 56′ W. 8 a.m. G.T. 6th.
1 a.m., 7th.	S., 5. Ditto. In 51° 33′ N., 12° 8′ W. -	48	29·20	51	Bound Ely. To { 51° 30′ N. 10° 19′ W. 8 a.m. G.T. 7th.

No. 20 is a case of a rising barometer, with a southerly wind, caused by her steaming to the eastward. As she approached our coasts she got finer weather and less wind, showing that probably the area of lowest pressure to the West was taking a northerly course.

	Wind.	Air.	Bar.	Sea.	
8 a.m.	S. by W., 11. Perfect hurricane with terrific squalls. - - - -	45°	28·22	48°	No. 6. S.S. "Nestorian."
10 a.m.	S. by W., 10. Stove-in fore part of smoking-room. - - - -	—	—	—	In { 55° 6′ N. 17° 46′ W. 8 a.m. G.T. 6th.
1.12 p.m.	S. by W., 9. In 55° 3′ N., 18° W.	44	28·44	49	Bound W.S.Wly.
2.12 p.m.	S.W. by S., 9. Hard gale; terrific squalls; very high sea. - - - -	—	—	—	To { 54° 23′ N. 20° 13′ W. 8 a.m. G.T. 7th.
5.12 p.m.	S.W. by W., 8. Gale moderating. 55° 0′ N., 18° 5′ W. - - - -	44	28·53	48	
1.12 a.m., 7th.	S.W. by W., 6. Heavy westerly sea. 54° 46′ N., 19° 15′ W. - - -	45	28·99	49	
6.12 a.m.	W. by S., 5. Sea very high. 54° 25′ N., 19° 50′ W. - - -	42	29·17	49	

At 8 a.m. of the 6th No. 6 seems to have been her nearest to the area of low pressure, which was so near to No. 35 at 8 p.m. of the 5th. The changes of wind indicate that No. 6 passed to the south of the lowest pressure. This would give it a very northerly course. The Diagrams of self-registering instruments, in the Quarterly Weather Report, show that the *lowest* pressure did not pass over these islands, so that it seems to have taken a more northerly direction. It will be seen that on the 7th, at 10.20 a.m., Iceland had a strong southerly gale, with the barometer down to 28·38. The direction of the wind shows that there must then have been a lower pressure to the west of Iceland, so that the lowest may have recurved in that direction, unless it was, as it were, merged in the area of depression, which prevails during winter in the centre of the Atlantic.

		Wind.				Air.	Bar.	Sea.
No. 45. Ship "Carl Georg." In { 47° 42′ N. 17° 51′ W. 8 a.m. G.T. 6th. Bound E. by Nly. To { 48° 58′ N. 13° 32′ W. 8 a.m. G.T. 7th.	8 a.m. 1.10 p.m. heavy rain. 1.10 a.m., 7th. squalls; wind changed to W. at 1 a.m. In 48° 32′ N., 15° 7′ W. 5.10 a.m.	S.W., 7. S.W., 8. Wind increasing; constant In 47° 48′ N., 17° 36′ W. S.W., 9. Several rain and snow West, 9. In 48° 47′ N., 14° 17′ W.	-	-	-	53° ? 29·65 54 29·54 57 29·30 58 29·23	54° 54 — 52

No. 45 was well to the south-eastward of the lowest pressure; her barometer seems unusually high when compared with ships near her, and it is curious that it fell as she went to the eastward, whilst Nos. 20, 25, and 49 had a rising barometer when going in the same direction. Her barometer would distort the isobars so much that it has not been used in drawing them.

		Wind.				Air.	Bar.	Sea.
No. 49. S.S. "Marathon." In { 51° 42′ N. 19° 4′ W. 8 a.m. G.T. 6th. Bound East. To { 51° 34′ N. 11° 42′ W. 8 a.m. G.T. 7th.	8 a.m. 1 p.m. 1 a.m., 7th. 13° 34′ W. 5 a.m. In 51° 39′ N., 12° 32′ W.	S.W. ½ W., 9. Heavy sea. S.W. ½ W., 7. In 52° 6′ N., 16° 38′ W. Variable. Gloomy. In 51° 46′ N., Variable, ? 6 Fresh head wind and gloomy.	-	-	-	43° ? 28·55 49 ? 28·60 47 ? 29·00 49 ? 29·12	56° 50 50 50

It is a pity that No. 49 gives no clue as to the direction of the variable wind between 1 and 5 a.m. of the 7th; at 11 a.m. of the 7th she seems to have had a strong breeze from S.E.

107

	Wind.		Air.	Bar.	Sea.	No. 25. S.S. "Cuban."
8 a.m.	S.S.W, 9. Daylight much vivid lightning in S.S.W. and W.N.W. Very high sea.		43°	29·31	—	46° 50′ N. In 19° 30′ W. 8 a.m. G.T. 6th. Bound E. by Nly. To 47° 55′ N. 14° 56′ W. 8 a.m. G.T. 7th.
1.10 p.m.	S.S.W., 8. Gale moderating; sea very high. In 47° 13′ N., 18° 17′ W.		—	29·33	—	
6.10 p.m.	W.N.W., 7. Heavy rain. In 47° 24 N., 17° 24′ W.		—	—	—	
1.10 a.m., 7th.	W.N.W., 7. In 47° 40′ N., 16° 10′ W.		—	29·43	—	

No. 25 was well to the southward, but had a strong gale. It will be seen that her wind was similar in direction to that of No. 6, a ship 500 miles to the north of her. This speaks for the elongated nature of the depression, deepening as it extends north. Very little to the westward of No. 25, at 8 a.m., the wind seems to have been westerly; she, going fast to the eastward, did not get the wind from that direction until about 6 p.m., showing that it took several hours to outstrip her.

	Wind.	Air.	Bar.	Sea.	No. 30. H.M.S. "Orontes."
8 a.m.	W. by S., 6 to 7. Still hove-to.	47°	28·82	49°	50° 25′ N. In 20° 16′ W. 8 a.m. G.T. 6th. Bound East. To 50° 32′ N. 15° 4′ W. 8 a.m. G.T. 7th.
11 a.m.	She bore up and proceeded on her voyage.				
1.20 p.m.	W. by N., 5. Squally; passing hail showers. In 50° 15′ N., 20° 3′ W.	47	29·00	48	
1.20 a.m., 7th.	W. by S., 3. Fine. In 50° 26′ N., 16° 55′ W.	50	29·19	51	
5.20 a.m.	N.N.E., 2. Overcast and drizzle. In 50° 29′ N., 15° 52′ W.	46	29·20	50	

	Wind.	Air.	Bar.	Sea.	No. 19. S.S. "England."
8 a.m.	S.W. by W. ½ W., 10 to 11. Tremendous gale; sea doing much damage.	48°	28·57	52°	51° 16′ N. In 21° 20′ W. 8 a.m. G.T. 6th. Bound West. To 51° 22′ N. 23° 41′ W. 8 a.m. G.T. 7th.
9.12 a.m.	W. ½ S., 9 to 10. More moderate.	—	—	—	
1.30 p.m.	W. ½ S., 9. Sea deluging the decks, fore and aft. In 51° 20′ N., 21° 40′ W.	47	28·89	50	
8.30 p.m.	W. by N. ¼ N., 7 to 8. Clear sky; heavy cross sea. In 51° 21′ N., 22° 36′ W.	—	—	—	
1.30 a.m., 7th.	W. by N. ¼ N., 7. Ditto. In 51° 21′ N., 23° 6′ W.	46	29·20	50	
5.30 a.m.	W. ½ N., 7 to 8. Hard squalls. In 51° 22′ N., 23° 30′ W.	48	29·31	52	

108

		Wind.		Air.	Bar.	Sea.
No. 53. S.S. "Weser." In {49° 47' N., 21° 57' W., 8 a.m. G.T. 6th. Bound East. To {49° 37' N., 14° 0' W., 8 a.m. G.T. 7th.	8 a.m. 1.20 p.m. 5.20 p.m. High S.W. and N.W. seas. 1.20 a.m., 7th. 5.20 a.m.	West, 7. West, 7. S.W., 5. S. 2. W.N.W., 1.	- In 49° 53' N., 20° 30' W. In 49° 50' N., 19° 8' W. - In 49° 45' N., 16° 23' W. In 49° 41' N., 15° 1' W.	43° 45 - 45 44 44	29·05 29·18 - 29·18 29·30 29·36	51° 51 - 51 52 52

No. 53 was about 1° 30' S. of No. 19, and steaming fast to the eastward It will be seen how quickly she decreased the force of her wind and brought it to back to the *southward* with a *rising* barometer, whilst No. 19, going west, had a hard gale, and brought the wind to veer to the *north-westward* with a rising barometer. These facts, together with the experience of No. 6, seem to show that the lowest pressure was going to the northward, and that the steepest gradient was near the area of lowest pressure. Diagram 2 gives a continuous record of the observations of No. 53.

		Wind.		Air.	Bar.	Sea.
No. 7. S.S. "Minnesota." In {51° 7' N., 22° 6' W., 8 a.m. G.T. 6th. Bound Westerly. To {50° 35' N., 26° 12' W., 8 a.m. G.T. 7th.	8 a.m. 1.30 p.m. 7.30 p.m. 1.30 a.m., 7th. 5.30 a.m.	West, 10. W. by S., 7 to 8. W. by N., 7. W. by N., 6. W. by N., 6.	Blowing very hard, with violent squalls, and a high sea. Moderate gale; hail squalls. In 51° 5' N., 22° 43' W. Strong wind and hail squalls; heavy westerly sea. In 50° 55' N., 23° 52' W. Strong breeze; hail squalls and rain. In 50° 45' N., 25° 0' W. Ditto, ditto. In 50° 38' N., 25° 45' W.	— — — — —	— ?28·73 — — —	— — — — —

		Wind.		Standard Instruments.		
No. 35. S.S. "Tarifa." In {51° 4' N., 24° 58' W., 8 a.m. G.T. 6th. Bound W. by Sly. To {50° 14' N., 28° 37' W., 8 a.m. G.T. 7th.	8 a.m. 1.45 p.m. 1.45 a.m., 7th.	W.S.W., 9. W. by N., 7. W. by S., 6.	Hail squalls. Passing showers and squalls. In 51° 12' N., 25° 39' W. Hail squalls. In 50° 34' N., 27° 4' W.	44° 44 46	27·93 28·89 29·34	50° 49 49

Diagram 3 gives a continuous record of this ship's observations. The sudden rise in the barometer of ·96 in 5 hrs. 45 mins., whilst there was a slight fall in the next four hours, makes it possible that the reading at 1.45 p.m. was 28·39; still the diagram shows that the wind did back a little, and that it was squally between 1.45 and 5.45 p.m., Greenwich time.

	Wind.	Air.	Bar.	Sea.	No. 1.

8 a.m.   N.W. by W., ? 6   Strong breeze and squally; high sea, but moderating. -   -   -   45°   29·00·   49°
1.30 p.m.   Variable, 4.   Cloudy; high swell. In 49° 55′ N., 23° 21′ W. -   -   -   48   29·08   50
1.30 a.m., 7th.   N.E. by E., 2.   Cloudy; high N.W. swell.   In 50° 27′ N., 19° 44′ W. -   -   -   41   29·24   49

No. 1.
S.S. "City of Antwerp."
In { 49° 52′ N.
    25° 4′ W.
    8 a.m. G.T. 6th.
Bound Easterly.
To { 50° 46′ N.
    17° 38′ W.
    8 a.m. G.T. 7th.

It will be seen that Nos. 1 and 35 were nearly north and south of each other at 8 a.m., distant about 72 miles, with an extremely steep gradient between them. No. 1 does not seem to have had strength of wind to correspond to such a gradient. All the ships bound East reported less wind as they progressed.

	Wind.	Air.	Bar.	Sea.	No. 26.

8 a.m.   W. by N., 9.   Strong gale; hard squalls. -   -   -   -   -   45°   29·12   —
1.40 p.m.   W. by N., 9.   Ditto, ditto. In 47° 26′ N., 25° 45′ W. -   -   -   50   29·15   —
1.40 a.m., 7th.   W. by N., 8.   Brisk gale. In 48° 3′ N., 22° 57′ W. -   -   -   —   29·24   —
2.40 a.m.   N.W. by W., 6.   Strong breeze and very squally. -   -   -   -   -

No. 26.
S.S. "Venezuelan."
In { 47° 0′ N.
    26° 59′ W.
    8 a.m. G.T. 6th.
Bound E. by Nly.
To { 48° 24′ N.
    21° 22′ W.
    8 a.m. G.T. 7th.

No. 26 was nearly 3° south of No. 1, and seems to have had the wind much stronger.

	Wind.	Air.	Bar.	Sea.	No. 13.

8 a.m.   W. by S., 6.   Smart breeze; heavy easterly swell. -   -   -   -   —   ? 28·86   —
2 p.m.   W. by S., 6.   Fresh breeze and fine. 52° 54′ N., 28° 57′ W. -   -   -   —   ? 28·94   —
2 a.m., 7th.   W. by N., 3.   Light breeze and fine. 53° 17′ N., 27° 11′ W. -   -   -   —   ? 29·08   —

No. 13.
S.S. "India."
In { 52° 37′ N.
    30° 26′ W.
    8 a.m. G.T. 6th.
Bound E. by Nly.
To { 53° 29′ N.
    26° 16′ W.
    8 a.m. G.T. 7th.

It will be remembered that No. 13 got her strongest breeze from N.N.W. about 6 p.m. of the 5th, which gradually backed to W.N.W. and W., indicating that the area of lowest pressure crossed her bow on its way to the North, and that the steepest gradient was a good distance to the East of her, as her strongest wind was only 7. She continued to feel the swell caused by the easterly wind on the northern side of the area of lowest pressure which had passed her.

110

		Wind.	Air.	Bar.	Sea.
No. 2. S.S. "City of Cork." In { 50° 5′ N. 31° 26′ W. 8 a.m. G.T. 6th. Bound Westerly. To { 49° 36′ N. 34° 19′ W. 8 a.m. G.T. 7th.	8 a.m. and hail. 2.8 p.m. and high sea. 3.8 p.m. .10.8 p.m. 2.8 a.m., 7th. and hail squalls; high sea.	W. by N., 8. Heavy squalls ; snow - - - - - W. by N., 8, 9. Very heavy squalls 50° N., 32° 1′ W. - N.W. by W., 9. Ditto, high cross sea W. by N., 8. Wind and sea modera- ting. 40° 50′ N., 32° 57′ W. - W. by S., 6. Moderate wind; snow 49° 44′ N., 33° 34′ W. -	38° 44 — 41 41	29·05 29·01 — 29·48 29·58	46° 50 — 50 50
No. 21. S.S. "Denmark." In { 49° 18′ N. 32° 44′ W. 8 a.m. G.T. 6th. Bound E. by Nly. To { 50° 13′ N. 26° 0′ W. 8 a.m. G.T. 7th.	8 a.m. with high sea. 2.4 p.m. 31° 3′ W. 3.4 p.m. of wind and hail; heavy sea, ship labouring heavily. 2.4 a.m. 7th. with rain showers, and high sea.	Wind. W. ½ N., 5. Fresh breeze and squally, - - - - W. ½ N. 5, Ditto ditto. 49° 38′ N., - - - - Variable, Wly., 7 to 8. Heavy squalls W. ½ N., 7. Fresh breeze, squally, 50° 2′ N., 27° 44′ W.	41° 44 44	?29·46 ?29·35 ?29·65	51° 51 50
No. 17. S.S. "Helvetia." In { 46° 47′ N. 39° 46′ W. 8 a.m. G.T. 6th. Bound Westerly. To { 46° 7′ N. 43° 8′ W. 8 a.m. G.T. 7th.	8 a.m. hard hail squalls; high sea, shipping large quan- tities of water over all. 2.40 p.m. weather. 46° 34′ N., 40° 14′ W. 2.40 a.m., 7th. fine, but very puffy, a high north-westerly swell. 46° 17′ N., 42° 3′ W.	Wind. N.W. by W., 8 to 9. Strong gale, - - - West, 6 to 7. Strong wind, thick - - N.W., 5 to 6. Fresh breeze and - - -	38° 46 39	29·66 29·79 —	53° 58 58
No. 39. S.S. "Westphalia." In { 46° 42′ N. 41° 4′ W. 8 a.m. G.T. 6th. Bound W. by Sly. To { 45° 23′ N. 46° 42′ W. 8 a.m. G.T. 7th.	8 a.m. 3 a.m. (see extracts for 5th) they say "Squalls, "reaching the violence of a hurricane," but here no remark. 2.50 p.m. 46° 30′ N., 41° 56′ W. 2.50 a.m., 7th.	Wind. W. by N. ½ N., 10. With hail. *At* - - - - W.N.W., 7. Cloudy, with hail. - - - W. by N., 4. 45° 43′ N., 45° 18′ W.	43° 41 34	29·75 29·88 30·01	55° 54 44

The wind seems to have lulled as No. 39 got into cooler water. Diagram 4 gives a continuous record of her observations.

111

Wind.
8 a.m.   N.N.E., 9 to 10. Hard squalls and rain; hove-to with a floating anchor, and engines going slow for more than 24 hours; no change of wind direction or force; carried away bulwarks, and stove starboard lifeboat.
2.45 p.m.   N.N.E., 10. Heavy squalls and rain. In 45° 38′ N., 41° 10′ W.
4.45 a.m., 7th. N.N.E., 7 to 8. Hove in floating anchor, and at 6.40 a.m. went full speed. In 45° 58′ N., 40° 28′ W.

No. 12.
S.S. "Dacian."
In { 45° 44′ N.
    { 41° 21′ W.
    { 8 a.m. G.T. 6th.
Bound E.N.Ely. very slowly, being hove-to.
To { 46° 0′ N.
    { 40° 16′ W.
    { 8 a.m. G.T. 7th.

It is very puzzling to see how No. 12 had a most remarkably steady but heavy N.N.E. gale, while ships to the north and south of her had the wind north-westerly. It will be seen that the same difficulty existed on the 5th. As already said, it is probable that she gave the magnetic instead of the true direction for the wind as reported in her log. No. 12 gives no instrumental readings.

Wind.
8 a.m.   W.N.W., 7. More moderate, and less sea.
2.50 p.m.   W.N.W., 6 to 7. Strong wind and squally, heavy westerly sea. 43° 34′ N. 42° 46′ W.
10.50 p.m.   Calm, cloudy. 43° 31′ N., 44° 9′ W.
2.50 a.m., 7th. Calm, gloomy. 43° 29′ N., 44° 51′ W.

No. 10.
S.S. "Manhattan."
In { 43° 56′ N.
    { 42° 10′ W.
    { 8 a.m. G.T. 6th.
Bound Westerly.
To { 43° 26′ N.
    { 45° 37′ W.
    { 8 a.m. G.T. 7th.

Wind.   Air.   Bar.   Sea.
8 a.m.   N.W. by W., 8 to 9. Unsteady wind; overcast and squally, with hail showers; heavy confused sea, shipping much water. -   -   —   29·78   —
2.54 p.m.   N.W. by W., 6 to 7. Unsteady wind; cloudy, but clear. 47° 34′ N., 43° 33′ W. -   —   29·90   —
2.54 a.m., 7th. W. by N., 5. Unsteady wind; clear blue sky. 46° 47′ N., 46° 12′ W.   -   -   32°   —   35°

No. 4.
S.S. "Prussian."
In { 47° 48′ N.
    { 42° 49′ W.
    { 8 a.m. G.T. 6th.
Bound W. by Sly.
To { 46° 28′ N.
    { 47° 29′ W.
    { 8 a.m. G.T. 7th.

Wind.
8 a.m.   W. by N., 8. Ship hove-to; wind inclining to moderate; sea very high. -   -   -   42°   —   48°
3 p.m.   W. by N., 6. Sea falling; engines full speed; looking very unsettled. 44° 40′ N. 44° 12′ W.   44   —   55
3 a.m., 7th. W. by N., 4 to 5. Moderate and fine. 44° 46′ N., 45° 42′ W.   -   -   -   -   38   —   47

No. 11.
S.S. "Iowa."
In { 44° 49′ N.
    { 43° 55′ W.
    { 8 a.m. G.T. 6th.
Bound Westerly.
To { 44° 50′ N.
    { 46° 53′ W.
    { 8 a.m. G.T. 7th.

No. 23.
S.S. "Atrato."
In { 37° 15′ N.
     43° 55′ W.
     8 a.m. G.T. 6th.
Bound N.Ely.
To { 39° 29′ N.
     40° 6′ W.
     8 a.m. G.T. 7th.

	Wind.	Air.	Bar.	Sea.
8 a.m.	Northerly, 2. Light variable wind; heavy confused swell. - - - -	—	?30·27	—
2.51 p.m.	South-easterly, 2. Ditto and overcast; north-north-westerly swell; heavy and confused. 37° 57′ N., 42° 43′ W. - - -	—	?30·28	—
2.51 a.m., 7th.	South-easterly, 3. N.N.W. swell. 39° 1′ N., 40° 54′ W. - - - -	—	?30·19	—

No. 23 is far south, and seems to have been caught up by a slight depression travelling to the eastward, as her barometer fell with a south-easterly wind increasing. She got the swell of the north-westerly wind to the N.W. of her.

No. 42.
Ship "Swea."
In { 31° 27′ N.
     49° 39′ W.
     8 a.m. G.T. 6th.
Bound E.N.Ely.
To { 32° 53′ N.
     46° 35′ W.
     8 a.m. G.T. 7th.

	Wind.	Air.	Bar.	Sea.
8 a.m.	S.W. by S., 4 - - - -	71°	30·08	68°
3.15 p.m.	S.W., 5. 31° 54′ N., 48° 45′ W. -	71	30·05	68
3.15 a.m., 7th.	S.W., 5. Stormy, with hard squalls. Rain for two hours and cloudy. 32° 36′ N., 47° 12′ W.	70	30·03	67

No. 42 is very far south, and has a light south-westerly wind, probably related to a low pressure to the N.W. of her, where there is a sea of a temperature over 70°. No. 38, to the W.N.W. of her, has a hard N.E. gale, which seems to be blowing between the same low pressure and the higher one over the cold land.

No. 9.
S.S. "Colorado."
In { 44° 43′ N.
     53° 27′ W.
     8 a.m. G.T. 6th.
Bound E.N.Ely.
To { 46° 27′ N.
     47° 12′ W.
     8 a.m. G.T. 7th.

	Wind.	Air.	Bar.	Sea.
8 a.m.	N.W. by N., 3. Light breeze; overcast and hazy. - - - - -	30°	—	37°
3.26 p.m.	N.W. by N., 3. Fine and clear; hard frost. 45° 16′ N., 51° 36′ W. - -	32	—	35
4.26 p.m.	N. by E., 2 to 3. Ditto, ditto. -	—	—	—
3.26 a.m., 7th.	N.W. by N., 3. Ditto, ditto, 46° 5′ N., 48° 30′ W. - - - -	30	—	30

No. 36.
S.S. "Palmyra."
In { 40° 19′ N.
     62° 51′ W.
     8 a.m. G.T. 6th.
Bound Easterly.
To { 40° 49′ N.
     58° 35′ W.
     8 a.m. G.T. 7th.

Standard Instruments.

	Wind.	Air.	Bar.	Sea.
8 a.m.	E.N.E., 5. Rain. - - -	57°	29·87	70°
4 p.m.	East, 5. Ditto. 40° 27′ N., 61° 31′ W.	59	29·86	70
4 a.m., 7th.	S.E., 5. Heavy rain. 40° 44′ N., 59° 10′ W. - - - - -	58	29·67	57

No. 36 had continuous rain with the cir.-s from S.S.E. and S. when the wind was E. and E.S.E.; the barometer eventually fell quickly, and

113

the wind went from S.E. to S., S.S.W., and N.N.W., showing that a wave of low pressure swept over her, having easting in its course. It will be remembered that on the 5th Bermuda had a southerly wind; the exact hour is not given, but it was probably related to that experienced by No. 36 at 4 a.m. of the 7th. The change in sea temperature is remarkable. The specific gravity was decidedly lower in the cold water. Diagram 5 gives a continuous record of this ship's observations.

The 6th was Sunday, and the only observation sent by General Lefroy was 4.18 p.m. G.T. Bar. 29·854. Wind N.W. 1.

	Wind.					
8 a.m.	N.E. by N., 3. Cloudy.					

No. 15.
S.S. "Moravian."
at Portland.
In { 43° 40' N.
     70° 20' W.
     8 a.m. G.T. 6th.
Bound Easterly.
To { 43° 12' N.
     66° 33' W.
     8 a.m. G.T. 7th.

	Wind.		Air.	Bar.	Sea.
8 a.m.	N.E. by N., 5 to 6. Misty and rain; easterly sea. - - - - -		38°	30·08	40°
4.36 p.m.	N.E. by E., 5 to 6. Rain; high easterly sea. 40° 41' N., 69° 11' W. - - -		40	30·07	42
4.36 a.m., 7th.	N. by E., 5 to 6. Ditto. 40° 55' N., 66° 19' W. - - - - -		38	29·93	40
5.36 a.m.	N.W. by W., 5 to 6. Overcast. 40° 56' N., 66° 6' W.				

No. 16.
S.S. "City of London."
In { 40° 36' N.
     70° 47' W.
     8 a.m. G.T. 6th.
Bound Easterly.
To { 40° 59' N.
     65° 26' W.
     8 a.m. G.T. 7th.

	Wind.				
8 a.m.	N.E. by N., 6 to 7. Overcast. -	-	39°?	30·25	45°
4.40 p.m.	Ditto. Ditto and drizzle. 40° 36' N., 69° 43' W. - - - - -		39?	30·15	45
5.40 p.m.	N. ½ E., 6 to 7. - - -	—	—	—	
4.40 a.m., 7th.	N. ½ E., 5 to 6. Cloudy. 40° 25' N., 67° 50' W. - - - - -		42?	30·15	46

No. 18.
S.S. "Virginia."
In { 40° 34' N.
     71° 13' W.
     8 a.m. G.T. 6th.
Bound Easterly.
To { 40° 19' N.
     67° 9' W.
     8 a.m. G.T. 7th.

	Wind.					
8 a.m.	N.E., 6.	Overcast.	-	-	34°	30·13	40°
4.37 p.m.	N.E., 7.	Ditto.	41° 29' N., 69° 14' W. -	-	40	30·01	39
4.37 a.m., 7th.	N.E., 6.	Ditto.	41° 20' N., 66° 50' W. -	-	37	29·99	39

No. 40.
S.S. "Deutschland."
In { 41° 29' N.
     71° 21' W.
     8 a.m. G.T. 6th.
Bound East.
To { 41° 17' N.
     66° 8' W.
     8 a.m. G.T. 7th.

		Wind.					Air.	Bar.	Sea.
No. 55. S.S. "Rhein." In { 40° 33' N. / 71° 52' W. / 8 a.m. G.T. 6th. Bound Westerly. To New York.	8 a.m. 0.22 p.m. 73° 51' W.	N.E., 5. N.N.E., 5. -	Rain. Rain; overcast. -	- 40° 27' N., -	- - -	- - -	38° 35	30·11 30·15	43° 42

		Wind.							
No. 38. Ship "Nicoline." In { 36° 34' N. / 72° 51' W. / 8 a.m. G.T. 6th. Bound N.Ely. To { 37° 0' N. / 71° 23' W. / 8 a.m. G.T. 7th.	8 a.m. 4.50 p.m. 72° 26' W. 4.50 a.m., 7th.	N.N.E., 10. N. by E., 9. - N. by E., 7.	Overcast. Ditto. - 37° 9' N.,	- 36° 57' N., - 71° 39' W.	- - -	- - -	56° 57 54	29·88 29·88 30·00	71° 72 72

This is the third day that the "Nicoline" has been struggling against a heavy N.E. gale, which indicates a lasting higher pressure to the N.W. of her over the cold land, and a lower to the S.E. over the warm sea.

		Wind.			Bar.
No. 3. S.S. "Etna." In New York.	A.M. P.M.	Northerly. North-westerly.	Moderate and clear. - Ditto.	-	?30·15

New York Observatory.
8 a.m. G.T. 6th.
To 8 a.m. G.T. 7th.

8 a.m. Wind N. ¼ E., *4 miles per hour.* Barometer 30·20; air 28°. The barometer oscillated slightly during the 24 hours.

The temperature decreased to 27° by 10 a.m., when it gradually rose to 34° by 2 a.m., 7th, falling to 30° by 4 a.m., rising to 36° by 5.15 a.m., and again falling to 29° by 6.15 a.m.

Very light airs continued throughout the 24 hours, the direction being steady at N. till 2 p.m., when it veered to N.E. by N. by 3 p.m., at which hour it commenced backing, and was W.N.W. at 6.15 p.m. It then veered to N. by E. by 8 p.m., where it remained for the next 12 hours.

GENERAL REMARKS ON THE CHART FOR 8 A.M., GREENWICH TIME, FEBRUARY 6TH, 1870.

The logs of 37 ships have been consulted, and the same system has been followed.

The southerly wind still prevails over the British Isles and Europe, amounting to a strong gale at Cork and in the Irish Channel. Shetland had a very heavy S.E. gale continuing at 9 a.m. of the 7th. At 9 p.m.

of the 6th, North Uist in the Hebrides, reports a southerly gale of hurricane force, continuing at 9 a.m. of the 7th. It was this gale which did so much damage to the harbour works at Wick.*

It will be remembered that there was a ridge of higher pressure to the west of Ireland on yesterday's Chart, having a north-westerly wind on its eastern side. This seems to have swept away to the eastward, leaving a southerly wind extending from 20° W. in the Atlantic to Norway.

Iceland reports a S.W. gale at Reykjavik, and a N.E. gale at Stykkisholm; these places are very near each other and appear to have an area of low pressure between them, which must have been the case if the winds are correct. The Chart for 8 a.m. of the 7th gives a somewhat similar local depression to the S.W. of Ireland.

In Cumberland Sound there is a light north-westerly wind. At Belle Isle the wind was north-westerly at 4 p.m., whilst at St. John's, Newfoundland there was a S.W. gale at 0.30 p.m., and at New York the wind was moderate northerly.

At Terceira there was a moderate westerly gale at 11 a.m., and at Madeira at 10 a.m. there was a light south-easterly air.

The hardest gale is now in 55° N. and 18° W., where No. 6, the "Nestorian," has the wind S.S.W., 11; this direction and force show that there was a lower pressure to the westward of her, and that she eventually passed to the south of it, because her wind shifted to S.W. and W. by S. Hence we may suppose that the low pressure experienced by No. 35 at 8 p.m. of the 5th, in about 51° N. and 24° W., had travelled quickly to the north-eastward, causing a steeper gradient for southerly winds over the British Islands, but keeping several degrees to the west of them.

The way in which the wind blows from the same direction over several degrees of latitude indicates the elongated shape of these depressions; for instance, from No. 6 in 55° N. 18° W. to No. 25 in 47° N. 19° W. the wind is about S.S.W., again from No. 7 in 51° N. 22° W. to Terceira in 39° N. 27° W. it is westerly, whilst from No. 2 in 50° N. 31° W. to No. 10 in 44° N. 42° W. it is W.N.W.

The general run of the isobars between Ireland and Newfoundland indicates the tendency of the air to move round a central area of lowest pressure; whilst the specially low pressure with which we have been dealing seems to be found where the northerly and southerly winds come nearest together. Perhaps the apparent motion of the area of depression to the north-eastward may be caused by the shifting of the point at which

---

* Plate VIII. of the Quarterly Weather Report shows that Aberdeen had a S. by E. gale, exceeding 50 miles an hour, at 5 p.m. of the 6th.

the two currents meet, the old depression being constantly in the process of being filled up and a new one formed in its stead.

The following Diagram is an attempt to illustrate my meaning. Suppose that a northerly wind exists on the western, and a southerly wind on the eastern side of the Atlantic, and that these winds are, as it were, closing with each other, or at any rate that one is pressing on the other, there will be a point C where they are in close contact, and an eddy will be formed there. (See the Chart for 8 a.m., February 5th, where the winds of a complete eddy are given.)*

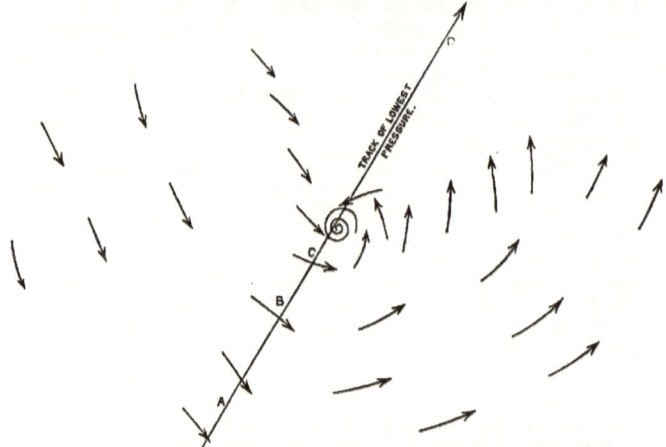

The lowest barometrical readings and the heaviest rain would probably be found at the actual point of contact of the two winds. If the closing of these currents went on, the eddy would *appear* to shift its position with the point of contact, but would really be formed afresh out of different air along the line of meeting. The direction of motion and apparent speed of the area of lowest pressure would depend upon the relative force and tendency to close of the two currents of air.

We may therefore suppose that eddies had formed along the line at A and B, and would eventually form at D, leaving in their rear the winds as represented by the arrows. (See the reductions of the four

---

* Some remarks on this subject by Capt. R. Inglis, of the Cunard line of steamers, will be found at p. 9 of " the Report on the Meteorology of the North Atlantic." (Non-official No. 2.)

Charts from February 5th, 8 a.m., to February 6th, 8 a.m., given on the last Chart, as illustrations of this idea.)

This theory seems to agree with the way in which some winds blow over large spaces of the sea, and has the advantage of not requiring that the air forming the cyclonic centre should be absolutely shifted 30 miles an hour over the earth's surface. It also supposes that the eddy is being continually re-formed from fresh air supplied by the opposing currents, which is a sufficient reason for the constant heavy rain at its centre.

The N.E. gale near New York seems to be related to another area of low pressure, which prevails over the Gulf Stream, having a southerly wind on its eastern side. Collisions between these currents of air seem to cause the frequent cyclonic gales travelling to the N.Ed. which are experienced on the coast of America during the winter months. The diagram on p. 116 seems also to illustrate them.

The winds of some ships and some isobars seem very irregular; but it has been thought better not to smooth the latter into curves. They are the nearest to the truth which could be drawn, and indicate what the curves probably were. They also show what an immense advantage it would be in such work if all instruments were standards, and all observers equally careful.

Extracts and Remarks to accompany the Chart for 8 a.m. Greenwich Time, February 7th, 1870.

The wind continues southerly over western Europe and most parts of the British Islands.

About 2° to the south-westward of Valencia there is an area of low pressure causing the wind to be easterly at that station. There seems to be a somewhat similar eddy off the Land's End, for Plymouth has a southerly wind, whilst St. Ann's Head has it easterly, and Penzance north-easterly. The isobars seem to incline round these eddies. Norway, Shetland, and the Hebrides, report a wind of nearly hurricane force, the former two from S.E., the latter from S.

		Standard Instruments.			No. 50.
Wind.		Air.	Bar.	Sea.	S.S. "Hotspur."
8 a.m. S.S.W. ¼ W., 2. Fine weather.		57·4°	30·15	57°	In { 36° 42′ N. 1° 23′ W. 8 a.m. G.T. 7th.
Noon. W.S.W., 3. Fine; sea smooth. In 36° 50′ N., 0° 44′ W.		60	30·13	57	Bound Easterly.
8 p.m. W.S.W.; 3. Fine weather; *heavy* dew. 37° 0′ N., 0° 33′ E.		57	30·10	—	To { 37° 15′ N. 2° 28′ E. 8 a.m. G.T. 8th.

No. 50 is far south, and in the Mediterranean.

118

No. 28.		Wind.	Air.	Bar.	Sea.
S.S. "West Indian."	8 a.m.	Variable between S.W. and E.S.E.			
In { 51° 48' N. 6° 31' W. 8 a.m. G.T. 7th.	4 to 5. Heavy south-westerly sea.		44°	29·48	—
Bound S.Wly.	0.30 p.m. S.S.E. 4. Heavy sea. 51° 15' N.,				
To { 49° 33' N. 9° 2' W. 8 a.m. G.T. 8th.	7° 10' W.		—	—	—
	9.30 p.m. S.W. by W., 5 to 6. Squally.				
	50° 28' N., 8° 2' W.		—	29·22	—
	11.30 p.m. W.N.W., 6 to 7. Squally. 50° 17' N.,				
	8° 14' W.		—	—	—
	1.30 a.m., 8th. W.N.W., 7. Violent squalls, heavy				
	south-westerly sea. 50° 7' N., 8° 20' W.		—	—	—

No. 28 seems to have passed through the area of low pressure which was to the south-westward of Valencia at 8 a.m. She got its W.N.W. wind (proving that the lowest pressure had passed her) at 11.30 p.m. in 50° 17' N., 8° 14' W. This shows that there was easting in its route.

No. 20.		Wind.	Air.	Bar.	Sea.
S.S. "The Queen."	8 a.m.	N.E. ¼ E., 5 to 6. Gloomy.	47°	29·24	40°
In { 51° 30' N. 10° 19' W. 8 a.m. G.T. 7th.	0.38 p.m. S.E. by E., 4 to 5. Heavy drizzle.				
	51° 30' N., 9° 36' W.		47	29·29	48
Bound E. by Nly.	4.38 p.m. North by easterly, 4 to 5. Cloudy.				
To { 52° 12' N. 6° 12' W. 8 a.m. G.T. 8th.	51° 33' N., 8° 48' W.		47	29·24	43
	8.38 p.m. South by westerly, 5. Heavy				
	showers. 51° 47' N., 8° 9' W.		47	29·19	44
	0.38 a.m., 8th. S.E. by S., 4. Heavy rain.				
	51° 55' N., 7° 30' W.		48	29·19	51
	4.38 a.m. East-south-easterly, 5. Heavy				
	showers. 52° 4' N., 6° 51' W.		—	29·29	—

No. 20 steamed to the eastward on the northern side of the area of low pressure and kept the wind unsteady, but generally easterly and moderate in force.

No. 49.		Wind.	Air.	Bar.	Sea.
S.S. "Marathon."	8 a.m.	Variable, ? 6 to 8, preceded by variable,			
In { 51° 34' N. 11° 42' W. 8 a.m. G.T. 7th.	followed by E. by S., gloomy.		50°	29·05	50°
	10.44 a.m. E. by S., ? 7. 51° 28' N., 10° 59' W.		—	—	—
Bound Easterly.	0.42 p.m. E. by S. ? 7. Rain. 51° 25' N.,10° 29' W.		52	29·03	50
To { Queenstown (Roche's Point.) 51° 45' N. 8° 20' W. 10.33 p.m. G.T. 7th.	4.42 p.m. E. by S., ?5. Cloudy, moderating.				
	51° 33' N., 9° 37' W.		40	29·05	41

No. 49, like No. 20, seems to have steamed to the eastward in front of the area of low pressure to the westward of her, keeping a nearly steady barometer. No. 28, bound W., had a falling barometer, and at 9.30 p.m. her wind shifted to S.W. by W.

	Wind.		Air.	Bar.	Sea.	
8 a.m.	West, 9.	Overcast; constant rain.	48°	29·39	52°	No. 41. S.S. "Hammonia."
1 p.m.	North, 9.	49° 59′ N., 13° 44′ W. -	47	29·47	52	In { 49° 54′ N. 12° 26′ W. 8 a.m. G.T. 7th.
1 a.m., 8th.	S.W., 7.	49° 41′ N., 17° 8′ W. -	47	29·60	52	Bound Westerly.
5 a.m.	W.N.W., 5.	49° 36′ N., 18° 17′ W. -	45	29·42	52	To { 49° 32′ N. 19° 5′ W. 8 a.m. G.T. 8th.

About 1 p.m. No. 41 seems to have steamed into the northerly wind which was to the westward of her at 8 a.m. Then again her wind backed quickly to S.W. with a falling barometer, until it shifted to W.N.W. These undulations in the pressure seem common just to the westward of Ireland.

It will be noticed how near this W. wind was to the E. wind at Valencia.

	Wind.		Air.	Bar.	Sea.	
8 a.m.	West, 8.	- - -	58°	29·29	52°	No. 45. Ship "Carl Georg."
0.50 p.m.	West, 6.	49° 16′ N., 12° 38′ W. -	57	29·31	52	In { 48° 58′ N. 13° 32′ W. 8 a.m. G.T. 7th.
4.50 p.m.	S.W., 6.	49° 18′ N., 12° 7′ W. -	53	29·30	—	Bound Easterly.
4.50 a.m., 8th.	South, 5.	Constant rain. 49° 26′ N., 10° 33′ W. - - - - -	53	29·26	—	To { 49° 28′ N. 10° 7′ W. 8 a.m. G.T. 8th.

At 1 p.m., No. 41 bound W., had a northerly wind which lasted for 12 hours, whilst No. 45 bound E., and only 61 miles to the S.E. of her, never got the northerly wind, but had it W. backing to S.W. and S. as she closed with the land.

	Wind.		Air.	Bar.	Sea.	
8 a.m.	N.W., 5.	Rain one hour. -	45°	29·38	51°	No. 53. S.S. "Weser."
0.49 p.m.	S.W., 7.	Rain three hours. 49° 32′ N., 12° 16′ W. - - - - -	44	29·29	52	In { 49° 37′ N. 14° 0′ W. 8 a.m. G.T. 7th. Bound East.

At 0.49 p.m. No. 53 was experiencing a S.W. wind, force 7, when No. 41, only 63 miles to the W.N.W. of her, had the wind N., 9, showing the small size of the area of low pressure between them. Diagram 2 gives a continuous record of the observations of this ship until noon ship's time of the 7th, when the log ends.

120

			Wind.		Air.	Bar.	Sea.
	No. 25.						
	S.S. "Cuban."	8 a.m.	W.N.W., 7. Moderating. Sea				
In	47° 55′ N. 14° 56′ W. 8 a.m. G.T. 7th.	confused. - - - - - -			40°	29·47	—
	Bound E. by Nly.	0.56 p.m.	W.N.W., 6, at 1.56, force 7. With				
To	49° 9′ N. 9° 58′ W. 8 a.m. G.T. 8th.	very heavy hail squalls. 48° 6′ N., 14° 3′ W. - 8.56 p.m. N.N.W., 8 to 9. 48° 32′ N., 12° 27′ W. -			40	—	—
		1.56 a.m., 8th. W.N.W., 7 to 8. Sea much confused. 48° 47′ N., 11° 20′ W. - - -			—	29·02	—

No. 25 seems to have steamed to the north-eastward on the S.W. side of the small area of low pressure already alluded to, keeping the wind north-westerly.

			Wind.		Air.	Bar.	Sea.
	No. 30.						
	H.M.S. "Orontes."	8 a.m.	N. by W., 3. Overcast; passing				
In	50° 32′ N. 15° 4′ W. 8 a.m. G.T. 7th.	showers. - - - - - -			45°	29·28	48°
	Bound Easterly.	0.55 p.m.	N.N.W., 7 to 8. Ditto and squally.				
To	51° 16′ N. 9° 43′ W. 8 a.m. G.T. 8th.	50° 37′ N., 13° 46′ W. - - - 1.55 p.m. N.W. by W., 7 to 9. Overcast; squally; raining. 50° 39′ N., 13° 30′ W. - -			45 45	29·23 29·23	47 49
		0.55 a.m., 8th. N.W. ½ W., 4 to 6. Squalls and showers. 51° 1′ N., 11° 15′ W. - - -			50	29·38	50
		1.55 a.m. West, 5 to 6. Some blue sky and squally. 51° 8′ N., 11° 4′ W. - - -			50	29·37	—

It is interesting to notice how No. 30, to the westward of an area of low pressure, and steaming to the eastward kept the wind northerly, whilst No. 20 to the northward of it and bound the same way, kept the wind easterly.

			Wind.		Air.	Bar.	Sea.
	No. 24.						
	S.S. "Nile."	8 a.m.	W. ½ S., 8 to 9. Heavy squalls and				
In	42° 5′ N. 16° 10′ W. 8 a.m. G.T. 7th.	sea, with rain. - - - - -			—	29·87	—
	Bound S.Wly.	1.6 p.m.	W. by S. ½ S., 8. Ditto with showers.				
To	39° 38′ N. 19° 1′ W. 8 a.m. G.T. 8th.	41° 41′ N., 16° 26′ W. - - - - 5.6 p.m. W. by S. ½ S., 6 to 7. Cloudy; heavy westerly swell. 41° 15′ N., 16° 59′ W. - -			— —	30·04 30·02	— —
		1.6 a.m., 8th. S.W., 4. Heavy N.W. swell. 40° 23′ N., 18° 5′ W. -			—	30·06	—

Nos. 24 and 25 seem to have had the wind stronger than Nos. 53 and 30, which latter ships were further North, and seemed to be affected by the northerly wind on the western side of the small area of low pressure to the S.W. of Valencia.

	Wind.				Air.	Bar.	Sea.	No. 1.
8 a.m.	N.W. by W., 2 to 3. Clear.			-	44°	29·42	49°	S.S. "City of Antwerp."
1 p.m.	Ditto, 4, 5. Ditto. 50° 59′ N., 16° 7′ W.				45	29·47	49	In { 50° 46′ N. / 17° 38′ W.
4 p.m.	N. ¼ W., 2 to 3. Cloudy. 51° 3′ N.,							8 a.m. G.T. 7th.
15° 10′ W.	-	-	-	-	45	29·46	50	Bound Easterly.
1 a.m., 8th.	N. by W. ½ W., 4 to 5. Ditto.							To { 51° 28′ N. / 10° 4′ W.
51° 10′ N., 12° 19′ W.	-	-	-	-	45	29·40	50	8 a.m. G.T. 9th.

No. 1 seems to have followed and kept company with the small area of lower pressure to the eastward of her, for she steamed to the eastward over a part of the sea where there seems to have been a strong westerly gale at 8 a.m.

	Wind.				Air.	Bar.	Sea.	No. 6.
8 a.m.	W. by S., 5. Sea still very high.			-	43°	29·27	49°	S.S. "Nestorian."
1.27 p.m.	W. by N., 3. Ditto. 54° 11′ N.,							In { 54° 23′ N. / 20° 13′ W.
21° 45′ W.	-	-	-	-	47	29·36	49	8 a.m. G.T. 7th.
1.27 a.m., 8th.	W. by N., 5. Showery. 53° 44′ N.,							Bound W. by Sly.
25° 2′ W.	-	-	-	-	40	29·62	46	To { 53° 30′ N. / 26° 31′ W.
5.27 a.m.	N.W. by W., 5. Frequent showers							8 a.m. G.T. 8th.
of sleet; cross sea. 53° 35′ N., 26° 7′ W.		-		-	39	29·68	43	

No. 6 makes the first mention of a *cross* sea at 5.27 a.m. of the 8th, as if she were getting into a part of the ocean over which the winds of both sides of the area of lowest pressure had passed. It will be remembered that she had a perfect hurricane from the southward on the 6th inst., and that Shetland and Norway had a south-easterly wind of hurricane force on the 7th at 8 a.m. (see the Chart).

	Wind.				Air.	Bar.	Sea.	No. 26.
8 a.m.	N.W. by W., 6 to 7. Hard squalls.				42°	29·50	—	S.S. "Venezuelan."
1.20 p.m.	N.W. by W., 6 to 7. Ditto.							In { 48° 24′ N. / 21° 22′ W.
48° 40′ N., 20° 8′ W.	-	-	-	-	50	29·61	—	8 a.m. G.T. 7th.
5.20 p.m.	S.W. by W., 3. Fine. 48° 53′ N.,							Bound E.N.Ely.
19° 19′ W.	-	-	-	-	—	29·60	—	To { 49° 43′ N. / 16° 16′ W.
1.20 a.m., 8th.	Variable, 2 to 3. 49° 20′ N.,							8 a.m. G.T. 8th.
17° 40′ W.	-	-	-	-	—	29·43	—	
2.20 a.m.	S. by W., 2. Unsteady.							
5.20 a.m.	W. by N., 2. Ditto. 49° 33′ N.,							
16° 51′ W.	-	-	-	-	46	29·38	—	
7.20 a.m.	N. by E., 3. Drizzle. 49° 40′ N.,							
16° 26′ W.	-	-	-	-	—	29·41	—	

122

No. 26 seems to have had an unsteady wind following after the small area of low pressure which was to the north-eastward of her at 8 a.m. of the 7th. Another slight depression seems to have passed over her before 7 a.m. of the 8th.

		Wind.	Air.	Bar.	Sea.
No. 19. S.S. "England." In {51° 22' N. 23° 41' W. 8 a.m. G.T. 7th. Bound W. by Sly. To {50° 38' N. 28° 4' W. 8 a.m. G.T. 8th.	8 a.m. 1.37 p.m. 1.37 a.m., 8th. 6.37 a.m.	W. ½ S., 7. High sea still running. W. ½ S., 5 to 6. Clear; high west-north-westerly swell. 51° 23' N., 24° 18' W. N.N.W., 5 to 6. Ditto ditto, 50° 53' N., 26° 47' W. - - - N.N.W., 6. 50° 41' N., 27° 50' W.	49° 50 49 49	29·33 29·40 29·61 29·74	51° 51 50 51
		Wind.			
No. 21. S.S. "Denmark." {50° 13' N. In {26° 0' W. 8 a.m. G.T. 7th. Bound E. by Nly. To {51° 13' N. 19° 31' W. 8 a.m. G.T. 8th.	8 a.m. 1.38 p.m. 6.38 p.m. 1.38 a.m., 8th.	W. ½ N., 4, to 5. Very unsteady; fine weather. - - - - W. by S., 3 to 4. Variable, S.W. by W. to W. by N.; looking squally. 50° 25' N., 24° 24' W. - - - - - Variable, S. by Westerly, 4. 50° 38' N., 23° 4' W. - Variable, Northerly, 4. Continued the same till 8 a.m. Cloudy. 50° 56' N., 21° 15' W.	44°? 45 ? — 41 ?	29·70 29·82 — 29·66	50° 54 — 48
		Wind.			
No. 7. S.S. "Minnesota." {50° 35' N. In {26° 12' W. 8 a.m. G.T. 7th. Bound W. by Sly. To {49° 41' N. 31° 29' W. 8 a.m. G.T. 8th.	8 a.m. 1.50 p.m. 2.50 p.m. 8.50 p.m. 1.50 a.m., 8th.	W. by N., 7. Heavy squalls. - — — — S.W. by W., 5. Squally with rain; heavy westerly sea. 50° 25' N., 27° 16' W. - W. by N., 6. Heavy hail and snow squalls. - - - - - W. by S. to N.W. by N., 6. High sea. 50° 8' N., 28° 55' W. - - Variable, 6. Heavy hail squalls. 49° 56' N., 30° 5' W. - - - -	— — — — —	— ?29·35 — — —	— — — — —
		Wind.			
No. 13. S.S. "India." {53° 29' N. In {26° 16' W. 8 a.m. G.T. 7th Bound E. by Nly. To {54° 21' N. 20° 20' W 8 a.m. G.T. 8th.	8 a.m. 1.42 p.m. 1.42 a.m., 8th. 3.42 a.m.	W. by N., 2. Fine. - - - Variable airs. Cloudy. 53° 40' N., 25° 25' W. - - - - - Variable airs. Gloomy. 54° 6' N., 22° 9' W. - - - - - N.W. by N., 4. 54° 11' N., 21° 34' W. - - - - -	— — — —	?29·36 — — —	— — — —

	Wind.		Air.	Bar.	Sea.	
			\multicolumn{3}{c}{Standard Instruments.}	
8 a.m.	West, 6. Cloudy; squally; hail.		45°	29·51	51°	No. 35.
2 p.m.	W. by S., 5. Ditto, ditto, snow.					S.S. "Tarifa."
49° 54′ N., 30° 11′ W.	- - -		46	29·48	50	In { 50° 14′ N. / 28° 37′ W. / 8 a.m. G.T. 7th.
6 p.m.	W. by N., 7. Frequent heavy					Bound W. by Sly.
squalls, and hail. 49° 43′ N., 30° 39′ W.			42	29·40	48	To { 49° 1′ N. / 33° 32′ W. / 8 a.m. G.T. 8th.
10 p.m.	N.W. by W., 6. Ditto, ditto.					
49° 32′ N., 31° 7′ W. -	- -		41	29·71	50	
2 a.m., 8th.	N.W. by N., 4. Fine, with blue sky					
prevailing. 49° 21′ N., 31° 34′ W. -	-		42	29·85	51	
4 a.m.	Variable, 3. 49° 14′ N., 32° 15′ W.		—	—	—	
6 a.m.	S.E. by E., 5. Fine, with blue sky					
prevailing. 49° 7′ N., 32° 56′ W. -	-		43	29·85	52	

Diagram 3 contains the data of the "Tarifa" for each four hourly entry between England and America. Our last extract at 6 a.m., Greenwich time, of the 8th shows No. 35 to be as it were on the top of a wave of high pressure with the barometer commencing to fall (see Diagram 3), and the wind gone to S.E. by E. The Diagram shows that although the barometer was moderately high and the weather fine she was going into an area of low pressure, and in four hours had a strong southerly gale. It will be seen how something similar happened early on the 5th, before the setting in of the great gale, the difference being that on the 5th the barometer was lower, and the wind was W. by S., instead of N.W., before the barometer began to fall; the weather was squally instead of being fine, and the barometer fell faster than on the 8th.

The number of waves experienced by No. 35, each accompanied by its system of wind, is worthy of notice, as also the tendency in the barometer to be higher over the cold water to the westward than over the warmer to the eastward.

No 7 was in 49° 34′ N., 32° 11′ W., at 10.50 a.m. of the 8th, when she got the S.E. by E. wind experienced by No. 35 at 6 a.m., which indicates the N.Ely. movement of the change.

	Wind.	Air.	Bar.	Sea.	
					No. 2.
					S.S. "City of Cork."
8 a.m.	W. by S. ½ S., 4. Squalls; snow; hail;	41°	29·58	50°	In { 49° 36′ N. / 34° 19′ W. / 8 a.m. G.T. 7th.
sea decreasing. - - - -					Bound W. by Sly.
2.20 p.m. W. by N., 6. Ditto, ditto, ditto; high					
sea. 49° 28′ N., 35° 7′ W. - - -		37	29·57	49	To { 48° 51′ N. / 38° 53′ W. / 8 a.m. G.T. 8th.

| | Wind. | | | Air. | Bar. | Sea. |

10.20 p.m.　　　N.W. by N., 3.　Fine, clear.
49° 15′ N., 36° 26′ W.　-　-　-　-　40°　29·87　49°
2.20 a.m., 8th.　S.W. by W., 2.　Ditto, ditto.
49° 9′ N., 37° 5′ W. -　-　-　-　-　40　29·83　52
4.50 a.m.　　　E. by S., 3.　Fine weather.
49° 1′ N., 37° 54′ W.　-　-　-　-　41　29·70　52

No. 2 was 5° to the W. of No. 35, and seems to have lost the N.W. by W. wind about 4 hrs. sooner than she did.

No. 12.
S.S. "Dacian."
In { 46° 0′ N.
　　 40° 16′ W.
　　 8 a.m. G.T. 7th.
Bound N.Ely.
To { 47° 26′ N.
　　 37° 58′ W.
　　 8 a.m. G.T. 8th.

　　　　　　　　　　　Wind.
8 a.m.　　　N.N.E., 7.　Very high cross sea. -　—　—　—
2.40 p.m.　　N.N.E., 7.　Ditto. In 46° 9′ N.,
39° 54′ W. -　-　-　-　-　-　—　—　—
10.40 p.m.　　N.E., 6.　Cloudy. 46° 45′ N.,
38° 59′ W. -　-　-　-　-　-　—　—　—
3.40 a.m., 8th.　S.E., 5.　Clear, very high cross sea.
47° 9′ N., 38° 25′ W.　-　-　-　-　—　—　—

The north-easterly wind reported by this ship still differs much from that of ships near her.

No. 23.
S.S. "Atrato."
In { 39° 29′ N.
　　 40° 6′ W.
　　 8 a.m. G.T. 7th.
Bound N.Ely.
To { 41° 49′ N.
　　 35° 37′ W.
　　 8 a.m. G.T. 8th.

| | Wind. | | | Air. | Bar. | Sea. |

8 a.m.　　　East-south-easterly, 4.　Overcast;
drizzle. -　-　-　-　-　-　— ? 30·16　—
2.36 p.m.　East-south-easterly, 4 to 5. Ditto, ditto.
40° 5′ N., 39° 5′ W. -　-　-　-　— ? 30·09　—
8.36 p.m.　South-easterly, 3 to 4.　Ditto, ditto;
considerable N.N.W. swell; 40° 40′ N., 37° 55′ W. -　— ? 29·97　—
3.36 a.m., 8th.　S.S.E., 5.　Squally, drizzle.
41° 21′ N., 36° 33′ W. -　-　-　-　— ? 29·81　—

No. 23 got the swell of the N.N.W. wind which had prevailed for some time to the N.W. of her position. At 8 a.m. she had the south-easterly wind, which was felt by ships to the north-eastward of her, later in the day.

No. 17.
S.S. "Helvetia."
In { 46° 7′ N.
　　 43° 8′ W.
　　 8 a.m. G.T. 7th.
Bound W. by Sly.
To { 45° 7′ N.
　　 47° 53′ W.
　　 8 a.m. G.T. 8th.

　　　　　　　　　　　Wind.　　　　　　　　　　　　Air.　Bar.　Sea.
8 a.m.　　　N.W., 4.　Fine; high northerly swell at
4 a.m. -　-　-　-　-　-　-　40°　29·94　58°
4 p.m.　Variable airs.　Fine. N.E. sea. 45° 54′ N.,
41° 30′ W. -　-　-　-　-　-　—　—　—
7 p.m.　　North-easterly.　-　-　-　40　29·86　52
9 p.m.　E. by S., 4 to 5.　45° 42′ N., 45° 28′ W. -　—　—　—
3 a.m., 8th.　Rising northerly swell.

	Wind.			Air.	Bar.	Sea.
5 a.m., 8th.	E. by S., 6 to 7.	Barometer falling rapidly.	-	—	—	—
6 a.m.	S.W. by W., 6 to 7.	High northerly swell. 45° 21′ N., 47° 11′ W.	-	48°	29·00	45°

No. 17 seems to have passed through a small area of low pressure with corresponding changes of wind. In four hours after our last extract the wind suddenly veered to north and blew a strong gale, at the same time the temperature of the water was falling, and by 7 p.m. of the 8th it was down to 33°. This looks like an eddy of air travelling along the boundary line of warm and cold water, having a northerly wind to the westward of it.

	Wind.	
8 a.m.	N.W. by W. Light airs; cloudy.	
11.5 a.m.	N.N.E., 4. 43° 25′ N., 46° 16′ W.	
4.9 p.m.	East, 5. Gloomy. 43° 20′ N., 47° 10′ W.	
11.9 p.m.	E.S.E., 6. (Heavy rain at 9 p.m.) 43° 2′ N., 48° 48′ W.	
0.9 a.m., 8th.	S.S.W., 6 to 7. 43° 0′ N., 49° 2′ W.	
4.9 a.m.	S.W., 7. Rain. 42° 50′ N., 49° 51′ W.	
7.9 a.m.	W.N.W., 7 to 8. 42° 46′ N., 50° 11′ W.	

No. 10.
S.S. "Manhattan."
In { 43° 26′ N.
45° 37′ W.
8 a.m. G.T. 7th.
Bound Westerly.
To { 42° 45′ N.
50° 19′ W.
8 a.m. G.T. 8th.

No. 10 gives no instrumental observations or remarks on the sea. She seems to have experienced similar changes to No. 17, only earlier, being to the S.W. of her.

	Wind.		Air.	Bar.	Sea.
8 a.m.	S.W., 5. Very heavy rain and high sea.	-	70°	29·97	67°
3 p.m.	W.S.W., 7. Very heavy rain; sea very high. 33° 25′ N., 45° 40′ W.	-	70	29·89	67
7 a.m., 8th.	W.S.W., 7. Light squalls. 34° 55′ N. 44° 16′ W.	-	71	29·70	66

No. 42.
Ship "Swea."
In { 32° 53′ N.
46° 35′ W.
8 a.m. G.T. 7th.
Bound N.Ely.
To { 34° 53′ N.
44° 10′ W.
8 a.m. G.T. 8th.

At 8 a.m. Nos. 42 and 23 seem to have had an area of low pressure to the westward of them which afterwards came over the ships to the north-eastward of them. For instance, by referring to Diagram 3, it will be seen that No. 35 steamed into an area of low pressure at 6 a.m. of the 8th, in about 49° N. and 33° W., but it is not quite clear that they were the same.

126

				Air.	Bar.	Sea.
No. 39. S.S. "Westphalia." In {45° 23' N. 46° 42' W. 8 a.m. G.T. 7th. Bound W.S.Wly. To {43° 30' N. 53° 0' W. 8 a.m. G.T. 8th.		Wind.				
	8 a.m.	W.N.W., 4.	- - - -	33°	30·02	39°
	11.10 a.m.	North, 4. 45° 11' N., 47° 32' W.		32	30·05	40
	3.15 p.m.	East, 4. 44° 50' N., 48° 40' W.		37	29·92	38
	11.15 p.m.	East, 7. Four hours snow and rain.				
	44° 15' N., 50° 46' W.	- - - -		37	29·25	35
	1.15 a.m., 8th.	- - - -		—	29·05	—
	3.15 a.m.	North, 10. Four hours snow; wind backed from E. to N.; heavy storm. 43° 55' N., 51° 49' W.	- - - -	33	29·17	32
	7.15. a.m.	N., 10. 43° 35' N. 52° 52' W.	-	32	29·64	32

No. 39 was about 4° to the West, and a degree to the South of No. 17. It will be remembered that No. 17 did not get the shift to north until about 10 a.m. of the 8th or nearly seven hours later.

Diagram 4 gives a continuous record of this ship's observations.

			Air.	Bar.	Sea.
No. 11. S.S. "Iowa." In {44° 50' N. 46° 53' W. 8 a.m. G.T. 7th. Bound W. by Sly. To {44° 1' N. 51° 34' W. 8 a.m. G.T. 8th.		Wind.			
	8 a.m.	W. by N., 4. Clear. -	36°	—	42°
	Noon.	N. by E., 4. 44° 53'N., 47° 30'. Saw a steamer going W. (most likely No. 39).	—	—	—
	2 p.m.	N.E. by N., 3. 44° 54' N., 47° 48' W.	—	—	—
	3.12 p.m.	N.E. by E., 3. 44° 55' N., 47° 58' W.	35	—	40
	4.12 p.m.	E. by N., 3. 44° 52' N., 48° 12' W.	—	—	—
	7.12 p.m.	E. by N., 3. Wind increasing with snow and sleet. - - - -	—	—	—
	0.12 a.m., 8th.	N.E. by E., 7. Mist and rain. 44° 23' N., 50° 5' W. - - - -	37	—	37
	3.12 a.m.	N. by W., 8. 44° 11' N., 50° 56' W.	38	—	37

No. 11 was very near No. 39, and experienced similar weather.

			Air.	Bar.	Sea.
No. 9. S.S. "Colorado." In {46° 27' N. 47° 12' W. 8 a.m. G.T. 7th. Bound E. by Nly. To {48° 1' N. 41° 22' W. 8 a.m. G.T. 8th.		Wind.			
	8 a.m.	N.W., 3. Cloudy; hard frost. -	30°	—	30°
	1.26 p.m.	North-easterly, 4. Cloudy. In 46° 46' N., 45° 55' W. -	—	—	—
	4 p.m.	E.N.E., 4. Cloudy. In 46° 58' N., 45° 9' W. - - - -	30	—	30
	11 p.m.	East, 4 to 5. Very cloudy. In 47° 28' N., 43° 22' W. - - - -	37	—	36

	Wind.		Air.	Bar.	Sea.
1 a.m., 8th.	S.E., 6.	In 47° 36′ N., 42° 52′ W. -	36°	—	35°
6 a.m.	E.N.E., 7 to 8.	Heavy squall. In 47° 54′ N., 41° 46′ W. - - - -	37	—	35

In two hours the wind veered to S.E. again, and increased to a strong gale, lasting 12 hours.

No. 9 seems to have carried the S.Ely. wind much longer than the ships bound to the westward.

	Wind.	Air.	Bar.	Sea.	
8 a.m.	W. by S., 4. Clear blue sky.	32°	30·04	45°	No. 4. S.S. "Prussian."
1 p.m.	North-easterly; variable, 2. Cloudy, but clear. In 46° 8′ N., 48° 28′ W.	—	—	—	In {46° 28′ N. / 47° 29′ W. / 8 a.m. G.T. 7th. Bound W.S.Wly.
3.16 p.m.	E. by S., 5. Cloudy, but clear. 45° 56′ N., 49° 8′ W. - - - -	46	—	—	To {44° 55′ N. / 53° 23′ W. / 8 a.m. G.T. 8th.
7.16 p.m.	E. by N., 6. Misty, and heavy snow. 45° 44′ N., 49° 57′ W. - -	32	29·89	38	
11.16 p.m.	N.E. by E., 7. Dense mist and ditto. 45° 28′ N., 51° 3′ W. - - -	30	29·71	40	
2.16 a.m., 8th.	N.E. by N., 8. Ditto, ditto. 45° 16′ N., 51° 52′ W. - - -	30	29·61	38	
4.16 a.m.	N. by E., 8. Ditto, ditto, 45° 8′ N., 52° 55′ W. - - - -	—	—	—	
7.16 a.m.	N.N.W., 7. Overcast, but clear. 44° 56′ N., 53° 15′ W. - - -	29	29·71	37	

Nos. 4 and 11 bound the same way seem to have had similar weather whilst No. 9 (bound East), and very near No. 4 at 8 a.m. of the 7th, eventually steamed into a south-easterly wind, when No. 4 had a change to N.W.

	Wind.	All Standard Instruments.			
		Air.	Bar.	Sea.	
8 a.m.	S.S.E., 6. Heavy rain; smooth sea.	61°	29·45	66°	No. 36. S.S. "Palmyra."
Noon.	S.S.W., 3. Ditto, and confused sea. In 40° 55′ N., 58° 0′ W. - -	61	29·38	65	In {40° 49′ N. / 58° 35′ W. / 8 a.m. G.T. 7th. Bound E. by Nly.
2 p.m.	N.N.W., 7. Passing showers. 40° 58′ N., 57° 43′ W. - - - -	—	29·41	—	To {41° 41′ N. / 53° 34′ W. / 8 a.m. G.T. 8th.
3.45 p.m.	N.N.W., 7. Ditto. In 41° 0′ N., 57° 25′ W. - - - - -	53	29·38	66	
3.45 a.m., 8th.	N.N.W., 8. Fine weather. A heavy confused sea from N.W. and N.N.E. In 41° 27′ N., 54° 32′ W. - - - -	42	29·61	56	
7.45 a.m.	N.N.W., 8. Ditto, ditto. In 41° 39′ N., 53° 40′ W. - - - -	38	29·69	53	

At 7.45 a.m., 8th., No. 36 was about 200 miles south of No. 4. They had the same wind, but very different temperatures, owing to the difference of sea temperature. No. 36 reports a current of S. 79° W., 52 miles, the result of careful observations; and Capt. Watson says his experience led him to expect it to have been as strong in the opposite direction. See Diagram 5 for a continuous record of this ship's observations.

The following Bermuda observations were sent by General Lefroy:
2.18 p.m., G.T.   Bar. 29·951; wind "generally" N.W., 5.

Unfortunately they came too late to be entered on the Chart, but it will be seen that the N.W. wind completes the cyclonic movement round the area of low pressure supposed to exist to the north-eastward of Bermuda.

		Wind.		Air.	Bar.	Sea.
No. 16. S.S. "City of London." In { 40° 59' N. 65° 26' W. 8 a.m. G.T. 7th. Bound E. by Nly. To { 42° 7' N. 59° 31' W. 8 a.m. G.T. 8th.	8 a.m. sea. 4.15 p.m. sea; cloudy. 41° 8' N., 63° 26' W. 4.15 a.m., 8th. N.N.W., 6 to 7. Ditto. 41° 52' N., 60° 30' W.	W.N.W., 5 to 6. Overcast; easterly N.N.W., 5 to 6. High E.N.Ely.		38° 40 40	29·92 29·99 30·04	40° 58 56
No. 40. S.S. "Deutschland." In { 41° 17' N. 66° 8' W. 8 a.m. G.T. 7th. Bound E. by Nly. To { 42° 19' N. 60° 32' W. 8 a.m. G.T. 8th.	8. a.m. 4.18 p.m. 41° 11' N., 64° 26' W. 8.18 p.m. overcast. 41° 28' N., 63° 27' W. 4.18 a.m., 8th.	N.E. by N., 6. Overcast. N.E. by E., 6. Cloudy. In North, 6. High N.E. sea; North, 6. 42° 2' N., 61° 31' W.		37° 37 32 30	29·99 30·01 30·11 30·18	52° 41 39 52

No. 40 was about one degree to the westward of No. 16, and as she was going the same way, kept so. It is curious to notice the difference in the direction of their winds, though the force was the same. No. 16 had had the wind N. by E., and at 5.30 a.m. of the 7th gives it Northwesterly.

		Wind.		Air.	Bar.	Sea.
No. 15. S.S. "Moravian." In { 43° 12' N. 66° 33' W. 8 a.m. G.T. 7th. Bound Easterly. To { 43° 2' N. 60° 51' W. 8 a.m. G.T. 8th.	8 a.m. N.W.; Easterly swell. 4.18 p.m. clear in N. In 42° 53' N., 64° 35' W. 8.18 p.m. topsail. 42° 55' N., 63° 39' W. 4.18 a.m., 8th. easterly swell. 43° 0' N., 61° 47' W.	N.E., 4. Heavy nimbus in N. by W., 4. Fine, and very ? Northerly, 4. Cloudy; set main ? Northerly, 4. Cloudy; heavy		31° 30 28 27	30·04 30·07 30·09 30·15	38° 36 38 35

At 8.18 p.m. the ship's log gives N. by E. for the direction of the wind, and continues that direction for nearly 24 hours. During the same time the log kept for this office gives N.W. by N. for its direction. I have therefore entered it as northerly. Curiously, the other ships (Nos. 16 and 40) which were near do not give a clue to explain this, as one agrees with one direction, and the other with the other.

	Wind.	— —	Air.	Bar.	Sea.	
8 a.m.	N., 5. Cloudy. - -		41°?	30·13	44°	No. 18. S.S. "Virginia."
4.23 p.m. 65° 45′ W. -	N.E. by N., 5. Cloudy. 40° 10′ N., - - - -		38?	30·15	47	In { 40° 19′ N. 67° 9′ W. 8 a.m. G.T. 7th. Bound Easterly.
4.23 a.m., 8th. ?N.E. by N. 5 to 6. Heavy easterly swell. 40° 35′ N., 63° 43′ W. - -			40?	30·45	65	To { 40° 47′ N. 62° 47′ W. 8 a.m. G.T. 8th.

At 2 a.m. of the 8th, the remarks say, "wind hauling to eastward, in square sail," but no change is given in the direction column.

	Wind.		Air.	Bar.	Sea.	
8 a.m.	N. by E., 7. Cloudy. -		54°	29·99	72°	No. 38. Ship "Nicoline."
4.43 p.m. 70° 53′ W. -	N., 6. Ditto. 37° 20′ N., - - - -		50	30·07	71	In { 37° 0′ N. 71° 23′ W. 8 a.m. G.T. 7th. Bound N.N.Wly.
8.43 p.m. 71° 16′ W. -	N.N.E., 5. Ditto. 37° 31′ N., - - - -		47	30·13	57	To { 38° 23′ N. 72° 22′ W. 8 a.m. G.T. 8th.
0.43 a.m., 8th. from W. In 37° 41′ N., 71° 39′ W.	N.E., 5. Cum. from N.E. Cir.-s. -		46	30·16	56	
4.43 a.m. In 38° 5′ N., 72° 3′ W. -	E.N.E., 4. Cir. from W. by S. - -		47	30·08	53	

At 4.43 p.m., it is remarked that "there is a thick bank of clouds rising in the West, a sign of an East gale in this district."

At 4.43 a.m., 8th., it is remarked "brisk breeze, with rapidly increasing wind and sea; barometer falling quickly."

This was followed in 8 hours by a terrific storm from E.S.E., with squalls of hurricane force, but they will be dealt with in the remarks on the 8th.

There can be little doubt but that No. 38 saw the dense clouds, forming part of a cyclonic gale, advancing from the west or south-westward, and as she was on the north-eastern side of it, the gale commenced from E.S.E.

I have heard from captains used to that part of the sea, that this type of gale is well known there, and it will be seen that several similar gales have been dealt with in discussing these Charts for only 11 days.

130

No. 3.
S.S. "Etna."
In New York.

Had a north-westerly wind throughout the day, with fine weather in the morning, and overcast in the afternoon.

It will be seen that on the 8th the wind and weather at New York were influenced by the same cyclonic gale which was experienced by No. 38. New York being to the westward, and No. 38 to the eastward of its point of lowest pressure, the direction of their winds was of course different.

New York Observatory.
8 a.m. G.T. 7th.
To 8 a.m. G.T. 8th.

8 a.m. Wind, N. by E. *3 miles per hour;* barometer 30·23; air 30°.

The barometer changed very little until 4 a.m., 8th, when it commenced falling.

The temperature oscillated considerably till 2 p.m., when it commenced rising. At 10 p.m. it was 41°, at which time it commenced falling.

The wind remained steady at N. till about 2.30 p.m., when it backed to N.W. ¼ W., veering to N. again two hours later, and to E. by S. by 9 p.m.: after which it backed two or three points. The force throughout the 24 hours was *very* light.

GENERAL REMARKS ON THE CHART FOR 8 A.M., GREENWICH TIME, FEBRUARY 7TH, 1870.

The logs of 35 ships have been consulted, and the same system has been followed.

The southerly wind still prevails over the British Isles and Europe. A south-easterly gale of nearly hurricane force is reported in Norway, at Shetland, and the Hebrides. A very strong South gale was blowing in Iceland at 10.30 a.m.

In Cumberland Sound the wind was moderate from N.W. at 8 a.m.; near Belleisle at 4 p.m. it was light north-westerly.

At the Azores it was moderate westerly at 11 a.m., whilst in Madeira there was a very light west-south-westerly air.

The Quarterly Weather Report for this day, Plate VIII., shows that the barometer at Valencia fell from about 8 a.m. of the 7th until 3 p.m., when it remained pretty steady until 1 a.m. of the 8th, at which time it commenced to rise. During this time the wind *backed* from E. to N. and then to W. by N.

At Falmouth during the same time, or, rather, between 7 a.m. of the 7th, and 2 a.m. of the 8th, the barometer fell slowly, and the wind *veered* from S.E. at 6 a.m. of the 7th to S. at 8 a.m., where it remained steady until 2 a.m. of the 8th, when it suddenly veered to W., and the barometer rose.

These facts lead to the conclusion that the wind of Valencia was affected by the western side, and that of Falmouth by the eastern side of an area of low pressure; but whether it was the same area which affected both places is doubtful; the isobars and directions of wind on the 8 a.m. Chart seem to indicate that there were local disturbances.

At Armagh, Stonyhurst, and Glasgow the wind backed to N.E. or E.; at Aberdeen and Kew it was steady from about S. by E., but freshened into a gale at Aberdeen. This tendency to blow harder from the southward at Aberdeen than at any other observatory, so different from the action of southerly winds which accompany areas of low pressure coming in from the westward, seems to indicate that this southerly wind was anti-cyclonic: the accompaniment of a high pressure to the eastward, working its way to the westward, rather than of a low pressure working its way to the eastward. Perhaps it may have been a sign of the prevailing easterly wind which followed, and lasted several days.

We have already remarked that at 8 a.m. of the 7th, Norway and Shetland were experiencing a furious S.E. gale, whilst the wind was light from south at Aberdeen; but by 9 p.m. it was nearly 50 miles an hour from S. by E. at Aberdeen, and continued steady in direction and force until 6 p.m. of the 8th, when the force decreased with a steadily rising barometer though the direction continued. These facts seem to prove that the gale was first felt in the N.E., and worked its way S.W. to Aberdeen.

It will be noticed that the barometer is down to 28·38 in Iceland, with a strong southerly gale blowing, which, according to Buys Ballot's law, indicates that a lower barometer exists to the westward of that island. This leads to the supposition that, although the area of extremely low pressure which was in 55° to 60° N. and 20° to 25° W. on the 6th (taken in connexion with the rising barometer in Norway) helped to increase the force of the winds in the Hebrides, Shetland, and Norway, it did not pass to the N.E., but turned off to the northward, and passed to the westward of Iceland.

A cursory view of the Chart shows that the same main features of wind and weather exist over the Atlantic, viz., a southerly wind on the eastern and northerly on the western side, with an area of low pressure between them, round which the wind blows. At the same time there is a local eddy of wind to the S.W. of Ireland.

There are also indications of other waves or areas of low pressure. For instance, No. 23, in 40° W., has a falling barometer and south-easterly wind, which, on the following day, freshens into a gale; and, as has been remarked, No. 35 to the N.E. of her got a strong S.E. gale on the 8th. This day's Chart shows the probable position of the area of low pressure which was related to this gale to be to the N.E. of Bermuda. The observations received from that island since the Charts were published, show that there was a north-westerly wind there, which completes the circuit of the wind round this area of low pressure. The 8 a.m. Chart of the 8th shows what was most probably the same area of low pressure to be to the S.E. of Newfoundland.

Then, again, No. 38, in about 71° W., saw a gale brewing to the westward of her, which, as her captain foretold, commenced at E.S.E. Her barometer had already commenced falling, and we shall see that early on the 8th it fell very fast, proving that an area of low pressure was advancing upon her from the westward.

The way in which the isobars curve round the high pressure in the N.E., with the wind blowing nearly at right angles to them, seems worthy of notice.

Extracts and Remarks to accompany the Chart for 8 a.m., Greenwich Time, February 8th, 1870.

The European observations indicate that the wind draws round an area of low pressure at the entrance of the Irish Channel, being northerly at the western, westerly at the southern, southerly at the eastern, and south-easterly at the north-eastern stations.

The strongest wind is still from S.E. at the north-eastern stations, where the barometer is high and rising. On consulting the Quarterly Weather Report, Plate VIII., we find that on this day a strong S.E. gale blew at Aberdeen, with a rising barometer. After the 8th, north-easterly and easterly winds prevailed at all the observatories for several days.

This being the last Chart, extracts have not been confined, as in the other cases, to the 24 hours between 8 a.m. Greenwich time of the given day and 8 a.m. Greenwich time of the next; but, where the 24 hours end, a line has been drawn, and then extracts and running quotations

133

have been continued in some cases for several days, so as to discover when various ships got the east wind which had set in on the eastern side of the Atlantic, with the object of proving whether or not it originated in the East and advanced towards the West.

	Wind.		Standard Instruments.			No. 50.
			Air.	Bar.	Sea.	S.S. "Hotspur."
8 a.m.	W. by S., 3. Fine. - - -		57°	30·04	57°	⎧ 37° 15' N.
Noon.	W. by S., 3. Fine. 37° 19' N., 3° 6' E.					In ⎨ 2° 28' E.
Sp. G. 1·0275	- - - - -		60	30·01	57	⎩ 8 a.m. G.T. 8th.
8 p.m.	W. by N., 4. Fork lightning in S.E.					Bound Easterly.
37° 21' N., 4° 40' E. -	- - - -		56	29·92	—	⎧ 37° 24' N.
						To ⎨ 7° 6' E.
						⎩ 8 a.m. G.T. 9th.

No. 50 was in the Mediterranean.

	Wind.	Air.	Bar.	Sea.	No. 28.
8 a.m.	Variable north-westerly, 6. -	50°	29·34	—	S.S. "West Indian."
1.39 p.m.	N.W., 3 to 4. Cloudy. 49° 2' N.,				⎧ 49° 33' N.
9° 39' W. -	- - - -	53	29·40	—	In ⎨ 9° 2' W.
4.39 p.m.	N.N.W., 4 to 5. Squally. 48° 44' N.,				⎩ 8 a.m. G.T. 8th.
10° 3' W.	- - - -	—	29·42	—	Bound S.Wly.
1.39 a.m., 9th.	N.W., 5 to 6. Showers. 47° 50' N.,				⎧ 47° 12' N.
11° 21' W. -	- - - -	—	—	—	To ⎨ 12° 15' W.
5.39 a.m.	Variable; decreasing. 47° 26' N.,				⎩ 8 a.m. G.T. 9th.
11° 55' W. -	- - - -	—	—	—	

	Wind.	Air.	Aneroid.		No. 30.
8 a.m.	W.N.W., 4. - - - -	50°	29·35	51°	H.M.S. "Orontes."
0.55 p.m.	N.W., 3 to 4. Fine. 51° 25' N.,				⎧ 51° 16' N.
8° 45' W. -	- - - -	49	29·32	51	In ⎨ 9° 43' W.
					⎩ 8 a.m. G.T. 8th.
					Bound to Queenstown.

The wind continued north-westerly, light, and weather fine, until she arrived at Queenstown at 3.55 p.m., the barometer having *fallen* ·02 in. since last observation.

This falling barometer, with the wind North-westerly, in a ship bound to the eastward, is worthy of notice as being most probably the effect of her easterly route.

	Wind.	Air.	Bar.	Sea.	No. 25.
8 a.m.	W.S.W., 4. - - -	40°?	29·62	—	S.S. "Cuban."
0.36 p.m.	Light baffling airs. 49° 26' N.,				⎧ 49° 9' N.
8° 59' W. -	- - - -	—	—	—	In ⎨ 9° 58' W.
11.36 p.m.	S.S.W., 3. Cloudy. 49° 37' N.,				⎩ 8 a.m. G.T. 8th.
6° 41' W. -	- - - -	—	—	—	Bound Easterly.
7.36 a.m., 9th.	S.S.W., 4. 49° 47' N., 5° 4' W. -	—	·—	—	⎧ 49° 47' N.
					To ⎨ 5° 7' W.
					⎩ 8 a.m. G.T. 9th.

At 9 a.m. of the 9th the wind backed to E.S.E.
At 1 p.m. it was E.N.E., increasing fast.
At 5 p.m. it was E.N.E.; a strong gale and high sea.

No. 45.
Ship "Carl Georg."
In { 49° 28′ N.
    10° 7′ W.
    8 a.m. G.T. 8th.
Bound Easterly.
To { 49° 42′ N.
    6° 28′ W.
    8 a.m. G.T. 9th.

	Wind.		Air.	Bar.	Sea.
8 a.m.	S., 5.	- - -	53°	29·30	—
0.38 p.m.	S., 5.	49° 31′ N., 9° 30′ W. -	52	29·34	—
4.38 p.m.	S.W., 5.	49° 33′ N., 8° 53′ W. -	52	29·29	—
8.38 p.m.	Variable, 5.	49° 35′ N., 8° 15′ W.	52	29·19	—
0.38 a.m., 9th.	N.N.E., 4.	49° 37′ N., 7° 38′ W.-	52	29·44	—
4.38 a.m.	N.W., 4.	49° 40′ N., 7° 1′ W. -	52	29·44	—

The wind continued N.W., 4, until noon of the 9th, when it shifted to W., 3, continuing so until 8 a.m., 10th, when it was S., 5, the barometer steadily rising.

	Wind.		Air.	Bar.	Sea.
At noon, 10th.	E.S.E., 6.	Wind increasing and getting easterly, with rain. 50° 0′ N., 3° 47′ W. -	51°	29·89	—

From this time the wind freshened, and at midnight of the 10th backed to east, freshening into a strong gale, which lasted until

	Wind.		Air.	Bar.	Sea.
Noon, 15th.	E.S.E., 10.	49° 25′ N., 6° 42′ W. -	48°	30·30	—

when the extract ends.

It will be seen that No. 45 got the easterly wind some days before ships to the westward of her. See remarks on No. 40, p. 147.

No. 26.
S.S. "Venezuelan."
In { 49° 43′ N.
    16° 16′ W.
    8 a.m. G.T. 8th.
Bound E. by Nly.
To { 50° 40′ N.
    11° 5′ W.
    8 a.m. G.T. 9th.

	Wind.		Air.	Bar.	Sea.
8 a.m.	North, 3 to 4.	Variable wind, and drizzle. - - - -	48°	29·42	—
1 p.m.	N. by E., 4.	49° 59′ N., 15° 12′ W.	50	29·30	—
5 p.m.	N.W. by N., 4.	50° 8′ N., 14° 21′ W.	—	29·65	—
9 p.m.	N.W. by N., 6.	Squally. 50° 16′ N., 13° 30′ W. - - - -	44	29·64	—
6 a.m., 9th.	N. by E., 6.	Clear. 50° 35′ N., 11° 35′ W. - - - -	39	29·64	—

At 1 p.m. of the 9th, in 51° 0′ N., 10° 20′ W., the wind veered to N.E. by E.

At 8 p.m. in 51° 10′ N., 9° 6′ W., it blew a fresh gale from N.E. by E., which veered to east, gale continuing.

It will be seen that No. 26, the most easterly ship, got the easterly gale first.

	Wind.				Bar.		No. 24. S.S. "Nile."
8 a.m.	S.W., 4.	Fine; heavy W. swell	—	30·14	—	In	39° 38' N. 19° 1' W. 8 a.m. G.T. 8th.
2.20 p.m. 39° 3' N., 19° 50' W.	W.S.W., 4.	Ditto,	ditto.	—	30·12	—	
9.20 p.m. 38° 25' N., 21° 14' W.	S.W., 4.	Squally;	ditto.	—	30·12	—	Bound W.S.Wly. To { 37° 33' N. 23° 15' W. 8 a.m. G.T. 9th.
5.20 a.m., 9th. S.W., 6 to 7. Heavy south-westerly sea; rainy; 37° 45' N., 22° 46' W.				—	29·95	—	

After noon of the 9th, the wind freshened into a gale from W.S.W., and after midnight it veered to west and N.W., still blowing a hard N.W. gale until 4 p.m. of the 10th, when it moderated, but continued north-westerly in direction.

No. 24 did not get the easterly wind which was to the N.E. of her on the 9th.

	Wind.	Air.	Bar.	Sea.	No. 41. S.S. "Hammonia."
8 a.m.	N.N.W., 7.	46°	29·46	51°	49° 32' N.
5.22 p.m.	North, 3. Sea somewhat decreasing.	48	29·96	52	In { 19° 5' W. 8 a.m. G.T. 8th.
9.22 p.m.	Variable, 1. 49° 13' N., 23° 7' W.	52	29·92	52	Bound Westerly.
1.22 a.m., 9th.	S.S.E., 3. 49° 7' N., 24° 24' W.	49	29·82	51	To { 49° 0' N. 26° 25' W.
5.22 a.m.	S.S.E., 4. 49° 1' N., 25° 41' W.	55	29·80	51	8 a.m. G.T. 9th.

At 1.53 p.m., 9th, No. 41 had a high wild sea from E.S.E., S., and S.W., though the wind was only S.S.E., 3.

The barometer fell to 28·90 at 5.53 p.m., when the wind changed from S.S.E., 3, to S., 2.

By 2 a.m., 10th, the wind had shifted to N., 3, and by 6 a.m. to N.N.W., 7, after which in 8 hours it lulled and backed to S.

Between noon (ship time) of the 10th, in 48° 9' N., 35° 33' W., and noon (ship time) of the 12th, in 45° 14' N., 49° 20' W., she passed through two other depressions, with the wind shifting from S. to N., or N.W. and back again; the strongest wind being S., 8, at 4 p.m. of the 11th. By referring to Diagram 3, it will be seen that No. 35 had several of these depressions, one on the 8th and 9th, in 36° to 38° W. being accompanied by a strong gale, shifting from S.E. to N.W., which seems to have been experienced later by No. 41. The log of No. 41 seems to show that the ships bound to the westward were not caught up by the easterly wind which was pressing itself to the westward over the Atlantic, and met the ships bound to the eastward.

136

No. 21. S.S. "Denmark."		Wind.		Air.	Bar.	Sea.
In { 51° 13' N. 19° 31' W. 8 a.m. G.T. 8th.	8 a.m.	N.Wly., 4 to 5. Wind variable.	-	42°	? 29·72	50°
Bound Easterly.	1.12 p.m.	N. by W., 6. Clear. 51° 26' N.,				
	18° 7' W. - - - - - -			44	? 29·76	51
To { 51° 29' N. 12° 56' W. 8 a.m. G.T. 9th.	8.12 a.m., 9th. N.E., 6 to 7. Gloomy. 51° 29' N., 12° 56' W. - - - - - -			—	—	—

At 4.42 p.m., 9th, No. 21 was off the Skelligs in 51° 40′ N., 10° 32′ W., with a strong easterly breeze, which freshened into a gale by midnight. By referring to Nos. 25 and 26 it will be seen that they were to the East of No. 21, and got the east gale before her.

No. 13. S.S. "India."		Wind.		Air.	Bar.	Sea.
In { 54° 21' N. 20° 20' W. 8 a.m. G.T. 8th.	8 a.m.	N.W. by N., 4 to 3. Fine.	-	—	? 29·66	—
Bound Easterly.	1.15 p.m.	N.W. by N., 3. Fine and clear.				
	54° 33' N. 18° 53' W. - - - - -			—	? 29·75	—
To { 54° 50' N. 14° 5' W. 8 a.m. G.T. 9th.	5.15 p.m. Northerly, 5. 54° 37' N., 17° 44' W.			—	rising	—
	8 a.m., 9th. N.E. by E., 5. Cloudy. 54° 50' N., 14° 5' W. - - - - - -			—	? 29·84	—

At 8 p.m. of the 9th the wind was fresh E.S.E. with a *rising* barometer.

At 11.30 p.m. it was S.E., fresh breeze and clear weather, where it seems to have continued until her arrival in port. This seems to have been a clear case of a S.E. wind caused by the high barometer to the north-eastward in Norway instead of being produced by an area of low pressure coming in from the westward.

No. 6. S.S. "Nestorian."		Wind.		Air.	Bar.	Sea.
In { 53° 30' N. 26° 31' W. 8 a.m. G.T. 8th.	8 a.m.	N.W. by W., 5. Cross sea; showers of sleet. - - - - -	-	39°	29·78	45°
Bound W. by Sly.	2 p.m.	W. by N., 4. Heavy ditto. 53° 16' N.,				
	28° 18' W. - - - - - -			41	29·98	47
To { 51° 58' N. 33° 59' W. 8 a.m. G.T. 9th.	6 p.m. S.E. by S., 2. Heavy northerly swell.					
	52° 58' N., 29° 35' W. - - - - -			36	29·79	46
	8 p.m. E. by S., 5. 52° 49' N., 30° 11' W. -			—	—	—
	10 p.m. E. by S., 7. Cloudy. 52° 36' N.,					
	31° 11' W. - - - - - -			41	29·64	45
	2 a.m., 9th. E. by S., 8. Strong gale and gloomy.					
	52° 23' N., 32° 9' W. - - - - - -			42	29·29	45
	6 a.m. E. by S., 7. Heavy confused sea.					
	52° 5' N., 33° 26' W. - - - - -			44	28·91	47

From this time the wind decreased until it was at—

	Air.	Bar.	Sea.
3.24 p.m., 9th. S.E. by S., 4., when the wind shifted suddenly to N. by W.	at 2.24 p.m., 9th 49°	28·75	48°
4.24 p.m. N. by W., 9. 51° 16′ N., 36° 27′ W.	—	—	—
6.24 p.m. N. by W., 10. Perfect hurricane; terrific squalls. 51° 1′ N., 36° 55′ W.	40	29·01	48

From this time the northerly gale moderated with a rising barometer, until 5 a.m. of the 10th, when it fell calm, and was followed by a southerly gale and falling barometer, the wind veering to N.W. as its force decreased.

It seems quite clear that No. 6 got the gale experienced by No. 35 on the 8th (see Diagram 3), but she had the wind more easterly, and after the shift it was more northerly; it must be remembered that she was more than 3° to the N. of No. 35. So far as I can estimate the facts of the case No. 6 (the north-eastern ship) got the changes about 12 hours after No. 35.

At 8 a.m., 8th, Nos. 6 and 13 were in nearly the same latitude, and about 6° apart, the former bound to the westward, went into a south-easterly wind, with a fast *falling* barometer, whilst No. 13, bound to the eastward, also got a south-easterly wind, but with a *rising* barometer. These facts illustrate well the two kinds of south-easterly wind experienced in these latitudes, the one on the north-eastern side of an area of low pressure, the other on the south-western side of an area of high pressure.

The way in which No. 6, bound W., in a high latitude, experienced frequent changes of wind and barometer, whilst No. 13, bound E., got a steady south-easterly wind, at the same time that a steady easterly wind had set in over the British Islands, looks as if these areas of low pressure took a more northerly course during our easterly winds, (being as it were fended off from these islands by the increased pressure existing over them,) and eventually merged into the central area of low pressure in the Atlantic, increasing the gradient for the south-easterly winds blowing at our northern stations.

	Wind.	Air.	Bar.	Sea.	
8 a.m.	W.N.W., 5. Cloudy; high sea.	48°	29·76	51°	No. 19. S.S. "England."
11 a.m. 28° 40′ W.	S.S.W., 3 to 4. Ditto. 50° 30′ N.,	46	29·82	50	In { 50° 38′ N. 28° 4′ W. 8 a.m. G.T. 8th.
Noon. 28° 52′ W. 29.539.	E.S.E., 4. Ditto. 50° 28′ N.,	—	—	—	Bound W. by Sly. To { 49° 39′ N. 33° 18′ W. 8 a.m. G.T. 9th.

No. 19.
S.S. "England"
—continued.

	Wind.		Air.	Bar.	Sea.
2 p.m.	E.S.E., 4 to 5. Ditto, high W.N.W. sea. 50° 23′ N., 29° 16′ W.	-	48°	29·78	50°
9 p.m.	S.	-	—	—	—
10 p.m.	S., 8. High sea. 50° 4′ N., 31° 5′ W.	—	—	—
11 p.m.	S.S.E., 8.	-	48	29·18	50
2 a.m. 9th.	S.S.E., 8. Sea filled the saloon. 49° 54′ N., 32° 0′ W.	-	48	29·08	50
8 a.m.	S.W., 9. 49° 39′ N., 33° 18′ W.	-	52	28·88	56

The barometer gradually fell, and the wind veered more to the westward, until it was at—

	Wind.		Air.	Bar.	Sea.
4 p.m., 9th.	W.N.W., 9; with tremendous squall of wind and hail. 49° 23′ N., 34° 57′ W.	-	—	—	—
7 p.m.	N.W., 9. Hove ship to.	-	51°	28·62 at 11.15 p.m.	54°
10 p.m.	N.N.W., 9.	-	-	46	28·65	50

At 10 a.m., 10th, the wind was N.N.W.; nearly calm. - - - - - 51 29·00 51

At 11 a.m. the wind was S.S.E.; increasing breeze. Barometer falling

The 8 a.m. chart for the 8th seems to show that the south-easterly, and afterwards north-westerly, winds experienced by No. 19 between noon of the 8th and 4 p.m. of the 9th, were actually blowing to the westward of her at 8 a.m. of the 8th. Other ships near her got similar changes.

The above extracts show that No. 19 continued to experience several changes of wind and corresponding changes of pressure. They will be seen depicted on Diagram 3 of the barometer, wind, &c. experienced by No. 35.

No. 35.
S.S. "Tarifa."
In { 49° 1′ N.
    { 33° 32′ W.
    { 8 a.m. G.T. 8th.
Bound W.S. Wly.
To { 47° 50′ N.
    { 36° 57′ W.
    { 8 a.m. G.T.

	Wind.		Standard Instruments.		
			Air.	Bar.	Sea.
8 a.m.	S.E. by E., 5	- - -	43°	29·81	51°
2.23 p.m.	S.E. by S., 8. Overcast; misty. 48° 40′ N., 35° 41′ W.	-	48	29·27	51
6.23 p.m.	S. by E., 9. Squally, with rain. 48° 26′ N., 35° 48′ W.	-	53	28·59	52
0.23 a.m., 9th.	S.W. by S.	- - -	—	—	—
2.23 a.m.	S.W. by W., 6. Squally; showery. 47° 59′ N., 36° 3′ W.	-	54	28·73	54

	Wind.				Standard Instruments.		
					Air.	Bar.	Sea.
6.23 a.m. 36° 42′ W.	W. by N., 3.	Fine.	47° 52′ N.		53°	28·70	56°
2.32 p.m., 9th. rain. 47° 38′ N., 38° 0′ W.	N.W. by N., 9.	Squally, with rain.			49	29·08	55

Diagram 3 gives a better idea of the changes than these extracts. Capt. Murphy remarks that this gale commenced at S. (magnetic) and ended at N., but that they usually commence at S.W. and end at N.W. It will be seen on Diagram 3 how No. 35 got the same oscillations as those which were experienced by Nos. 19 and 6, but earlier.

By consulting the extracts from Nos. 6, 19, and 35, we are led to suppose that the strength of the north-westerly wind was greater with the more northern ships. No. 35 passed through four other atmospheric waves before she arrived at Boston (see Diagram 3).

	Wind.	Air.	Bar.	Sea.	No. 23. S.S. "Atrato."
8 a.m. squalls; rain.	Southerly, 7. Overcast; heavy squalls; rain.	—	?29·66	—	In { 41° 49′ N 35° 37′ W. 8 a.m. G.T. 8th.
2.17 p.m. 34° 22′ W.	S.S.W., 7. Fine. 42° 26′ N.,	—	?29·44	—	Bound E.N.Ely.
2.17 a.m., 9th. eastward. 43° 20′ N., 31° 41′ W.	S.Wly., 8. Lightning to south-	—	?29·19	—	To { 43° 57′ N. 30° 21′ W. 8 a.m. G.T. 9th.
8.17 a.m.	S.S.Wly., 8. 43° 57′ N., 30° 21′ W.	—	?29·07	—	

4 p.m., 9th. 44° 35′ N., 28° 35′ W.	North-westerly, 6. Decreasing.		—	?28·84	—

After 4 p.m. the barometer rose and the wind decreased.

1.45 a.m., 10th. westerly swell. 45° 14′ N., 26° 30′ W.	N. by E., 4 to 5. Fine; heavy		—	?29·08	—

The extract ends at 1.30 a.m., 11th, in 46° 44′ N. 21° 50′ W., when there was a north-easterly gale and high easterly sea; barometer rising.

140

No. 12.
S.S. "Dacian."
In {47° 26' N.
      37° 58' W.
      8 a.m. G.T. 8th.
Bound N.Ely.
To {49° 19' N.
      35° 29' W.
      8 a.m. G.T. 9th.

Time	Wind.
8 a.m.	S.E., 6. Ship labouring heavily.
8.30 a.m.	E.S.E., 7. Slowed engines at 10.30 a.m.
2.30 p.m.	S.E., 8. Very high sea. 47° 58' N., 37° 11' W.
5.30 p.m.	S.E., 7. Set on full speed.
8.30 p.m.	E., 7. 48° 16' N., 36° 48' W.
2.30 a.m., 9th.	Variable, 6. Gloomy. 48° 53' N., 36° 2' W.

After the above extracts No. 12 records a variable wind for 24 hours, then gives N., 6, at 1 a.m. of the 10th. No barometer or other instrumental readings are given, so that there is no clue as to the prevailing direction of the strong variable wind.

No. 2.
S.S. "City of Cork."
In {48° 51' N.
      38° 53' W.
      8 a.m. G.T. 8th.
Bound W. by Sly.
To {47° 38' N.
      43° 10' W.
      8 a.m. G.T. 9th.

Time	Wind.	Air.	Bar.	Sea.
8 a.m.	E. by S., 5 to 6. Squally.	42°	20·52	52°
9.37 a.m.	S.E. by E., 7. Frequent squalls. 48° 48' N., 39° 14' W.	—	—	—
2.40 p.m.	S.E. by E., 8. 48° 37' N., 40° 18' W.	48	29·21	53
4.40 p.m.	S.E. by S., 7. 48° 30' N., 40° 38' W.	49	29·09	54
5.40 p.m.	S.W., 6. Dull. 48° 27' N., 40° 48' W.	50	28·91	54
7.40 p.m.	S. by W., 5.	—	—	—
10.40 p.m.	S.W. by W., 3. Dull. 48° 9' N., 41° 38' W.	51	28·47	54
11.40 p.m.	W. by S., 11. Suddenly increased to a hurricane. 48° 6' N., 41° 48' W.	—	—	—
0.40 a.m., 9th.	N.W. by N., 10. Very heavy squalls. 48° 3' N., 41° 58' W.	50	28·–?*	52
7.40 a.m.	N.W. by W., 8. 47° 38' N., 43° 10' W.	39	29·42	41

The wind continued to blow a moderate gale from the north-westward until 3 p.m. of the 9th in 47° 14' N., 44° 18' W., when it backed to the westward; at 7 p.m. the barometer began to fall, and at 11 p.m. the wind was S.E., freshening fast, with a fast falling barometer.

* A blank space was left, so that it is not known whether 28 inches was meant for the reading or not.

By referring to Diagram 3 it will be seen that No. 35 got the same changes, but several hours after No. 2, because she was to the eastward of her.

On the 9th No. 2 went into sea water at a temperature of 34°, and air 29°, so that the heavy westerly gale was near the line where the warm and cold waters meet.

No. 2 seems to have got the gale as strong as No. 6, and stronger than Nos. 19 and 35; this looks as if the western part of the area of low pressure passed well to the westward of the last two ships, having a very northerly course, so that No. 6 coming to the westward in a much higher latitude came in for its full force.

	Wind.					Air.	Bar.	Sea.	No. 9.
8 a.m.	S.E., 8.	Heavy rain; high sea.			-	37°	—	35°	S.S. "Colorado."
2.40 p.m.	S.E., 9.	Overcast; rain; high south-easterly sea.	48° 16′ N., 40° 26′ W.	-	-	38	—	36	In { 48° 1′ N. 41° 22′ W. 8 a.m. G.T. 8th. Bound E. by Nly.
6.40 p.m.		Light variable airs; high sea. 48° 26′ N., 39° 40′ W.		-	-	38	—	36	To { 49° 10′ N. 36° 32′ W. 8 a.m. G.T. 9th.
2.40 a.m., 9th.		Calm; heavy rain. 48° 48′ N., 38° 7′ W.		-	-	40	—	38	
8 a.m.		W., 3. 40° 10′ N., 36° 32′ W.		-	-	—	—	—	

10.40 a.m., 9th.	W., 6.	40° 17′ N. 36° 0′ W.	-	50	—	46

The strong westerly breeze with fine weather continued until about 5 p.m. of the 9th, in 40° 41′ N., 34° 16′ W., when the wind backed to the south-eastward, blowing a strong breeze, and the weather still continued fine. Here the extract ceases. It is worthy of notice that at this very time (5 p.m.) No. 6 was about 130 miles to the N.W. of No. 9, and was experiencing a heavy N. by W. gale, with squalls of hurricane force.

This sudden subsiding of the S.E. gale, and continuance of light airs and calms for several hours looks as if the worst of the gale had gone to the northward, whilst No. 9 was going to the eastward, so that she only got a strong westerly breeze, the result of a low pressure far to the north of her, which agrees with the last remark on No. 2.

	Wind.					Air.	Bar.	Sea.	No. 42.
8 a.m.	West, 7.		-	-	-	71°	29·72	66°	Ship "Swea." In { 34° 53′ N. 44° 10′ W. 8 a.m. G.T. 8th.
2.50 p.m.	W.N.W., 8.	Misty. 35° 34′ N., 43° 30′ W.	-	-	-	67	29·73	65	Bound E.N.Ely.
6.50 p.m.	W.N.W., 10.	Heavy increasing sea. 35° 40′ N., 42° 51′ W.	-	-	-	67	29·78	64	To { 35° 55′ N. 40 39′ W. 8 a.m. G.T. 9th.

	Wind.		Air.	Bar.	Sea.
6.50 a.m., 9th.	N.W., 9 to 8. Wind decreasing.				
35° 53′ N., 40° 51′ W.	-	-	64°	29·93	63°

It will be noticed that this ship is far to the southward.

About midnight of the 9th the wind was light, N.N.W. Barometer at its highest, 30·03. From this time the wind backed to the westward, and freshened a little with a slightly falling barometer.

No. 42 seems to have sailed to the N.E. in company with an area of low pressure to the northward of her, which eventually passed her. She got the wind S. by E., 10, at 2 a.m., 13th in 40° 57′ N., 31° 56′ W., and it continued so until 10 p.m., when it veered to S.E., and remained easterly until the 15th, when the extract ends.

No. 17.
S.S. "Helvetia."
In { 45° 7′ N.
47° 53′ W.
8 a.m. G.T. 8th.
Bound W. by Sly.
To { 44° 28′ N.
51° 56′ W.
8 a.m. G.T. 9th.

	Wind.		Air.	Bar.	Sea.
8 a.m.	S.W. by W., 7. High N.E. swell.		45°	28·99	44°
10.14 a.m.	N. by W., 8 to 9. Confused sea.				
45° 2′ N., 48° 28′ W.	-	-	—	—	—
3.15 p.m.	N.W. by N., 7 to 8. Heavy sea.				
44° 58′ N., 48° 57′ W.	-	-	35	29·45	40
3.15 a.m., 9th. N.W. by N., 5. Fine. 44° 42′ N.,					
50° 37′ W.	-	-	—	29·99	—
7.15 a.m.	N.W. by N., 3. Overcast. 44° 36′ N.,				
51° 46′ W.	-	-	33	30·03	37

9.15 a.m., 9th. N.E. by Ely., 3. Misty. 44° 29′ N.,					
51° 57′ W.	-	-	—	—	—
0.15 p.m.	E. by S., ? 44° 22′ N., 52° 37′ W.		—	—	—
3.33 p.m.	E. by S., 7. Overcast; hail.				
44° 15′ N., 53° 17′ W.	-	-	—	—	—
6.33 p.m.	South-easterly, 9. 44° 5′ N., 53° 48′ W		—	—	—
7.33 p.m.	S.W. by W., ? 44° 2′ N., 53° 58′ W.		44	29·13	40

After 7.33 p.m. of the 9th the wind drew more northerly, and decreased with a rising barometer.

It will be remembered that at *5 a.m.* of the 8th, No. 17 had a shift of wind from E. by S. to S.W. by W. Here, again, at 7.33 p.m. of the 9th, she has a similar change. By referring to Diagram 3 it will be seen that No. 35 had similar changes on the 10th and 11th. It seems probable that these were the same depressions which had travelled to the eastward between the times of passing No. 17 and reaching No. 35.

143

	Wind.				No. 10.
8 a.m.	W.N.W., 8.	Rising sea.			S.S. "Manhattan."
3.25 p.m.	W.N.W., 9.	Confused sea.	42° 30′ N., 51° 8′ W.	In	⎧ 42° 45′ N. ⎨ 50° 19′ W. ⎩ 8 a.m. G.T. 8th.
11.25 p.m.	Light and variable.		42° 25′ N., 52° 54′ W.		Bound Westerly.
4. 25 a.m., 9th.	S. by E.		42° 19′ N., 54° 0′ W.	To	⎧ 42° 15′ N. ⎨ 54° 44′ W. ⎩ 8 a.m. G.T. 9th.

11.25 a.m., 9th. S. by E., 7. High sea.   42° 9′ N., 55° 33′ W.
3.46 p.m.   S.W., 7.   Rising sea. 42° 4′ N., 56° 26′ W.

It will be remembered that about midnight of the 7th, No. 10 had a change of wind from S. to S.W. and W. Here, on the 9th, we have her passing through a similar change. We have already remarked that Diagram 3 shows No. 35 to have had similar, perhaps the same, changes on the 10th and 11th.

	Wind.				Air.	Bar.	Sea.	No. 11.
8 a.m.	N.W. by N., 9.	Squally; rain.			33°	—	39°	S.S. "Iowa."
3.30 p.m.	N.W., 7.	43° 45′ N., 52° 40′ W.			29	—	33	In ⎧ 44° 1′ N. ⎨ 51° 34′ W. ⎩ 8 a.m. G.T. 8th.
7.30 p.m.	N.W. by W., 6.	Sea falling.						Bound W. by Sly.
43° 38′ N., 53° 23′ W.	-	-	-	-	29	—	32	To ⎧ 43° 18′ N. ⎨ 55° 37′ W. ⎩ 8 a.m. G.T. 9th.
3.30 a.m., 9th.	Light baffling.	43° 25′ N.,						
54° 50′ W. -	-	-	-	-	32	—	40	
7.30 a.m.	E. by S., ? 5.	43° 18′ N., 55° 33′ W.			35	—	42	

11.30 a.m., 9th. E. by S., 7 to 8. Misty; raining.
43° 11′ N., 56° 17′ W.   -   -   -   -   42°   —   46°
3.48 p.m.   S. by E., 6 to 7. Heavy beam sea.
43° 4′ N., 57° 0′ W.   -   -   -   -   57   —   57

About 9 p.m. the wind shifted to S.W. by W.

About midnight it shifted to W. by S. Strong breeze, and weather clearing.

It will be noticed that No. 11 had similar changes to those of No. 10, but they seemed to come rather later. Now, No. 11 was the more northern ship of the two, which indicates that the weather changes had northing in their route, though it is pretty certain that they went to the eastward also.

			Air.	Bar.	Sea.
No. 39.	8 a.m.	Wind. N.W., 10. - - -	32°	29·07	33°
S.S. "Westphalia."	3.40 p.m.	N.W., 9 to 8. 42° 53' N., 54° 58' W.	33	29·94	38
In { 43° 30' N. 53° 0' W. 8 a.m. G.T. 8th.	7.40 p.m.	N.W., 5. 42° 40' N., 56° 8' W. -	36	30·13	50
Bound W. by Sly.	11.40 p.m.	Calm. 42° 27' N., 57° 18' W. -	38	30·07	54
To { 42° 0' N. 59° 37' W. 8 a.m. G.T. 9th.	3.40 a.m., 9th.	S.E., 5. 42° 13' N., 58° 27' W. -	44	29·84	54
	7.40 a.m.	S.S.E., 10 to 11. 42° 0' N.,			
	59° 37' W. -	- - - -	56	29·15	66
	Noon, 9th.	S. to N.W., 10 to 4. 41° 47' N.,			
	60° 47' W. -	- - - -	58°	29·18	64°
	4 p.m.	W.S.W., 7. 41° 33' N., 61° 56' W.	55	29·05	57

After 4 p.m., 9th, the wind was W. by S. to W., increasing to force 10, with a slowly rising barometer.

This is well shown in Diagram 4.

It will be noticed that this ship records a change in the temperature of the sea of 33° in 24 hours.

At 6 a.m. of the 8th, ship's time (or about 9.30 a.m., Greenwich time), Nos. 39 and 36 were in longitude 53° 17' W., being N. and S. of each other about 100 miles apart (see Diagrams 4 and 5), No. 39 being the more northern ship. Their records are as follows :—

	Wind.	Air.	Bar.	Sea.
No. 39. N.W., 10. Snow and rain. 43° 20' N., 53° 17' W. - - - - -		31°	29·75	35°
No. 36. N.W., 7. Blue sky and cloud. 41° 40' N., 53° 17' W. - - - - -		38	29·75	54

Here there was a difference of 19° in the temperature of the sea, the warmer water having less wind and finer weather. In 18 hours No. 39 bound W. went into a very heavy south-easterly gale, whilst No. 36 bound E. kept a steady N.W. wind and fine weather for 30 hours. (See remark to No. 38, p. 153, for an estimate of the speed with which this south-easterly gale moved to the north-eastward.)

			Air.	Bar.	Sea.
No. 4.	8 a.m.	Wind. N.N.W., 7. Overcast. -	29°	29·76	37°
S.S. "Prussian."	10.16 a.m.	N.W., 6. 44° 45' N., 54° 5' W.	—	—	—
In { 44° 55' N. 53° 23' W. 8 a.m. G.T. 8th.	3.42 p.m.	N.W., 6. Cloudy, but clear.			
Bound W. by Sly.		44° 25' N., 55° 27' W. - - -	35	30·02	37
To { 43° 35' N. 59° 27' W. 8 a.m. G.T. 9th.	7.42 p.m.	N.W., 5. Ditto. 44° 13' N.,			
	56° 27' W. -	- - - -	32	30·15	40

	Wind.			Air.	Bar.	Sea.
11.42 p.m.	W.S.W., 4.	44° 0' N., 57° 27' W.		34°	—	39°
3.42 a.m., 9th.	S.S.E., 3.	Rain and mist. 43° 48'N.,				
58° 27' W.	-	- - - -	-	34	30·03	—
5.42 a.m.	E.S.E., 6;	43° 42' N., 58° 57' W.		—	—	—
8 a.m.	E.S.E., 7.	Heavy rain; 43° 35' N.,				
59° 27' W.	-	- - - -	-	40	29·51	43

From this time the wind gradually changed to S.W., and W., falling lighter until p.m. of the 9th, when the barometer was 29·22, and the wind freshened to 7 from W.S.W. It then veered more northerly with a rising barometer.

No. 4 was about 90 miles north of No. 39, and seems to have had lighter winds and better weather. They seem to have got the S.Ely. wind simultaneously in about the same longitude.

	Wind.			Standard Instruments.				No. 36.
				Air.	Bar.	Sea.		S.S. "Palmyra."
8 a.m.	N.N.W., 7 to 8.	Fine.	N.W.					⎧ 41° 41' N.
and N.N.E. sea.	-	- - -	-	38°	29·76	53°	In ⎨ 53° 34' W.
3.28 p.m.	N.W. by N, 7.	Ditto, ditto.						⎩ 8 a.m. G.T. 8th.
42° 4' N., 51° 56' W.	Sp. gr. 1·0255.	-	-	34	29·82	51		Bound E. by Nly.
11.28 p.m.	N.N.W., 6.	Ditto,	ditto.					⎧ 43° 9' N.
42° 35' N., 50° 12' W.	-	-	-	30	29·92	34	To ⎨ 48° 44' W.
3.28 a.m., 9th.	N.N.W., 5.	Ditto,	ditto.					⎩ 8 a.m. G.T. 9th.
42° 50' N., 40° 20' W.	-	-	-	31	29·96	38		
7.28 a.m.	N.N.W., 5.	North sea; clouds						
from N.N.E.	43° 6' N., 48° 50' W.	-	-	32	29·98	42		

3.11 p.m., 9th.	W. by N., 2.	43° 37' N.,			
47° 50' W. -	- - - -	-	39	29·98	44

From this time the wind gradually backed, and the barometer fell until

10.51 a.m., 10th.	S., 7. Heavy rain. 45° 45' N.,			
42° 45' W. -	- - - - -	55	29·26	55

When the wind veered to W. with a rising barometer.

At 2.23 p.m., G.T., of the 11th, in 48° N. and 35° 48' W., the wind had backed to S.S.E, 4, and continued easterly until she arrived in England on the 17th.

See the remarks to No. 39, p. 144, for a comparison with No. 36, and Diagram 5, which contains the meteorological data recorded by No. 36.

No. 16.
S.S. "City of London."
In { 42° 7′ N.
    59° 31′ W.
    8 a.m. G.T. 8th.
Bound E.N.Ely.
To { 44° 17′ N.
    53° 58′ W.
    8 a.m. G.T. 9th.

Time	Wind	Air.	Bar.	Sea
8 a.m.	N.N.W., 5. High easterly sea and cloudy.	39° ?	30·09	59°
3.50 p.m.	N.N.W., 3. Easterly sea and cloudy. 42° 36′ N., 57° 34′ W.	34 ?	30·13	50
7.50 p.m.	N.N.E., 4. Ditto, ditto. 42° 58′ N., 56° 42′ W.	34 ?	30·19	48
3.50 a.m., 9th.	E.N.E., 4. Ditto, ditto. 43° 42′ N., 54° 57′ W.	34 ?	30·10	40

9.50 a.m., 9th.	E.S.E, 3. 44° 15′ N., 53° 38′ W.	34 ?	29·97	34

From this time the wind freshened, with snow squalls, until

| 1.50 p.m., 9th. | S.E., 8. Heavy squalls and showers; 45° 30′ N., 50° 22′ W. | 37 ? | 29·10 | 35 |

From this time instrumental readings were not given for twelve hours, but the wind drew to S.S.E. and S.W., decreasing in force, with a rising barometer after 3 p.m. of the 10th.

No. 40.
S.S. "Deutschland."
In { 42° 19′ N.
    60° 32′ W.
    8 a.m. G.T. 8th.
Bound E.N.Ely.
To { 44° 4′ N.
    54° 35′ W.
    8 a.m. G.T. 9th.

Time	Wind	Air.	Bar.	Sea.
8 a.m.	N., 6 to 5. Cloudy; sea decreasing.	31°	30·16	50°
3.54 p.m.	N., 5. Cloudy; sea rather high. 42° 53′ N., 58° 35′ W.	30	30·19	42
11.54 p.m.	E., 4. Cloudy. 43° 28′ N., 56° 38′ W.	31	30·13	41
3.54 a.m., 9th.	N.N.E., 5. Cloudy. 43° 45′ N., 55° 39′ W.	32	30·06	39

11.54 a.m., 9th.	E.S.E., 6. Overcast; thick snow. 44° 20′ N., 53° 42′ W.	30	29·89	37
7.27 p.m.	S.E., 9. First, snow, then hail and rain. 44° 54′ N., 51° 50′ W.	32	29·36	36
11.27 p.m.	S.E., 9. 45° 9′ N., 50° 55′ W.	36·5	29·13	36·5

From this time the wind veered to S. and W., decreasing with a rising barometer, which soon began to fall.

| | Wind. | | | Air. | Bar. | Sea. |

2.42 p.m., 11th.   S., 7.   48° 7′ N., 40° 27′ W. -   54°·5 29·43 54°·5
In four hours the southerly wind freshened to force 8, and then decreased with a rising barometer.
2.14 p.m., 12th.   S.S.E., 9 to 10.   49° 14′ N.,
33° 31′ W. -   -   -   -   -   -   53   29·76   53

The wind continued S.S.E., 10 to 9, for 20 hours, barometer rising fast; on the 13th she had a fresh easterly wind, which lasted until her arrival in England on the 17th, the barometer being very steady about 30·07, though on the 13th it had been up to 30·34, and gradually fell.

By referring to Diagram 5 it will be seen that No. 36, the "Palmyra," experienced a similarly rising barometer about the same time and place, with a fresh S.E. wind, which settled into a steady N.E. to E. breeze, and the barometer on the 13th was up to 30·38, gradually falling with a strong N.E. wind.

Between the 13th and 17th the "Palmyra" continued in about 51° 20′ N., whilst No. 40 was in about 50° N. As would be expected in an easterly wind, the most northern ship had the higher barometer: the more southern ship had, however, the hardest gale from S.E., at the setting in of the easterly wind.

This S.E. wind to the *westward* of an area of *high* pressure, which seemed to work itself to the south-westward over the Atlantic, differed materially in weather and the following wind changes, from the S.E. wind to the *north-eastward* of an area of *low* pressure advancing from the south-westward.

We say the easterly wind seemed to be working to the westward, because the following extracts from logs appear to prove that this was the case :

		Highest Bar.	Wind.
No. 36 "Palmyra,"* 13th, 3.27 p.m., G.T. 51° 20′ N., 24° 0′ W. - - -		30·38	East 4
No. 40 "Deutschland," 13th, 9.46 p.m., G.T. 50° 10′ N., 26° 28′ W. - - - -		30·34	East 5
No. 15 "Moravian," 14th, 2 a.m., G.T. 52° 19′ N., 29° 30′ W. - - - -		30·42	E. by N. 4
No. 18 "Virginian," 14th, 2.14 p.m., G.T. 49° 11′ N., 33° 26′ W. - - -		?30·21	E. by S. 5

* See also Diagram 5, which gives a continuous record of the Meteorological data on board the S.S. "Palmyra."

With all ships the wind drew N. of E. as the barometer commenced falling! It will be seen that No. 18 was 9° 26′ to the Wd. of No. 36 when she got the crest of the wave of highest pressure, and it passed over her 23 hours after it had passed over No. 36; thus seeming to prove that the E. wind was working its way to the south-westward, whereas the ordinary changes travel to the north-eastward. This gives the easterly wind a progress to the westward of about 16 miles an hour.

See also the remarks on No. 45 (p. 134), which ship got the easterly wind on the 10th at noon in 50° 0′ N., and 3° 47′ W.

		Wind.		Air.	Bar.	Sea.
No. 15. S.S. "Moravian." In { 43° 2′ N. 60° 51′ W. 8 a.m. G.T. 8th. Bound Easterly. To { 43° 10′ N. 55° 29′ W. 8 a.m. G T. 9th.	8. a.m.	N., 4.	Heavy easterly swell.	26°	30·16	30°
	4 p.m.	N., 4.	Ditto. In 43° 7′ N., 58° 59′ W. - - - - -	29	30·18	30
	8 p.m.		N.E. by E., 2. Cloudy, but clear. In 43° 8′ N., 58° 6′ W. -	31	30·16	40
	4 a.m., 9th.	E. by S., 4.	Gloomy; ugly. At 3.15 a.m. wind suddenly freshened, and increased gradually till 3.35 p.m. In 43° 9′ N., 56° 23′ W. -	34	30·01	48
	8 a.m.		E.S.E., 6. In 43°10′ N., 55° 28′ W.	36	29·97	43

3.35 p.m., 9th.	S.E. by S., 9.	Ugly, with drizzle. 43° 11′ N., 53° 48′ W. - - -		39	29·52	43
7.35 p.m.	S.S.E., 9.	Misty drizzle. 43° 18′ N., 52° 59′ W. - - - - -		40	29·35	36
11.35 p.m.	S.S.W., 3.	Fog; rain; wind veering and backing. 43° 25′ N., 52° 10′ W. -		42	29·17	34

From this time the wind was light, veering to S.W. at 7 p.m. of the 10th, with a rising barometer, then backing to S.S.E., and again veering at—

3 p.m., 11th, to S.S.W., 7. Ugly; rainy weather. 45° 53′ N., 43° 23′ W. - - - - 56 29·41 56

It then lulled and gradually veered to N., but again backed, and was by—

2.30 p.m., 12th, S.S.E., 5. Fine, but misty. 48° 24′ N., 36° 55′ W. - - - 58 29·52 56

From this time the wind continued steady in direction, but freshened whilst the barometer rose, until it was at—

2.20 a.m. 13th. S.S.E., 9. Gloomy; squally and rain. 50° 2′ N., 34° 43′ W. - - - - 54 29·69 52

149

Afterwards the wind was steady, but decreased with a rising barometer, and was at—

	Wind.		Air.	Bar.	Sea.
2 p.m. 13th.	S.S.E., 6.	Cloudy, but clear.			
51° 40′ N., 32° 30′ W.	-	-	51°	30·10	52°

The wind then gradually backed to the eastward with a fast rising barometer. At 8 p.m. there were ponderous cum. in the E.S.E. when the wind was E.S.E., 4. She then came to her highest barometer.

	Wind.		Air.	Bar.	Sea.
2 a.m., 14th.	E. by N. 4.	Squally; showery.			
52° 19′ N., 29° 30′ W.	-	-	50°	30·42	52°

The barometer continued steady for 4 hours, and the wind went to E.N.E., 4, where it continued with a slowly falling barometer.

From this time until the ship's arrival at Tory Island on the 17th, the wind continued easterly, and was at—

	Wind.		Air.	Bar.	Sea.
0.40 p.m. 17th.	E., 3.	Cloudy, but clear.			
55° 16′ N., 10° 15′ W.	-	-	47°	30·28	48°

We have given the particulars carefully up to her arrival, because they record the way in which this ship came upon, as it were, a bank of high pressure, accompanying an easterly wind. The strong southerly gale which she and others experienced as they steamed up the western edge of this bank, and the slight depression common to them all after they had crossed the ridge of high pressure on its western edge, seem worthy of remark. See Diagram 5 for a section of this ridge in the case of No. 36 (the "Palmyra") on the 13th February, and the remarks on No. 40 (p. 147), where No. 15 is alluded to.

	Wind.		Air.	Bar.	Sea.	
8 a.m.	N.E. by N., 5.	Cloudy; easterly swell. 40° 47′ N., 62° 47′ W.	42° ?30·34	65°		No. 18. S.S. "Virginia." In { 40° 47′ N. / 62° 47′ W. / 8 a.m. G.T. 8th.
4 p.m.	E. by N., 4.	Variable breeze. 41° 6′ N., 61° 13′ W.	42 ?30·46	55		Bound E.N.Ely.
3 a.m., 9th.	S.E. by E.	Increasing breeze and puffy.	—	—	—	To { 42° 24′ N. / 58° 54′ W. / 8 a.m. G.T. 9th.
4 a.m.	S.E. by E., 8 to 9.	Rain. 42° 5′ N., 59° 29′ W.	52 ?29·67	62		

No. 18.
S.S. "Virginia"
—continued.

	Wind.	Air.	Bar.	Air.
Noon, 9th.	E.S.E., 7 to 8., moderating. Heavy rain; very heavy southerly sea.	52°?	29·19	48°
0.53 p.m.	S.S.E., 7	—	—	—
3.53 p.m. and rain. 43° 3′ N., 57° 44′ W.	S.S.W. 7. Very heavy cross sea	52?	29·21	47

After this the wind backed to S.E., with a falling barometer; then it veered again, and was at 11.53 p.m., 9th, S.S.W., 5 to 6. Cloudy. - - - 52? 29·01 48

From this time the wind varied from a moderate to fresh south-westerly breeze, with a rising barometer for 24 hours; it was then variable and light.

	Wind.			
3.14 p.m., 11th. 40° 2′ N., 48° 37′ W.	W. by N., 5 to 6. Cloudy.	40°?	29·36	36°
2.53 p.m., 12th. 47° 14′ N., 43° 21′ W.	N.W. by W., 8. Cloudy.	39?	29·30	44

This freshened into a strong gale at 10.40 p.m.

2.30 p.m., 13th. N. by Easterly, 5 to 6. Rain.
48° 1′ N., 30° 44′ W. - - - - 54? 29·85 58

From this time the wind was E. by S., with the barometer rising rather fast: this was the slope on the western edge of the high pressure working to the westward. See Diagram 5 for the barometer on board No. 36 on the 12th and 13th. No. 18 records her highest pressure at 2.14 p.m. next day as follows :

	Wind.	Air.	Bar.	Sea.
2.14 p.m., 14th.* 49° 11′ N., 33° 26′ W.	E. by S. and variable, 5.	55°?	30·21	53°

From this time the wind backed to E.N.E., fresh breeze, with a falling barometer, until it got to 29·80, when it gradually rose to about 29·90, where it remained steady until she drew near the land, the wind falling lighter. As she approached the land the barometer rose, and when she made the land, the state of things was as follows :

	Wind.	Air.	Bar.	Sea.
0.33 p.m., 20th. 8° 20′ W.	N.E., 3. Fine. 51° 50′ N.,	48°?	30·17	50°

After this the wind shifted to a moderate breeze from the North-westward, and fine weather.

---

* This observation is quoted on p. 147.

151

Since sending the Charts to press, the following Bermuda observations have been received from General Lefroy :

2.18 p.m., G.T., 8th, Bar. 30·111; wind "generally" S., 6.   Stormy night.
Ditto, ditto, 9th   „   29·651 ;   „   „   S.W.–N.W., 8.   Stormy day.
Ditto, ditto, 10th „   29·761 ;   „   „   W., 8.   Stormy weather and hard squalls.
Ditto, ditto, 11th „   29·961 ;   „   „   N.W., 8.
Ditto, ditto, 12th „   30·201 ;   „   „   S.S.W., 4.

If the reader will pencil S. 6. on the Chart of the 8th for the Bermuda wind, he will see how, in accordance with Buys Ballot's law, it indicates that there was an area of low pressure to the westward of that island, whilst the following wind-changes show that the lowest pressure in the area passed between Bermuda and the main land. On page 152 it will be seen how it eventually passed over No. 38 and the ships to the north-eastward of her. The long continuance of westerly gales at Bermuda, whilst an E. wind was working to the south-westward from our coasts, looks as if they may have had a similar cause.

	Wind.	Standard Instruments. Air.	Bar.
a.m.	Light easterly and north-easterly airs; appearance of snow.	—	—
10.40 a.m., 8th	-	20°	30·13
11.40 p.m.	North-easterly, 8. Thick snow.	—	—
4.40 a.m., 9th	North-easterly, 9. Thick falls of snow.	—	29·25
6.40 a.m.	N.E. by N., 9. Violent squalls and heavy falls of snow.	—	29·03
0.40 p.m., 9th.	N. by E., 6. Fine.	28	29·10

No. 37.
S.S. "Austrian."
In { Portland.
43° 39′ N.
70° 15′ W.
Moored at a Wharf.

From this time the wind backed to N.W. and W., with fine weather and a rising barometer.

On the 12th a.m. S.W., light. Cloudy, with rain, barometer falling; it then veered to N.W., a moderate breeze; and fine weather.

On the 13th, wind N.W. by W., moderate and fine. Started from Portland.

	Wind.	Air.	Bar.	Sea.
6.51 p.m., 17th.	S.S.E., 5. 46°41′ N., 42° 43′ W.	52°	29·75	55°

The above wind gradually freshened and drew more easterly, with a rising barometer after 6.40 a.m. of the 18th.

	Wind.				Air.	Bar.	Sea.
10.40 a.m., 18th.	E. by N., 8	-	-	-	51°	29·62	55°

From this time the wind continued easterly with a rising barometer until—

	Wind.				Air.	Bar.	Sea.
1.36 a.m., 21st. 24° 2′ W.	E.N.E., 3. Fine.	52° 55′ N., -	-	-	47°	30·40	51°
1.22 p.m., 21st. 53° 38′ N., 20° 38′ W.	N.W. by W., 3. Cloudy.	-	-	-	48	30·35	50

The wind continued light north-westerly, with a falling barometer, until the ship got to Liverpool, where she was—

	Wind.		Air.	Bar.	Sea.
Noon, 24th.	North-westerly. Fresh breeze and showery.	- - -	—	29·26	—

It will be seen that No. 36 got the S.S.E. wind, which drew more easterly, (and continued so until she arrived in England,) at 2.23 p.m. 11th, in 48° N., and 35° 48′ W., whilst No. 37 got it at 6.51 p.m. 17th, in 46° 41′ N., 42° 43′ W., showing that it had worked its way to the westward. A similar westerly movement in the south-south-easterly wind, changing to east, is shown by comparing No. 15 with the above, as she first had it at 2.30 p.m. 12th, in 48° 24′ N., 36° 55′ W.*

The N.E. gale and heavy snow experienced by No. 37 at Portland on the 9th seem to have been related to the area of low pressure which was just coming upon No. 38 at 8 a.m. of the 8th. See the Chart of that date, which gives the probable position of this area of low pressure. The difference in the wind-changes experienced by Nos. 37 and 38 indicates that the lowest part of this area of low pressure passed between them.

No. 38.
Ship "Nicoline."
In { 38° 23′ N.
    72° 22′ W.
    8 a.m. G.T. 8th.
Bound Westerly very slowly.
To { 38° 31′ N.
    72° 50′ W.
    8 a.m. G.T. 9th.

	Wind.		Air.	Bar.	Sea.
8 a.m.	E.S.E., 5.	Rapidly increasing wind. -	50°	29·85	53°
0.51 p.m.	E.S.E., 10.	Constant rain; terrific storm from E. to E.S.E. 38° 31′ N., 72° 53′ W. -	54	29·56	56
4.53 p.m.	South, 11.	Extremely heavy rain; hurricane squalls from S.E.; calm between them; high cross sea from N.E. to S.E. 38° 33′ N., 73° 18′ W. -	54	29·25	56

---

* These comparisons between the positions of the first of the easterly wind on the 11th or 12th and 17th only give it a progress of two miles an hour to the westward; whilst those on p. 147 give it 16 miles an hour between the 13th and 14th, indicating that its progress to the westward decreased in speed as it advanced.

	Wind.			Air.	Bar.	Sea.
6.53 p.m. Wind burst like a hurricane from S.W.; sea mountains high; lowest barometer (it fell an inch in 16 hours) -				—	29·15	—
8.53 p.m.	S.W., 11.	Rain.	38° 35′ N., 73° 11′ W. -	53°	29·15	55°
0.53 a.m., 9th.	W., 11.	Quite a hurricane. 38° 36′ N., 73° 3′ W.		50	29·17	55
4.53 a.m.	W., 11.	38° 33′ N., 72° 56′ W. -		—	29·26	—
8.53 a.m., 9th.	W.N.W., 11.	Hail and rain squalls. 38° 30′ N., 72° 49′ W.		48	29·28	54

From this time the wind continued N.W., 11, for four hours, when it gradually decreased, with a slowly rising barometer, until it was at—

	Wind.					
4.51 p.m., 11th.	N.W., 6.	38° 6′ N., 73° 14′ W. -		38	30·12	54

After this it backed to S.E., with a fast falling barometer.

It will be seen that about 5 p.m., when No. 38 logs the wind S., 11, No. 3 in New York (about 135 miles to the N. by W. ¼ W.,) has it N.E., 9, and by the self-recording anemometer at the observatory it is N.E. *31 miles an hour*. At the same time the barometer at New York was ·25 higher than it was with No. 38, and no doubt a lower pressure existed between these places. No. 38 got her lowest barometer at 6.53 p.m., whilst New York did not get it until 11.30 p.m. This looks as if the area of lowest pressure extended in a westerly or west-north-westerly direction, its south-eastern end passing No. 38 some time before its north-western end passed New York.

Here we have another of those areas of low pressure which are so common in this part of the sea. It will be seen that after 4.51 p.m. of the 11th, this ship was just entering another, for the wind had backed to S.E., and the barometer was falling fast, when the extract from the log closed.

It will be remembered that at 8 a.m. Greenwich time, of the 9th, in 42° 0′ N., 59° 37′ W., No. 39 was in a very heavy S.S.E. gale, whilst here we have No. 38 in a very heavy E.S.E. gale at 1 p.m. of the 8th, in 38° 31′ N., 72° 53′ W.

Now, by examining this day's Chart it will be seen that there was a considerable number of ships between Nos. 39 and 38, at 8 a.m., and that No. 38 was the only vessel with a south-easterly wind, hence it seems probable that this wind advanced to the north-eastward about 630 miles in 19 hours, or at the rate of about 33 miles an hour, the most westerly ships getting it first in all cases.

It will be remembered that a similar speed was made out for the area of extremely low pressure in the middle of the Atlantic on the 5th inst., as well as for that experienced by the "Austrian" (No. 37), and several other ships on the 30th of January.

No. 3.
S.S. "Etna."
In { New York
40° 43′ N.
74° 1′ W.
8 a.m. G.T. 8th.

	Wind.				Bar.
8 a.m.	N., 4.	Passing snow showers.	In New York.		? 30 · 14
10.56 a.m.	N.N.E.	Heavy snow.	Ditto	-	? 30 · 00
1.56 p.m.	N.E.	Ditto,	Ditto	-	? 29 · 73
4.56 p.m.	N.E., 9.	Heavy snow and sleet.		-	? 29 · 65
6.56 p.m.	N.E., 8 to 9.	Heavy snow.		-	? 29 · 55
8.40 p.m. at Castle Garden.		-	-	-	—
10.56 p.m.	No entry.	Ditto	-	-	? 29 · 20
2 a.m., 9th.	Wind backed to N.N.W.	Weather cleared.	-		—

From this time she experienced a fresh north-westerly wind with slowly rising barometer, until 4.15 p.m. of the 11th, when she was,

	Air.	Bar.	Sea.
In 44° 12′ N., 63° 53′ W. Where the extract ends.	30°	?29 · 70	36°

It seems clear that the lowest point of an area of low pressure passed between No. 38 and No. 3 in New York, which gave No. 38 a fearful gale from E.S.E., changing by S. to S.W. and N.W., whilst New York had a heavy N.E. gale, backing to N.W. It is worthy of notice that both ships had a N.W. wind after the gale.

It will be remembered that No. 37 in Portland got a N.E. gale at 11.40 p.m. of the 8th, whilst No. 3 in New York had it at 4.56 p.m.: the exact time of the commencement of the gale is not given in either log, but the difference between the hours given indicates the north-easterly route of the area of low pressure. These ports being about N.E. and S.W., 240 miles apart, we have a speed of about 34 miles an hour, agreeing remarkably with other estimates.

New York Observatory.
8 a.m. G.T 8th.
to 8 a.m. G.T. 9th.

8 a.m. Wind, E. by N. ½ N., *9 miles per hour.* Barometer 30·11; air 33°.

The decrease in pressure which commenced yesterday continued until 11.30 p.m., when the lowest reading (29·13) was recorded. From this time it rose, being 29·43 at 8 a.m., 9th.

There was but little variation in the temperature during the 24 hours, though it fell slightly as the barometer rose.

The north-easterly wind freshened to *26 miles per hour* by 1 p.m., and to *34 miles per hour* by 6 p.m., from which time it gradually diminished in force.

At 8 p.m. its direction was N.E. by E. It then gradually backed, and was W. by N., *19 miles per hour*, at 8 a.m., 9th.

A considerable amount of snow fell during the 24 hours.

These observations seem to agree very well with those of No. 3 (a ship in New York), with the one exception of wind force, the ship recording 9 of Beaufort's scale, *i.e.*, a close-reefed topsail breeze, whilst the observatory only got a speed of 34 miles an hour, which is supposed to equal 6 of Beaufort's scale, *i.e.*, a single-reefed topsail breeze. Hence it seems probable that the observatory is partially protected from the wind.

All records agree in showing that an area of low pressure swept quickly along the coast, its lowest point passing between No. 38 on one side, and New York and Portland on the other, showing that their north-easterly snow storms were related to her south and south-westerly gale.

General Remarks on the Chart for 8 a.m., Greenwich Time, February 8th, 1870.

The logs of 31 ships have been consulted, and the same system followed, excepting that the extracts in many cases extend over several days, as already remarked.

The southerly wind still prevails in Western Europe, though in the South of Ireland the direction is northerly.

A S.E. gale prevails in Norway, and at our most northern stations, whilst the wind is southerly in Iceland, where the barometer has risen nearly an inch.

The p.m. observations at Belleisle and in Newfoundland show light variable airs.

At the Azores at 11 a.m. the wind was fresh south-westerly, whilst at Madeira it was calm.

On this Chart we have signs of three distinct systems of wind related to separate areas of low pressure.

Two have their south-easterly and north-westerly winds represented at 8 a.m., whilst the most western one, causing a S. wind at Bermuda, and a S.E. wind with No. 38, is proved by the extracts to have crossed over her and several other ships to the north-eastward of her, in the course of a few hours.

The various extracts show that an easterly wind appeared in the English Channel on the 9th, and gradually worked its way to the south-westward, being met with, later and later, by those ships which were the furthest west.

The Charts show that the barometer had been rising in Norway for some days; hence, the cause of the easterly wind which followed seems to have been this accumulation of air to the N. It will be seen that the Chart for the 8th does not indicate an easterly wind coming in from the westward.

It seems probable that the large amount of air which had risen over the lower pressure in the centre of the Atlantic, during the long prevalence of southerly wind, had settled down over the cooler land, and formed the reservoir for the coming E. wind. The way in which the isobars curve round the high pressure in Norway seems to indicate that this mass of air was forcing its way to the south-westward. We have elsewhere stated that the barometer at St. Petersburg was up to 30·99! on the 5th.

It seems most probable that the system of low pressure which existed to the southward of Halifax on the 7th, has now advanced to the S.E. of Newfoundland.

The variations in the force of the wind indicate that more barometric observations would materially modify the distribution of the isobaric curves, for there is little doubt but that they were actually much closer where the wind is very strong, and further apart where it is relatively light.

The strong N.E. gale experienced by No. 3 at 4.56 p.m. of the 8th in New York, with heavy snow, whilst No. 38, only 135 miles to the S. by W. of that port, was experiencing a hurricane from S., seems to prove their close connection with the same area of low pressure. The speed with which this gale came upon ships to the north-eastward of No. 38, and the fact that New York, Portland, and No. 38 got a north-westerly wind after the gale had passed, are interesting to seamen in forming a judgment of what is coming. (See the remarks accompanying extracts from Nos. 3, 37, and 38, pages 151 to 154.)

Then, again, the fact that after 4.51 p.m. of the 11th No. 38 got the S.E. wind of another area of low pressure to the south-westward of her, proves how constant they are at this season, and with what caution the first indications of a south-easterly wind should be dealt with in these parts.

On the Charts for these 11 days we have signs of seven areas of low pressure having formed to the westward and passed rapidly to the north-eastward.

By referring to Plate VIII. in the Quarterly Weather Report for the data on the 8th and following days at the various observatories, it will be seen that the southerly wind which appears on this day's Chart in longitude 30° to 35° W. does not seem to have worked its way to any of the observatories, but that they all had a steadily rising barometer with the wind eventually going to E.

Conclusions derived from the Study of the Fourteen Charts for the Eleven Days from January 29th to February 8th, 1870, inclusive.

It has already been said, that it is believed the reader will learn most about the Atlantic weather at this time by carefully reading the extracts and remarks for each day, consulting the Charts as he goes on, for it has been thought better to call attention to facts at the time than merely to generalize on the whole. To make this more easy, the Charts and letter-press have been bound separately.

It seems right, however, to say a few words on the various conclusions suggested by a careful study of these data.

1st. As to the origin of the numerous gales experienced during the 11 days with which we have been dealing. *Origin of gales.*

By referring to the Charts it will be seen that almost invariably there was a northerly wind on the American coast, and a southerly wind at some distance to the eastward of that coast. This state of the wind, considered in connection with Buys Ballot's law, requires that there should be a trough of low pressure between two high pressures. Buchan's* monthly Charts of isobars, giving the mean pressure over the globe, show that the above is the case in the months of January and February. The January Chart shows the isobar of 30·2 over the American land, and again over the sea just to the northward of the N.E. trades, and we know that between these high pressures the hot Gulf Stream flows, which may well be supposed to cause an unusually low pressure, for,

---

* The Mean Pressure of the Atmosphere and the Prevailing Winds over the Globe for the Months and for the Year. By A. Buchan, M.A., F.R.S.E. Transactions of the Royal Society, Edinburgh, vol. xxv., printed in 1869.

other circumstances being the same, it is found that the barometer is lower over warm than over cold water. For instance, the meteorological data of the 10° square between the equator and 10° N., and from 20° to 30° W., which is now being discussed by this office, show that the lowest pressure exists over the hottest water. The conclusions derived from a study of the data for this region for January will be found in the Report of the Meteorological Committee of the Royal Society for 1871.

Bermuda seems to be peculiarly placed with regard to the winds of which we are speaking, for the observations given in the first number of the publications by this office, as well as those given by Buchan, together with others sent by General Lefroy, which are quoted in this paper, show that the island is subject to alternations of northerly and southerly winds in winter, whilst in summer scarcely any northerly wind is recorded.

The fact of this alternation between northerly and southerly winds in winter seems to show that the position of this area of low pressure may be variable, and that it may sometimes lie to the eastward, sometimes to the westward of the island.

When summer sets in, and an area of low pressure takes the place of the high pressure over the land, the element for a northerly wind is taken away, so that Bermuda and the American coast are subject to southerly winds.

It will be readily understood how this alternation of high and low barometer over the land in winter and summer accounts for the extremes of cold and heat experienced by the East coast of America, whilst we on the eastern side of the Atlantic are, in accordance with Buys Ballot's law, subject to southerly winds in winter, the highest barometer being then to the eastward of us.

To return to our subject: if the trough of low pressure cannot be shown to change its position, we have strong proof that frequent collisions take place between the northerly and southerly winds which blow in its neighbourhood, causing eddies similar to the one we have tried to illustrate on page 116, and that these eddies pass over Bermuda on a north-easterly route, producing first a south-easterly and then a north-westerly wind. We are thus led to the conclusion that these gales are caused by a collision between opposing currents of air.

The few storms dealt with in this paper support the idea that most of the winter snow storms of the coast of America are connected with these gales. (See the Chart of 8 a.m., 30th January, and Mr. Allison's remarks on p. 30; also p. 156 for remarks on the winds experienced by New York, Portland, and No. 38.) Besides the trough of low pressure over the Gulf Stream to which we have alluded, Buchan's Charts show a larger area of depression in the neighbourhood of Iceland at this season of the year, which is related to the prevailing winds of winter. It is probable that this low pressure is frequently intensified by the areas of low pressure which travel towards it from the East coast of America, and that these areas of low pressure, taken in conjunction with the very high pressures which generally exist over the land in winter, are the causes of our winter gales.

We will next consider the tracks of these gales. All the evidence gained by studying the data for these 11 days shows that they move to the north-eastward, and probably at a mean rate of nearly 30 miles an hour. *Tracks of gales.*

To give a graphic representation of their progress, the last Chart has been constructed; it contains reductions of the whole 14, placed under each other in the order of time. There it will be seen that the gale of the 30th of January was south of Halifax at 8 a.m., had advanced towards Newfoundland by 6 p.m., and was half across the Atlantic by 8 a.m. of the 31st, when it seemed to be lost in the normal area of low pressure over the centre of the Atlantic.

A similar gale appeared on the 2d February; it advanced to the north-eastward and was lost by the 4th. On the 4th a N.E. gale was blowing on the American coast, and a moderate S.E. wind in 32° N. and 51° W. Unfortunately there was a large space of sea in the south-western quarter of the Chart without ships, so that we have not such clear evidence of the progress of this gale; still on the 5th we find a very heavy gale and remarkably low pressure in the middle of the Atlantic, with a heavy N.E. gale blowing in Iceland and on the American coast, and an equally heavy S.W. gale in about 30° W. There are reductions of three Charts for the 5th, viz., at 8 a.m., 3 p.m., and 8 p.m. These show the north-easterly progress of the area of lowest pressure.

On the Charts of the 6th and 7th the direction of the wind indicates that another area of low pressure was advancing from the south-westward, which showed itself to the south-eastward of Newfoundland on the 8th. On this last Chart three areas of low pressure are shown, the last just appearing on the south-western corner of the Chart; this the extracts prove to have been very severe, and to have advanced to the north-eastward. It again was followed by another before our extracts end.

On page 116 we have given a figure, and said a few words to illustrate the idea, that the point of lowest pressure and complete eddy may be formed just where the counter currents of air are in close contact, and that its apparent motion may be caused by the closing in on each other of these currents of air, by which means the eddy is being constantly re-formed at the new point of contact. The Chart of 8 a.m., February 5th, is supposed to illustrate this idea.

If we consult Buchan's isobars of mean pressure for these months, we find that they trend to the north-eastward from the coast of America to England, and that the prevailing wind follows them, drawing rather towards the area of lowest pressure in the neighbourhood of Iceland. Hence, it seems fair to suppose that the tracks of these occasional eddies may be influenced by the main stream of air which seems to be flowing to the north-eastward round and into the area of lowest pressure, just as an eddy in a river is carried along by the main stream.

The data we have been dealing with proves that the points of *lowest* pressure in these areas of low pressure do not generally cross the British Islands; for instance, at 8 p.m., February 5th, the barometer was down to 27·38 in about 51° N. and 25° W., and at 8 a.m. of the 6th it was 28·22 in about 55° N. and 18° W., with a hurricane blowing from S.S.W. This direction of the wind indicates that there was a lower pressure to the westward, hence we may conclude that the area of *lowest* pressure took a very northerly course. Still, its influence was felt at all the self-registering observatories, taking Valencia first, and passing on to Aberdeen.

In the general remarks following the extracts for February 5th, we have pointed out how the gale which Valencia experienced later in the day is pictured on our 8 a.m. Chart. The reader will do well to study the remarks published in the Quarterly Weather Report for February 4th to the 7th, as well as its Plate VIII. There it is shown on p. 10 how at 8 a.m. of the 5th, "neither the daily Chart nor the barograms showed any very serious sign of disturbance." On p. 11 there is the following remark : " The facts appear to show that the gale which ensued on our " coast was to the full as much to be attributed to the advance of the " high pressure westwards from Russia, as to that of the low pressure " eastwards from the Atlantic." The isobars on our Charts for the 6th, 7th, and 8th seem to prove the force of this remark.

Whatever may be the cause of these areas of lowest pressure, the five diagrams which follow the Charts, as well as a large number of others received from the commanders of steamers to and from America, who are observing for this office, show that very many of them are experienced in the Atlantic, and the difference between the barometer curves of outward and homeward bound steamers, as well as the extracts from logs, show that they are travelling to the north-eastward. We have, then, two important facts : viz., 1st, by consulting Buchan's isobars, we find that during the winter months the normal state of pressure is high over the land on each side, and low over the sea in the 'central part of the Atlantic, also that the pressure gets lower as you go north from the Azores. Let the line A B C be supposed to represent a section of the normal state of pressure across the Atlantic, with a lower pressure to the N. than to the S. then the arrows may be supposed to represent the normal direction of the wind.

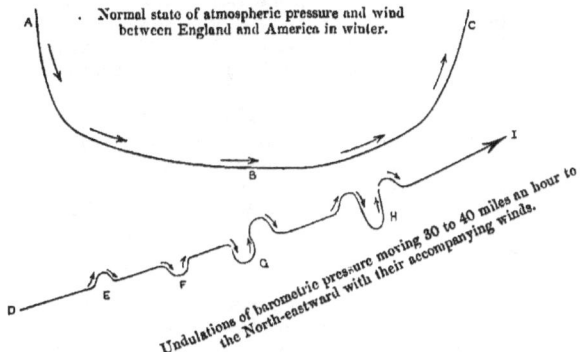

2ndly. Besides this normal state, we have, as it were, the crests and hollows of waves of pressure moving to the north-eastward. These (the diagrams show) sometimes follow each other very closely, and may be represented by the line D I. Keeping Buys Ballot's law in mind, let us suppose that a *ridge* of high pressure (E) be experienced travelling to the north-eastward, we know that it would be accompanied by corresponding winds, viz. northerly followed by southerly.

If merely a *depression* (F), then southerly winds would precede northerly.

If a *ridge and depression* (G), then northerly, southerly and northerly, would be the order of the winds.

If a *ridge and depression be followed by another ridge* (H), then northerly and southerly changes would be twice experienced.

Now it is hardly possible to look at the diagrams which accompany this paper without perceiving that they give sections of disturbances which could be explained by some one of the above cases. We may also suppose that after they have passed over a ship, the winds will be inclined to take up the normal direction as shewn on the line A B C.

If the reader can suppose such changes of pressure as are represented by the line D I to be travelling to the north-eastward over a sea which has its normal pressure represented by the line A B C, he will get the idea we wish to convey.

In the course of this paper it has been frequently remarked that with a steamer *bound to the eastward*, the barometer was falling with a northerly and rising with a southerly wind. Now it is quite clear that this would *always* be the case with a steamer steering to the eastward, if the atmospheric pressure over the Atlantic were always in the normal state represented by the line A B C, and this order of rise and fall would be reversed with a steamer bound to the westward.

Again, suppose it were possible that a steamer could go to the north-eastward faster than an atmospheric disturbance represented by the depression F, and so cut through it, then it is clear that she would have a falling barometer with a northerly, and a rising barometer with a southerly wind, but if these disturbances move at a speed of 30 miles an hour, it is clear that a steamer could not outstrip them, but only keep longer under their influence when steaming fast to the north-eastward, than when standing still, or going to the westward. Hence we may conclude that when the barometer falls with a northerly and rises with a southerly wind, as a ship steams to the eastward, she is experiencing, either the normal state of pressure, or a slowly moving disturbance.

We give only two instances of the barometer falling in a northerly wind, with a ship steaming to the westward, and they were both in the great gale of February 5th. They seem to indicate that the depression was increasing in intensity faster than the ships could move away from it. Such cases should be considered as important warnings.

What takes place when an easterly wind is working to the south-westward.

The various extracts which follow the 8th of February, when an easterly wind set in on the north-eastern part of the Chart, and worked its way to the south-westward, seem to show that such a state of things does not check the formation of cyclonic gales off the coast of America, for they were still experienced, and judging from the Bermuda* data the north-westerly winds were stronger. The routes which the gales took seemed, however, to be more northerly, as if the easterly wind interfered with their usual progress to the north-eastward.

Practical hints.

Considering the normal state of the wind, it seems clear that *in so far as the direction of the wind* is concerned, a sailing ship, bound from

* See p. 151 for the Bermuda observations from the 8th to the 12th and the remarks upon them.

England to America at this season of the year, should keep her yards well in, and gain good way, even though she may get driven to the northward by the south-westerly winds which prevail on the eastern side of the Atlantic, for there is good reason to expect that the wind will draw to the northward of W. as she gets over to the westward. The chances of meeting with ice, and other risks, would of course need careful consideration.

The very little progress made during the eleven days by No. 38, bound from Santos to New York, makes it probable that she would have gained by making her northing several degrees further to the eastward, where the Charts show that a southerly wind prevailed ; instead of closing with the land, where there was an almost constant fresh northerly wind.

This paper gives sufficient evidence of the caution needed when a S.E. wind sets in with a falling barometer. Captains used to the trade know these gales well. See Capt. Heim's remark, p. 129, ship No. 38.

It is not necessary to repeat here what has already been said in the Barometer Manual, published by this office, on the use of the barometer to seamen, and its various action depending on a ship's course and speed.

Mr. Meldrum, the meteorologist of the Mauritius, is pursuing a similar enquiry with regard to the weather in the Southern Indian Ocean. There he finds that waves of high and low pressure follow each other on an easterly course at an average speed of about 20 miles per hour. *Mr. Meldrum's researches in the same direction.*

It will be remembered that we find these waves to travel at the rate of 30 or 40 miles per hour. When we consider how the northern part of the North Atlantic is much more surrounded by land than the southern part of the Indian Ocean, causing more sudden differences of temperature, we may well suppose that the differences of pressure will be greater in the North Atlantic, giving more activity to the changes of weather.

Mr. Meldrum also finds that the hurricanes of the Southern Indian Ocean take their origin in the district lying between the N.W. monsoon and S.E. trade, where the barometer is generally lower than to the northward and southward, just as we have already stated that the winter gales off the coast of North America take their origin over a lower pressure between two areas of higher pressure.

The numerous reports of bad weather which were received in this office about the time that the "City of Boston" was lost led to this enquiry ; it gives sufficient evidence that she must have experienced one very severe gale. (See the extracts and remarks for the 30th January, p. 23.) *Final remarks.*

This paper only deals with eleven days of rather exceptional weather, when a southerly wind prevailed on our coasts. It can only be considered as a first attempt at the style of work which is needed to connect the excellent observations now being taken in America with those of Europe.

Perhaps enough has been done to prove that a larger number of observations is needed for this part of the sea than were available for the construction of the "Atlas des Mouvements généraux de l'Atmosphère," published by the Observatory of Paris, and that copious extracts from logs are also needed to connect the Chart of one day with that of the next, otherwise the progress of important changes is lost.

I would here remark that we have felt the want of a larger number of observations, and the frequent irregularity of the isobars shows how much better the work would have been if all ships had been observing with standard instruments. We have specially suffered from the frequent absence of information as to the exact times of wind-changes, and from uncertainty as to whether an entry related to the given time only, or to the time elapsed since the last entry.

If the commanders and owners of our large lines of steamers traversing the Atlantic would take up the subject, accept the offer of the loan of standard instruments from the Committee of the Royal Society who manage this Office, and, for at least a year, record careful observations, we might hope for first-rate results. I may add that if the keeping of an extra log on board steamers, so constantly in port, were thought too much trouble, we should be satisfied with the loan of the ship's log, recording observations of our standard instruments.

LONDON:
Printed by GEORGE E. EYRE and WILLIAM SPOTTISWOODE,
Printers to the Queen's most Excellent Majesty.
For Her Majesty's Stationery Office.
[3476.—750.}
[P. 808.—250.] 6/72.]

LIST OF PUBLICATIONS, &c.

ISSUED UNDER

The Authority of the Meteorological Committee.

OFFICIAL.

No. 1. Report for 1867. Presented to Parliament. Price 1s.
2. Instructions for Meteorological Telegraphy. Price 6d.
3. Fishery Barometer Manual. Price 6d.
4. Charts of Surface Temperature, South Atlantic Ocean. Price 2s. 6d.
5. Report for 1868. Presented to Parliament. Price 5d.
6. Report for 1869. Presented to Parliament. Price 10d.
7. Quarterly Weather Report for 1869.—Parts I. to IV. Price 5s. each. [Published by Stanford, Charing Cross.]
8. Barometer Manual. Price 1s.
9. Quarterly Weather Report for 1870.—Parts I. to IV. Price 5s. each. [Stanford.]
10. Report for 1870. Presented to Parliament. Price 10d.
11. Contributions to our Knowledge of the Meteorology of Cape Horn and the West Coast of South America. Price 2s. 6d. [Stanford.]
12. Currents and Surface Temperature of the North Atlantic Ocean, from the Equator to Latitude 40° N., for each Month of the Year. With a General Current Chart. Price 2s. 6d. [Stanford.]
13. A Discussion of the Meteorology of the Part of the Atlantic lying North of 30° N. for the Eleven days ending 8th February 1870. Price 2s. 6d. [Stanford.]
14. Quarterly Weather Report for 1871.—Part I. January-March. Price 5s. [Stanford.]

NON-OFFICIAL.

No. 1. Report to the Committee on the Connexion between Strong Winds and Barometrical Differences.—By Robert H. Scott, Director of the Office. Price 6d.
2. Report to the Committee on the Meteorology of the North Atlantic. — By Captain H. Toynbee, Marine Superintendent. Price 1s.
3. Report to the Committee on the Use of Isobaric Curves.—By Captain H. Toynbee, Marine Superintendent. Price 1s.
4. Routes for Steamers from Aden to the Straits of Sunda and Back. Price 6d.
5. On the Winds, &c. of the North Atlantic along the Tracks of Steamers from the Channel to New York. Price 6d.

Sold by POTTER, 31, Poultry, and STANFORD, Charing Cross.
The Annual Reports may be obtained of all Parliamentary Booksellers.

CHARTS AND DIAGRAMS

TO ACCOMPANY THE

PAPER ON THE METEOROLOGY OF THE PART OF THE ATLANTIC WHICH LIES NORTH OF 30° N.

FOR THE ELEVEN DAYS ENDING FEB. 8, 1870.

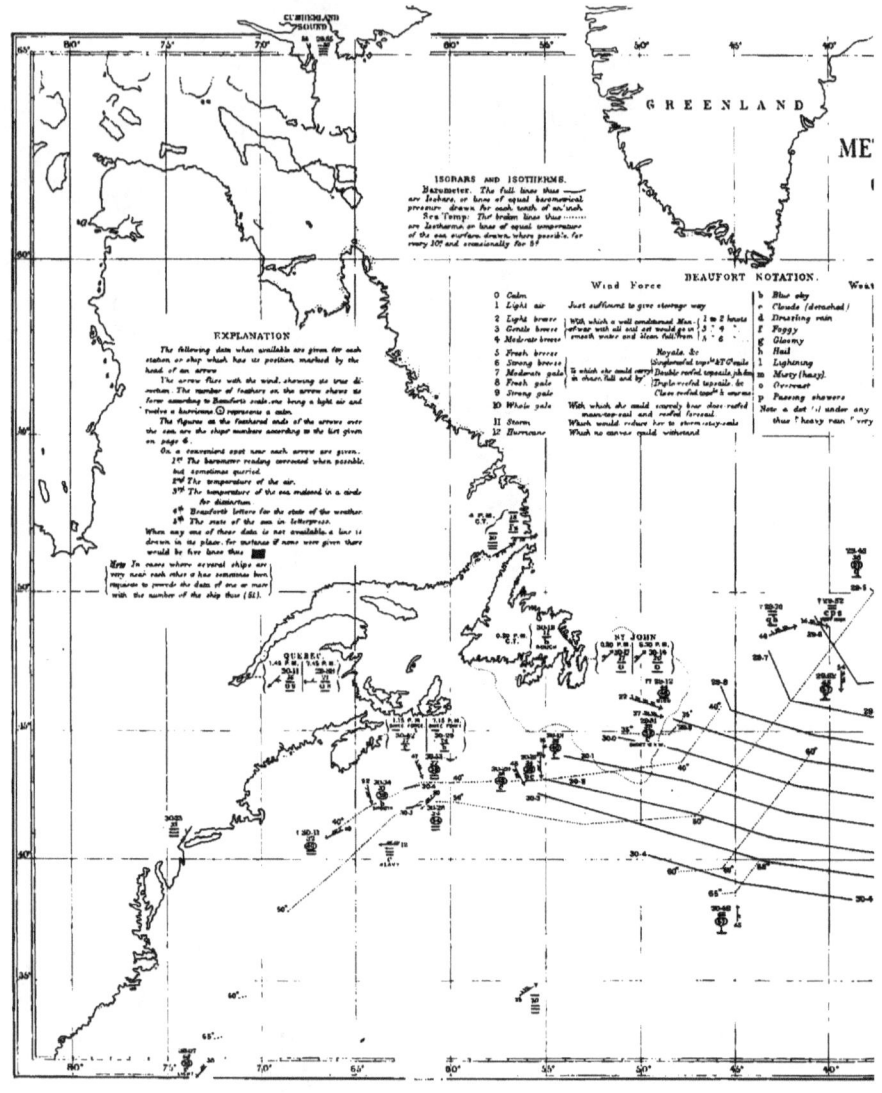

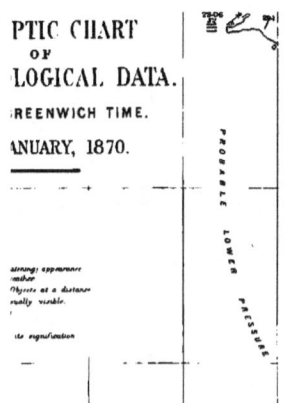

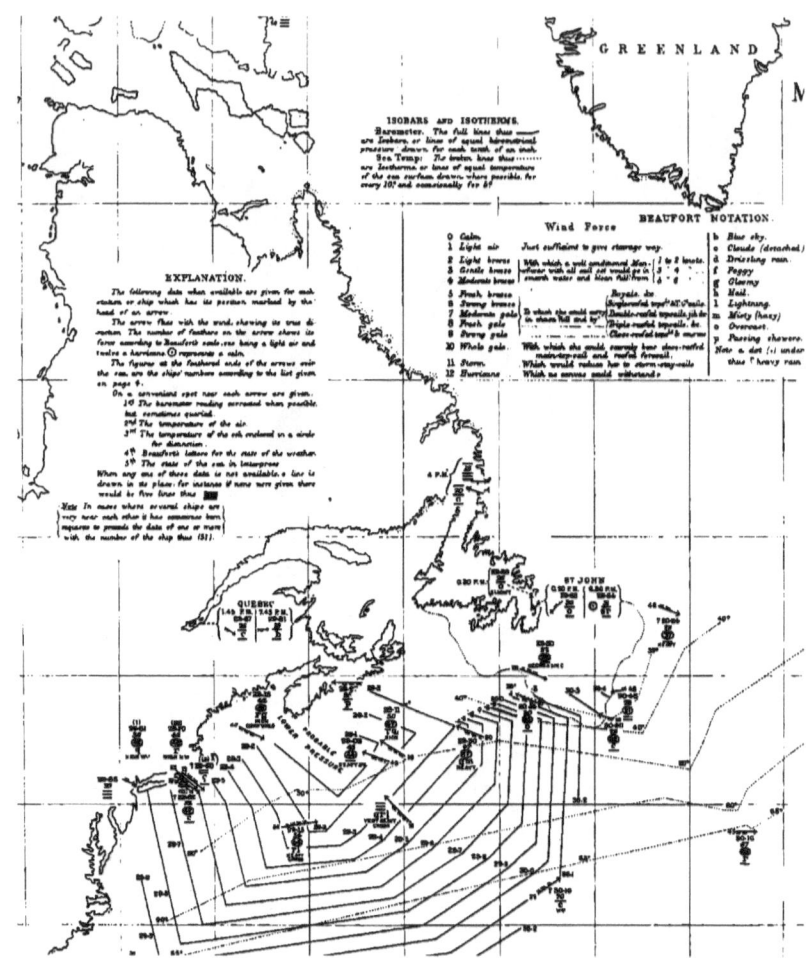

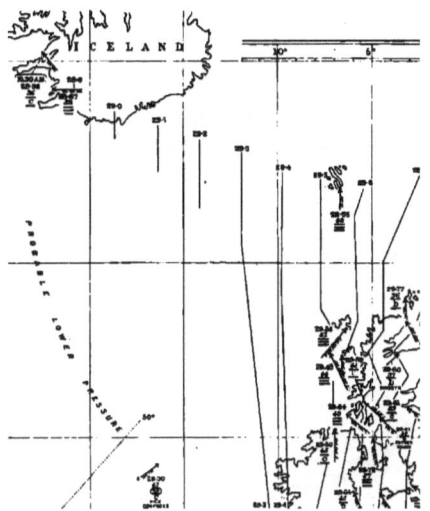

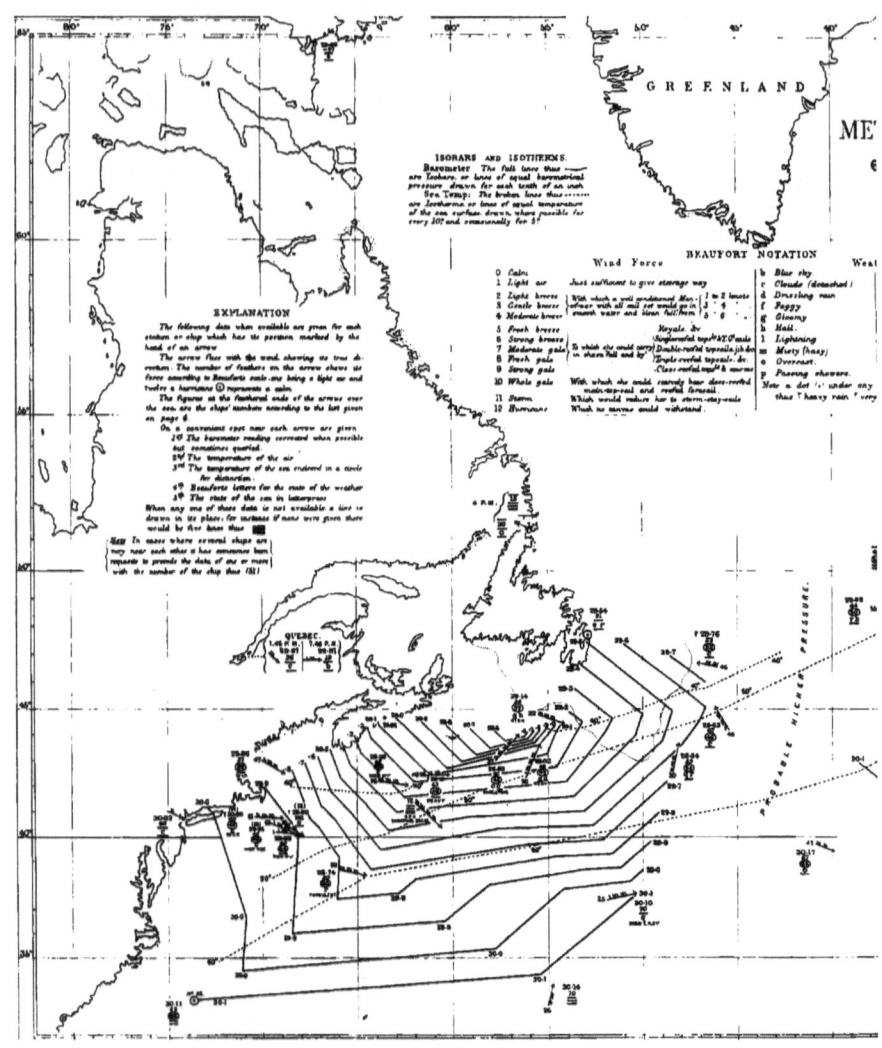

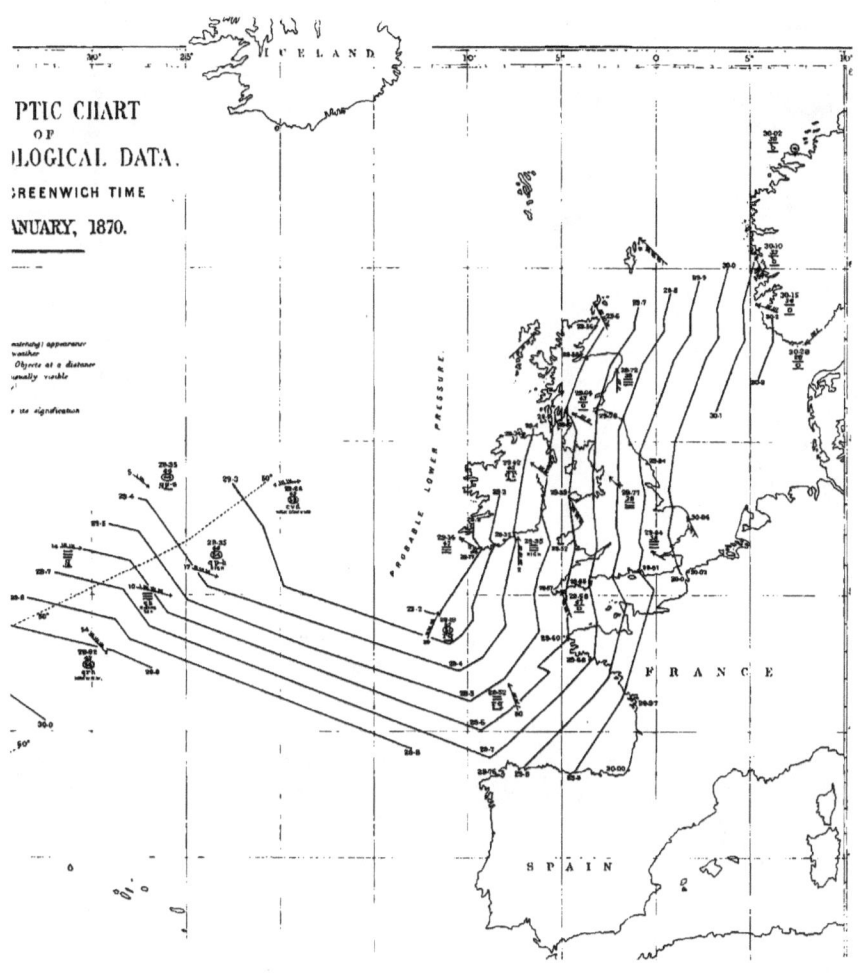

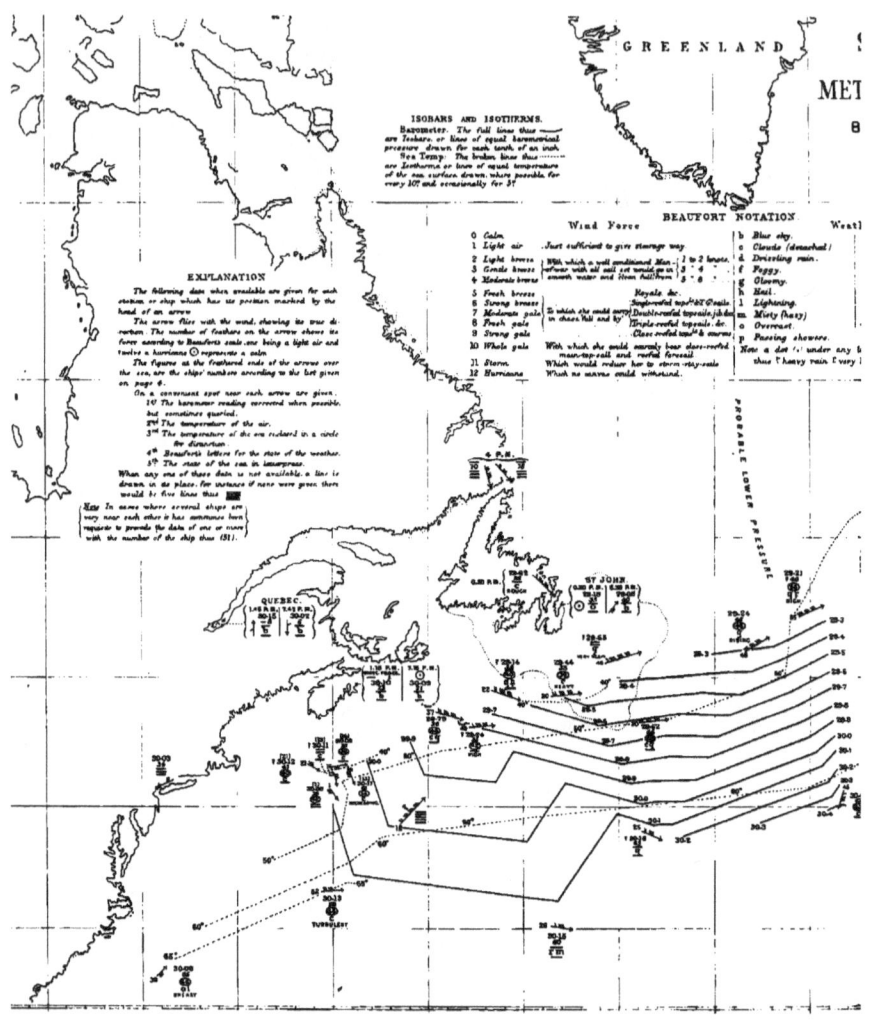

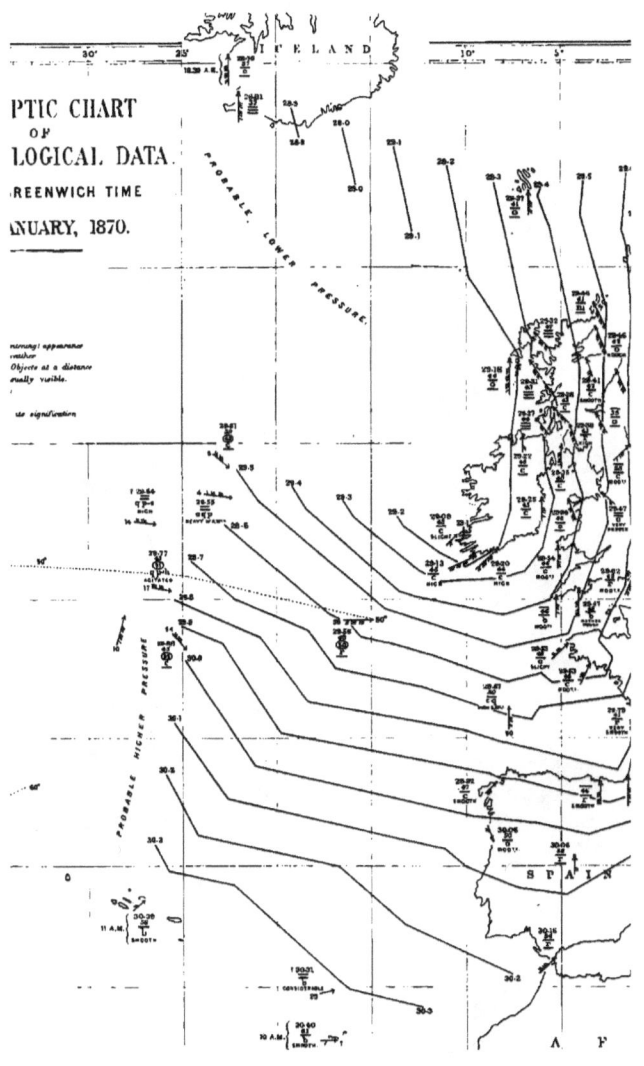

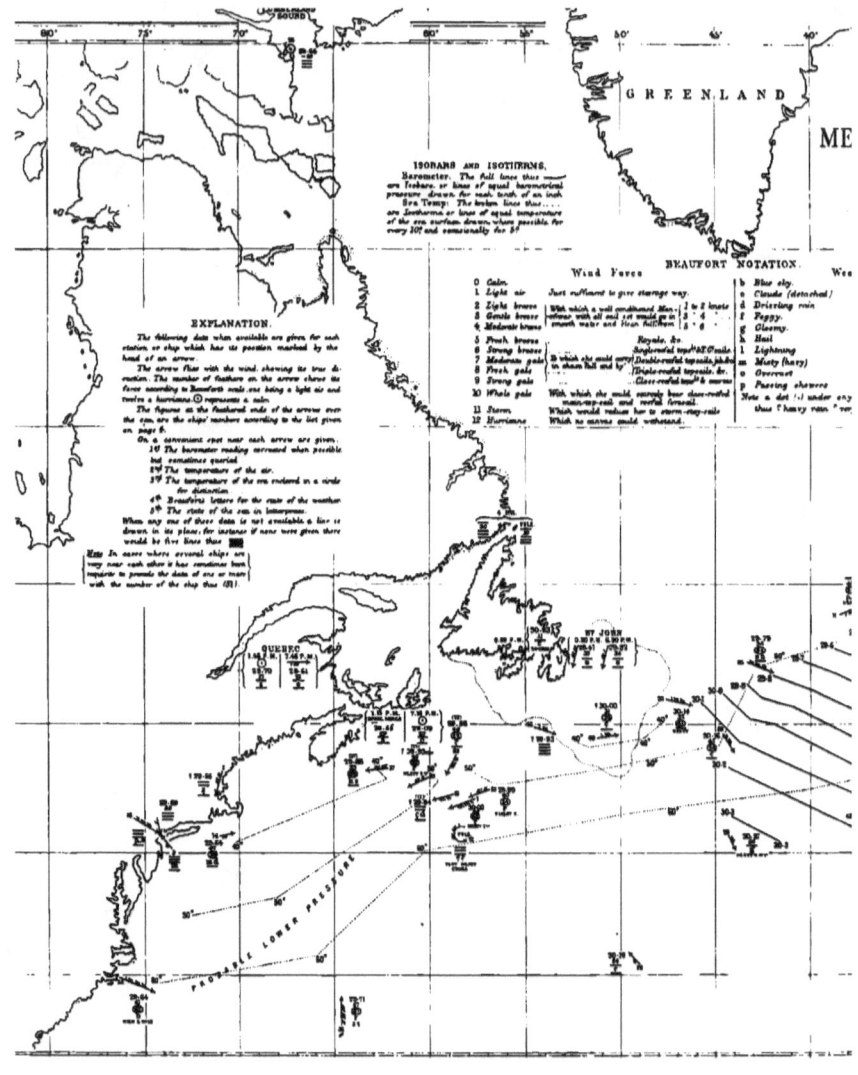

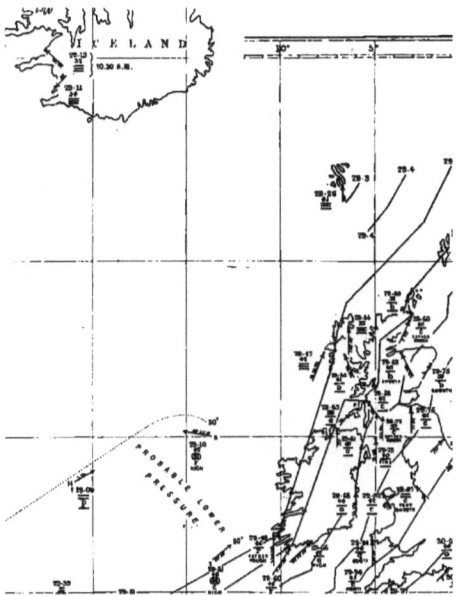

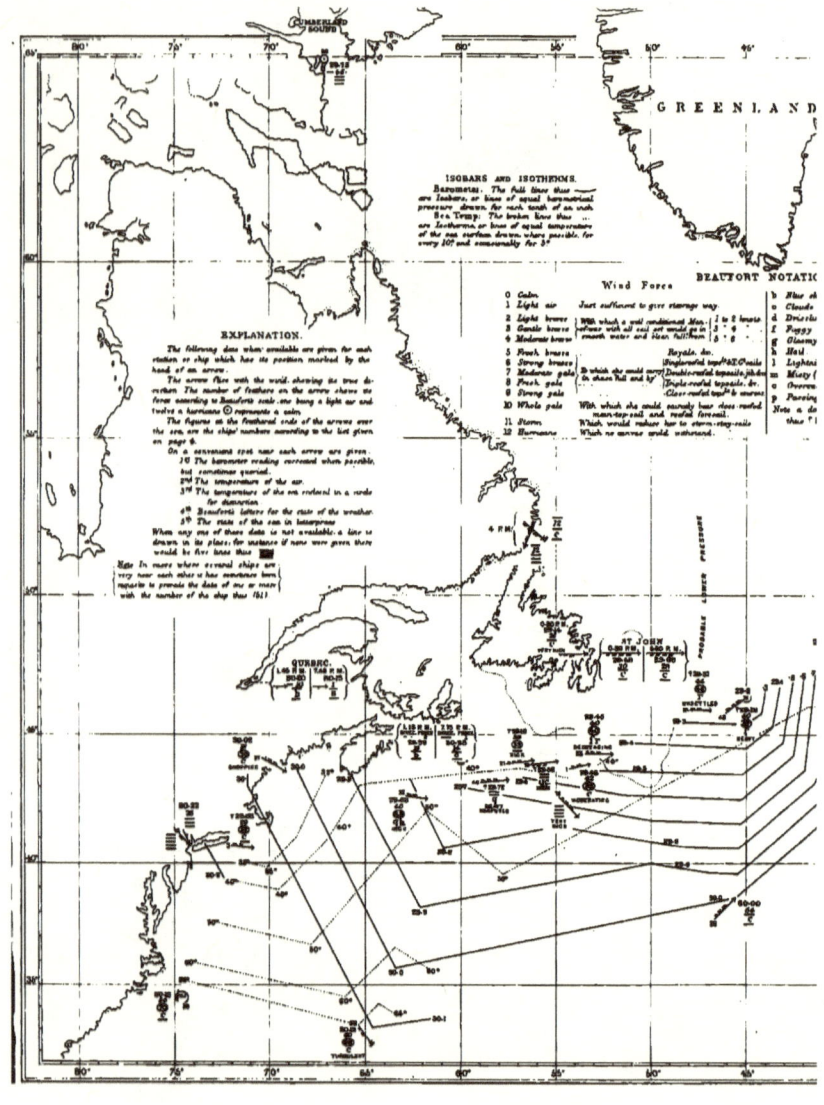

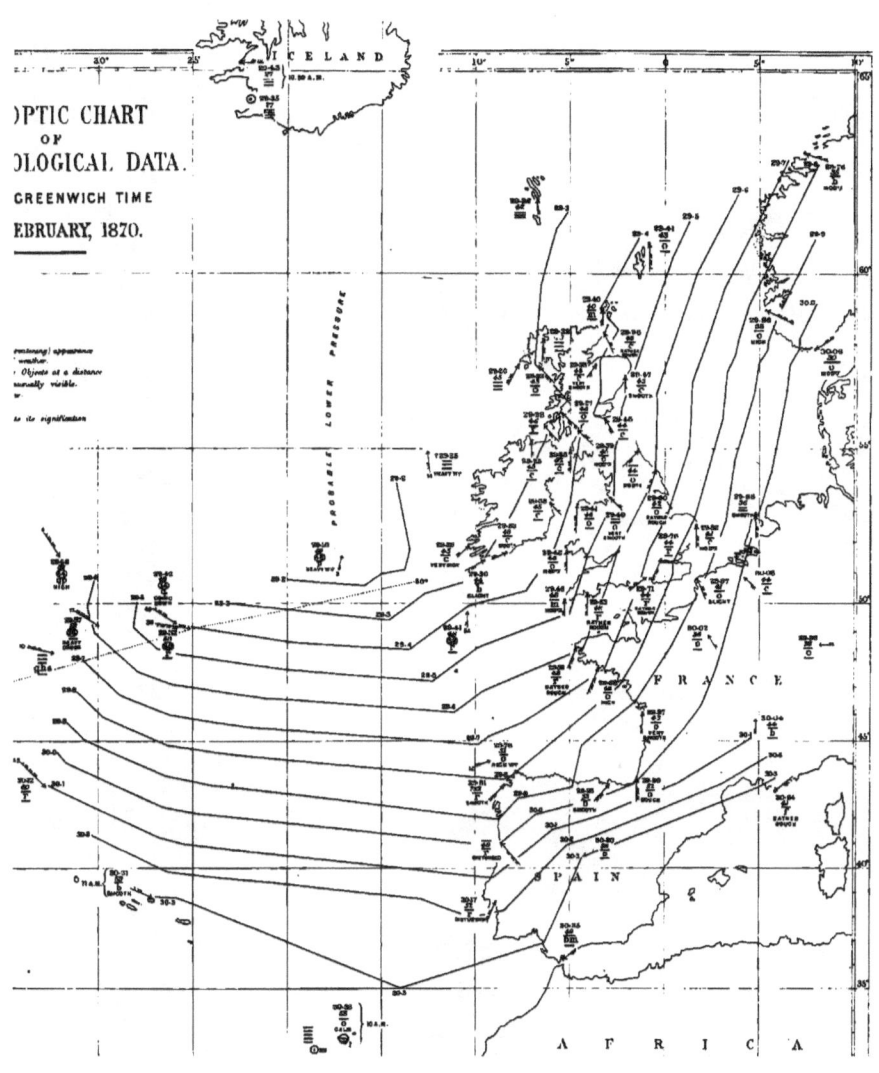

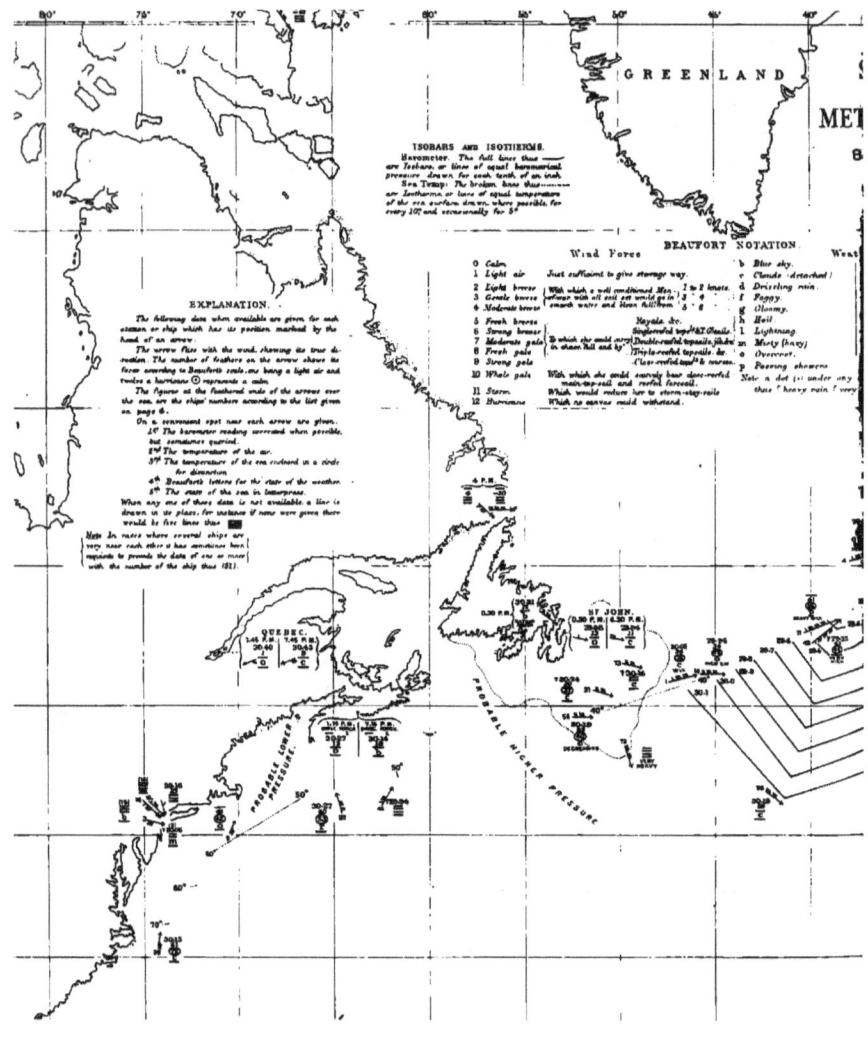

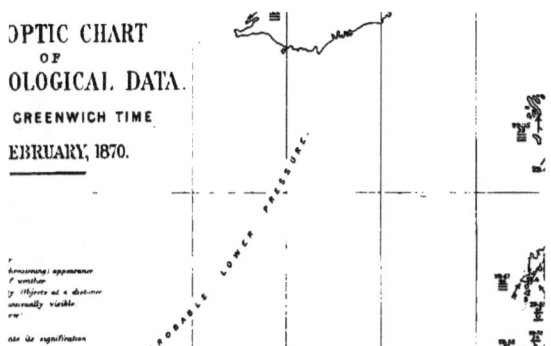

)PTIC CHART
OF
OLOGICAL DATA.

GREENWICH TIME

EBRUARY, 1870.

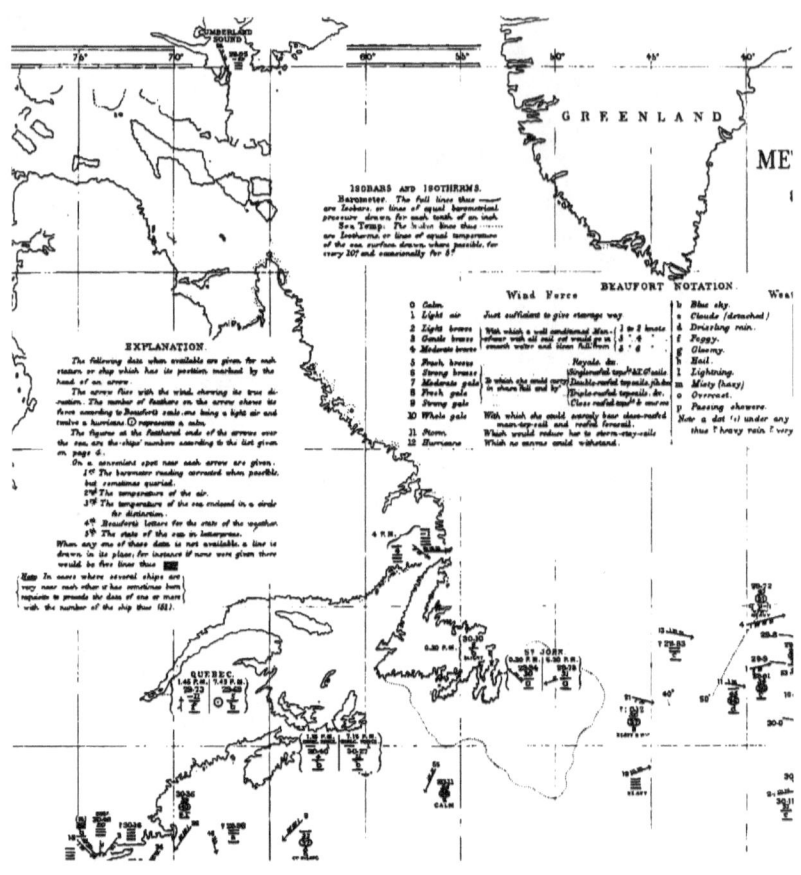

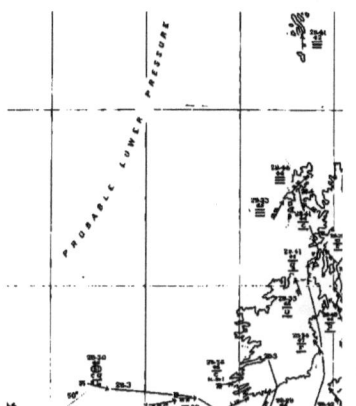

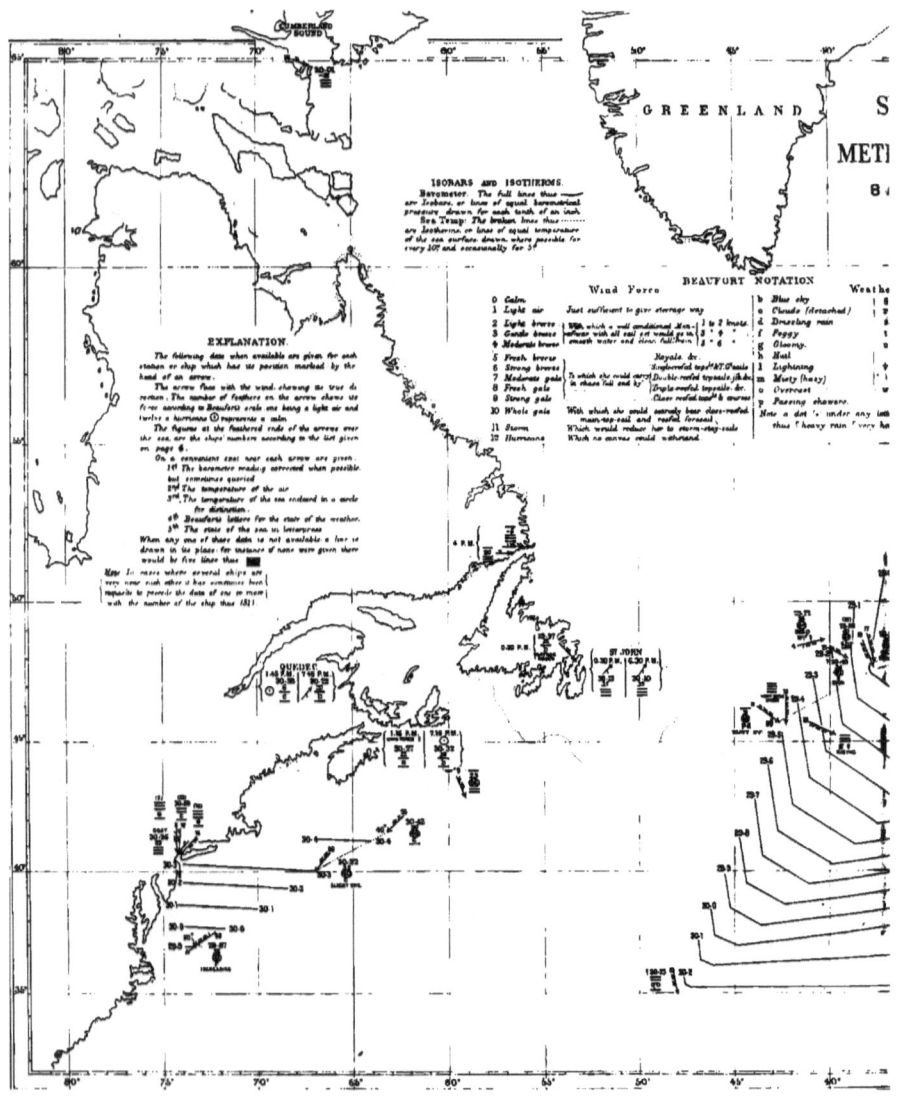

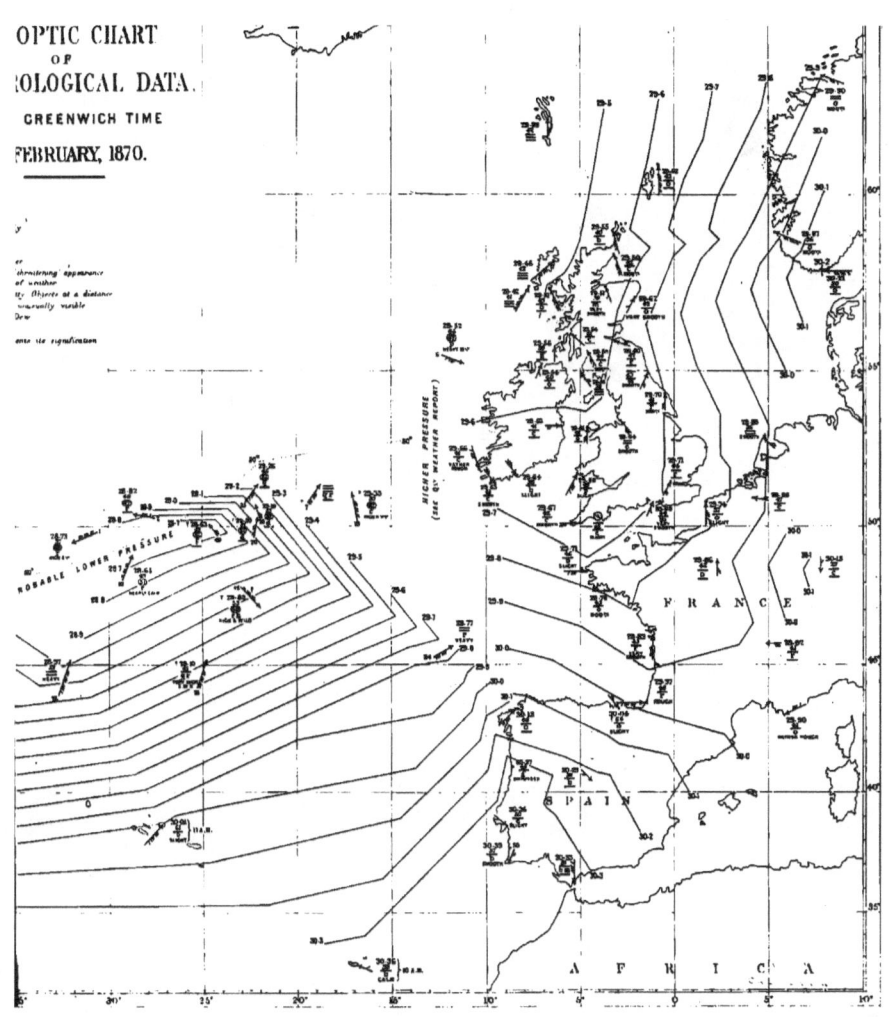

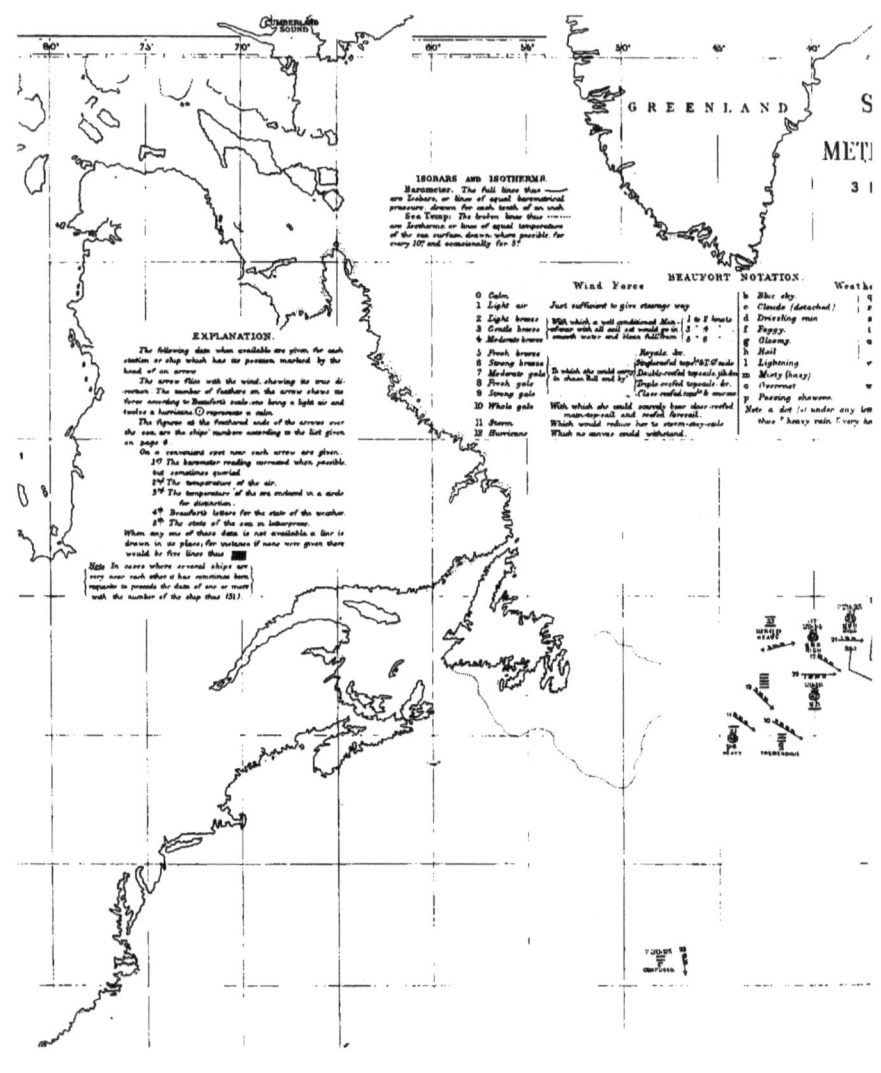

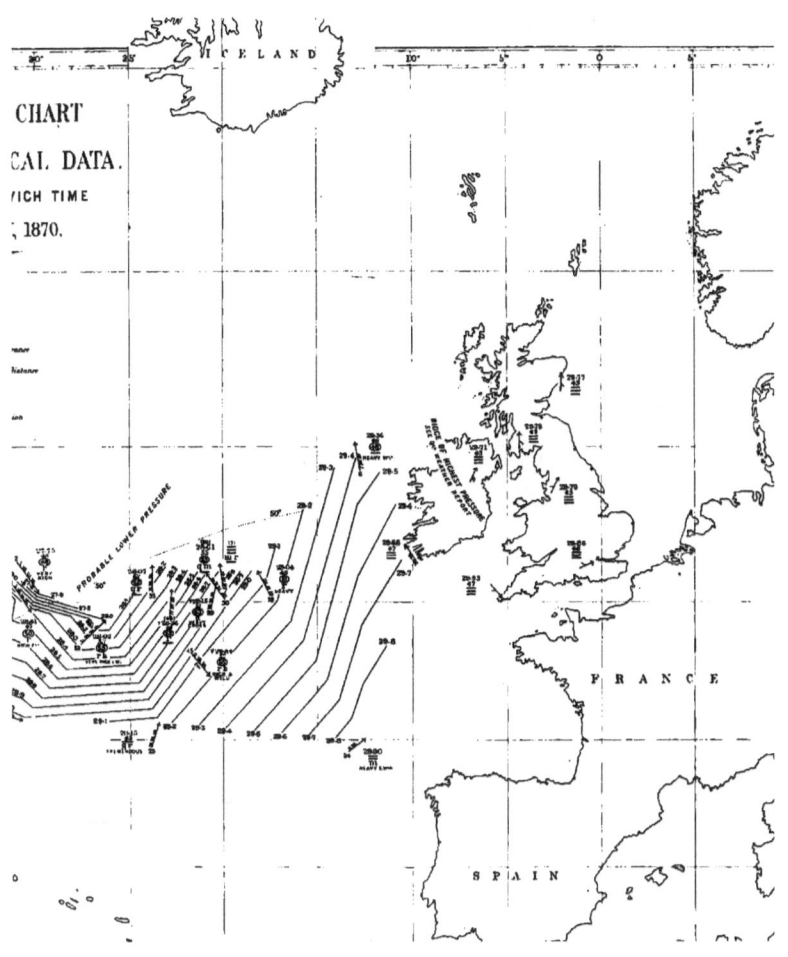

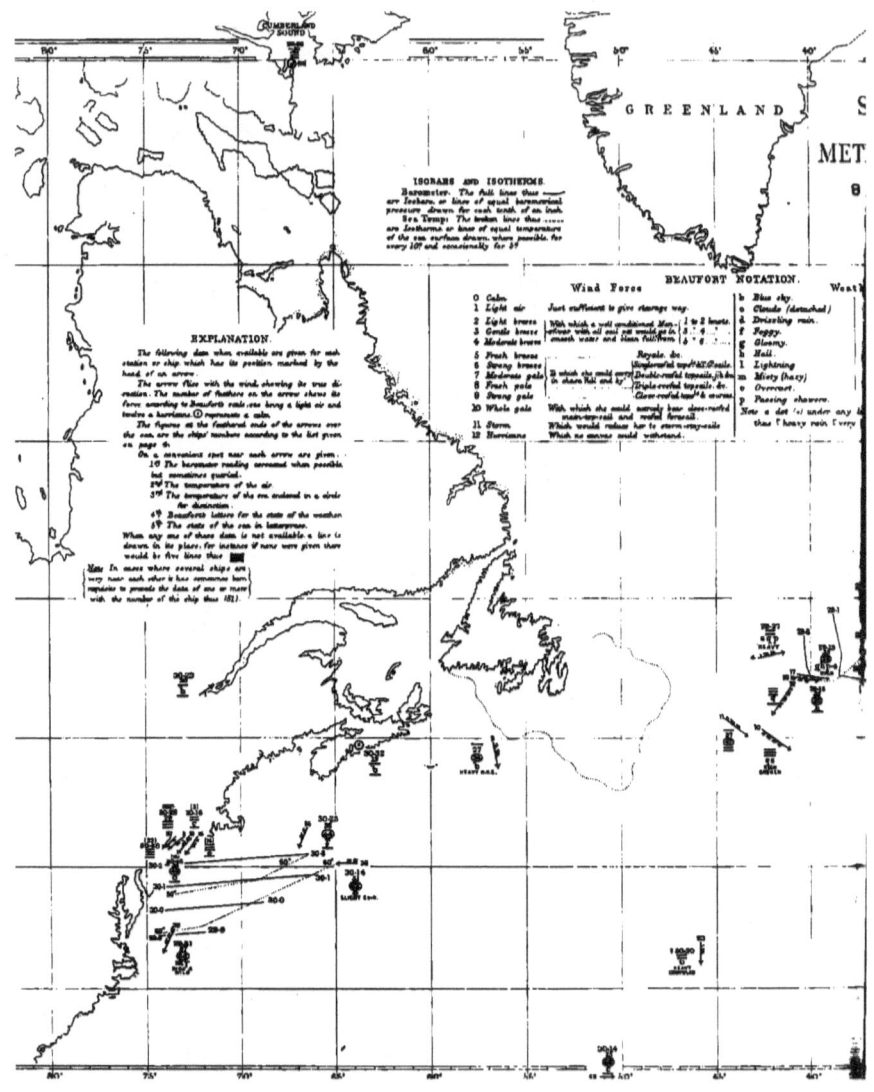

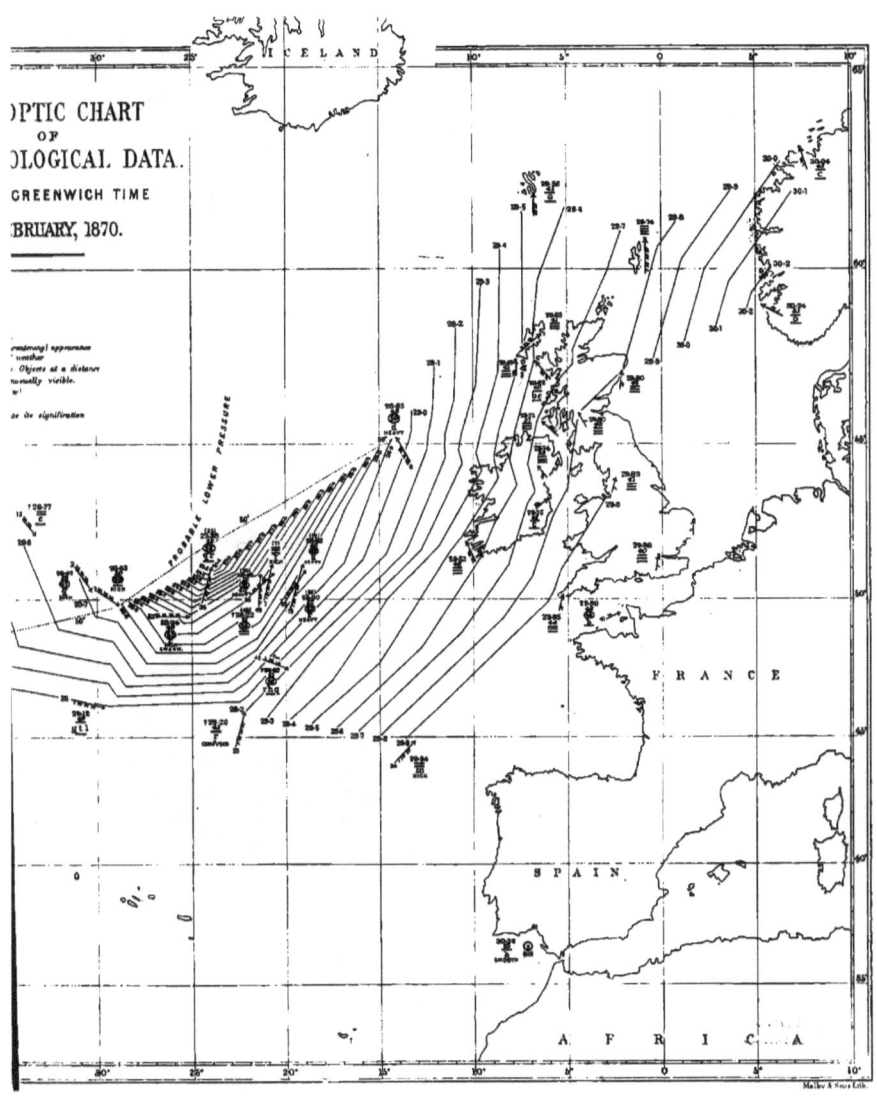

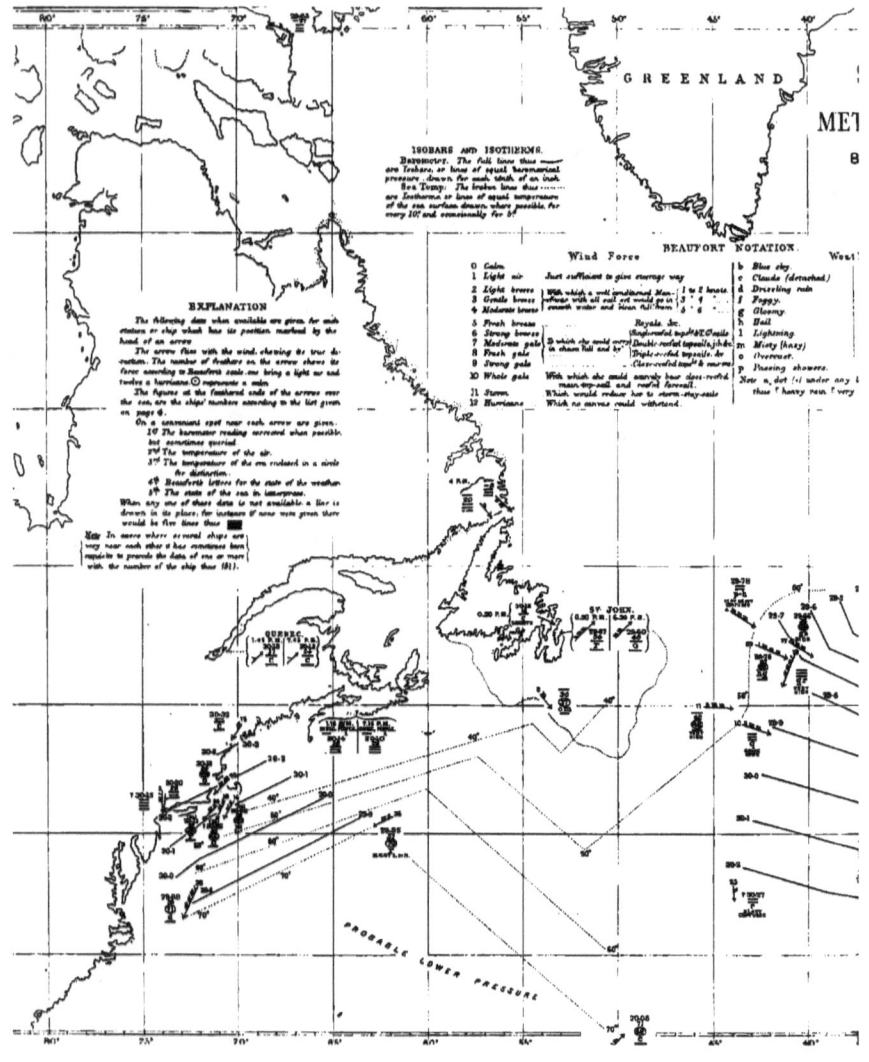

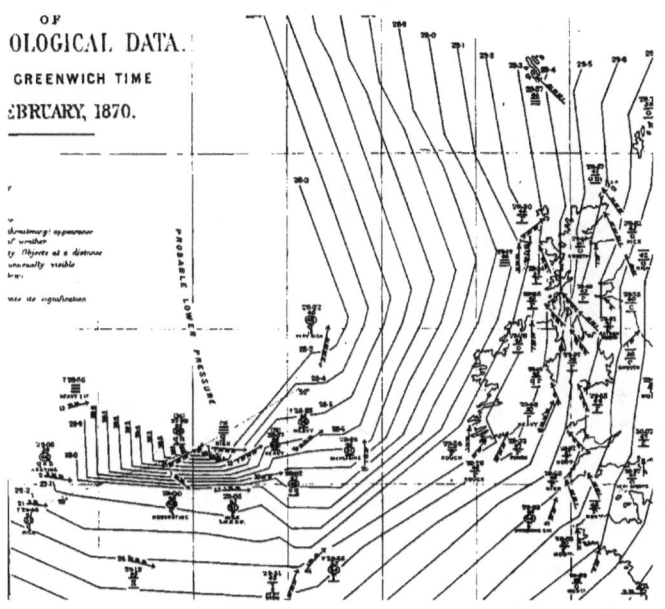

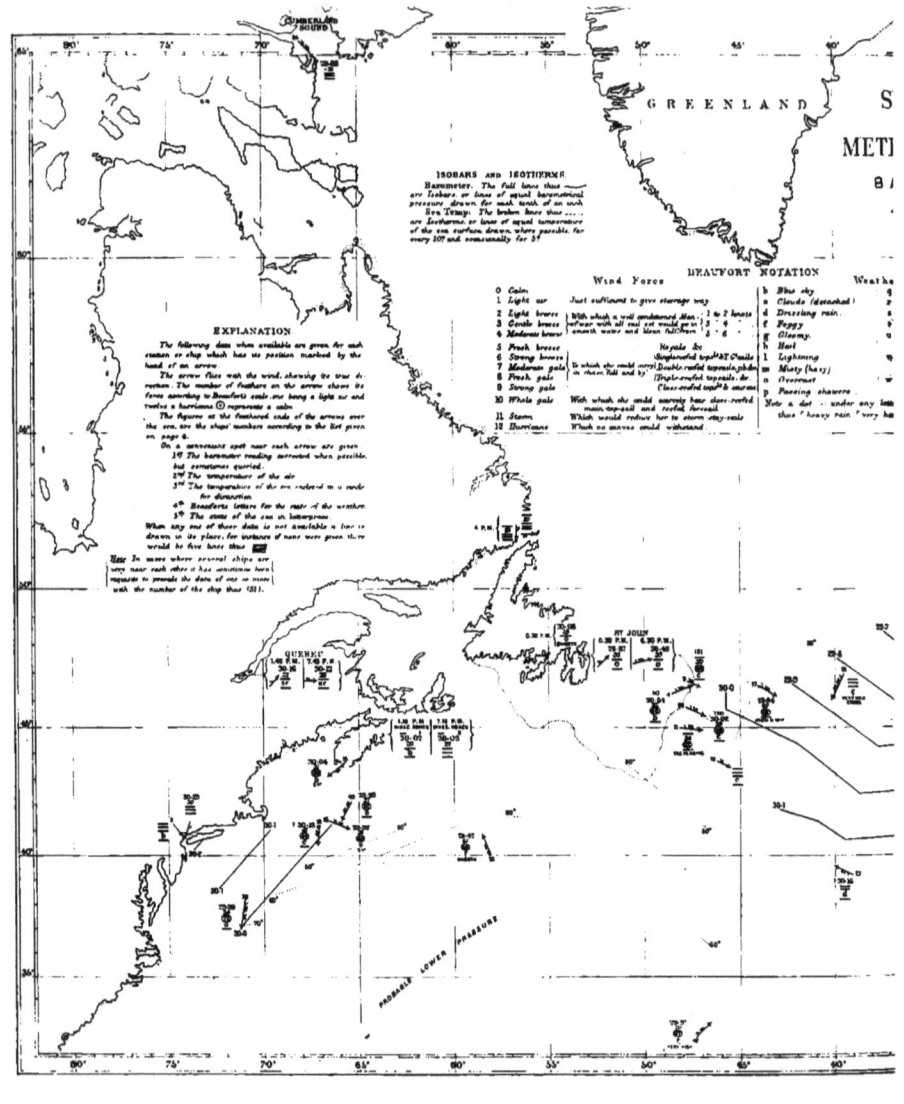

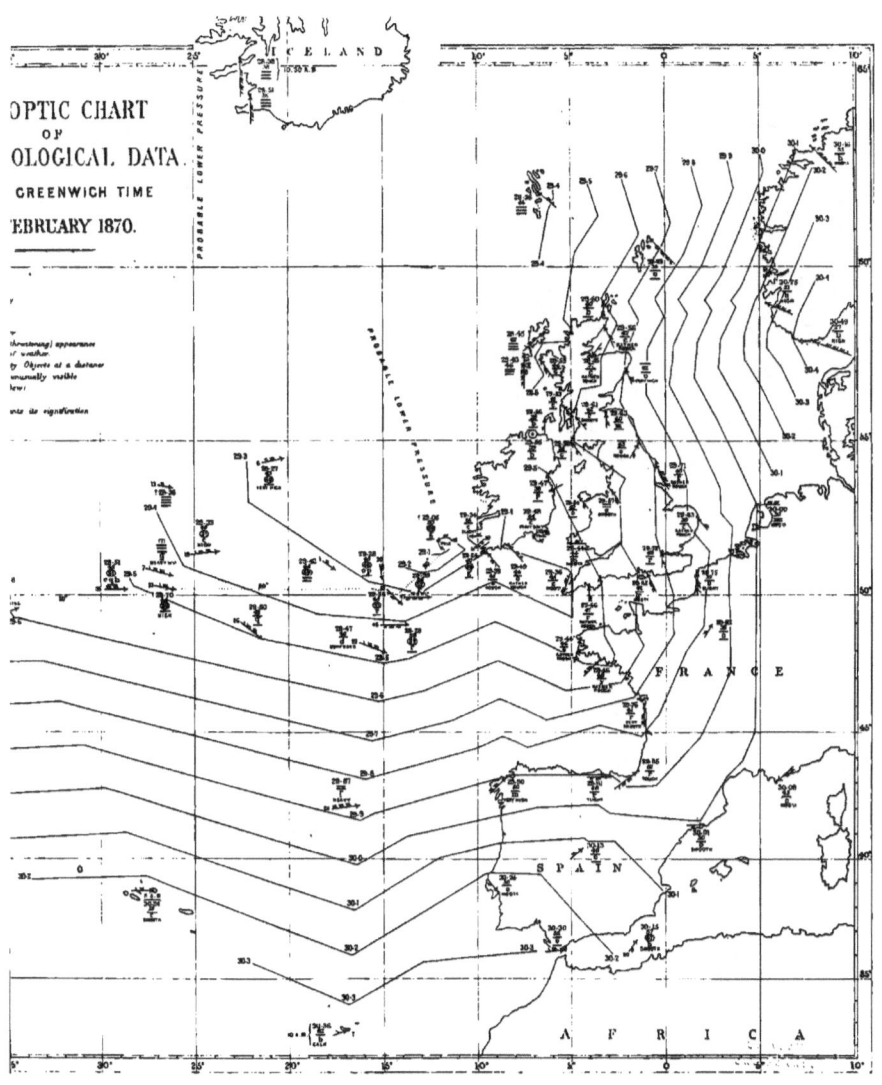

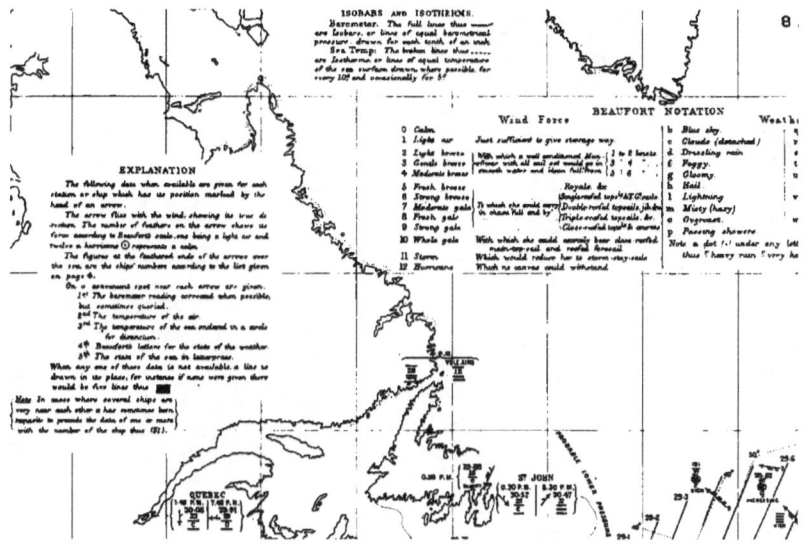

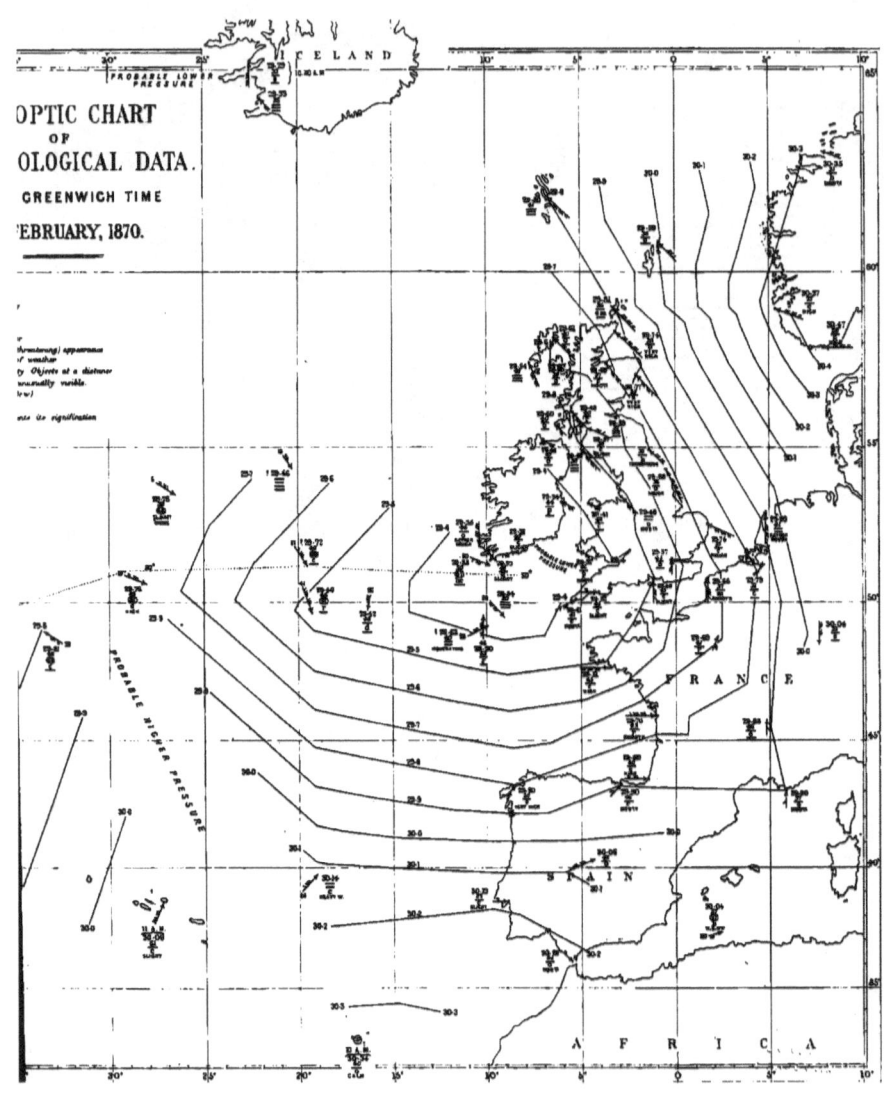

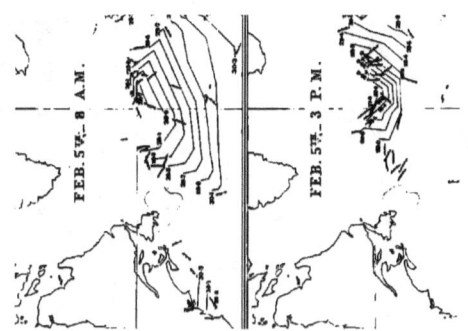

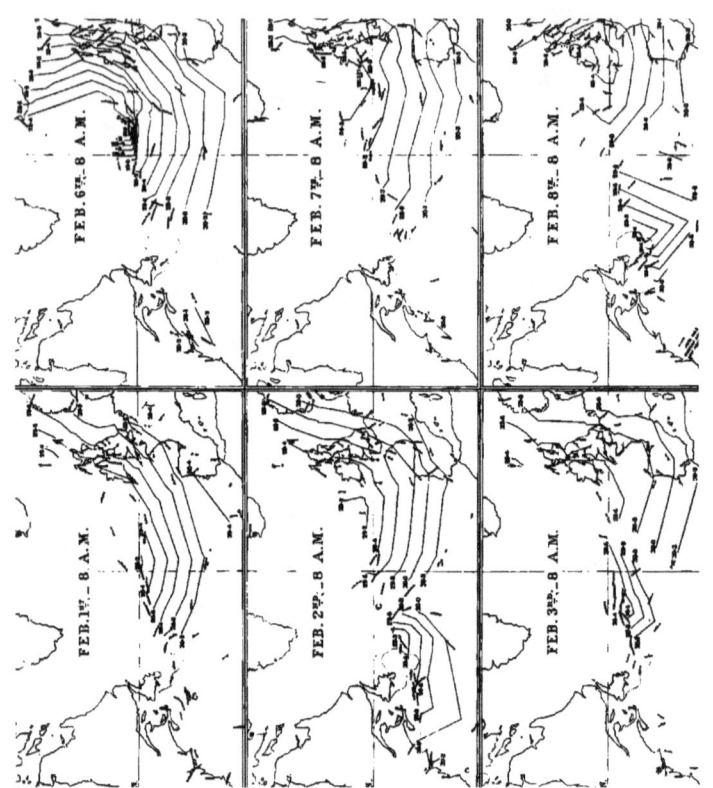

EXPLANATION OF DIAGRAMS.

On the upper part of these diagrams are the forces of wind by Beaufort's scale* expressed in figures 1 to 12, and its true direction. The arrow is supposed to fly with the wind, thus (↑), which means south. Then comes the weather by Beaufort's notation.* The wind and weather are supposed to be the average of what has prevailed in the four hours between the given hours. Next come the curve of four-hourly barometer readings, reduced for temperature and height of cistern, and the curves of sea surface and air temperatures. Near to the more sea temperature is written the specific gravity when available, which it will be noticed is generally lowest in the cold water, on the western side of the Atlantic.

On the lower part of the diagram is the track of the ship with a dot at her noon position of latitude, allowing each square to be a degree.

The longitude at noon is given immediately below that hour, between the day and hour lines.

Then, as all our quotations are for Greenwich time, and each square represents four hours of local time, the longitude in time is written above the noon hour. This is to be added to the given hour to find its corresponding Greenwich time, and as ships in general only alter their time keepers after noon each day, the longitude in time of the noon of a given day must be added to all four-hourly entries until noon of the following day. When comparing these diagrams with the observatory plates in the Quarterly Weather Report it must be remembered that the diagrams give the space of four hours, and the Quarterly Weather Report only that of one and a half hours to a tenth of an inch of the barometer. Hence the same amount of barometer range will show much more on the diagrams, than on the observatory plates.

* See thin scale and notation on each Chart.

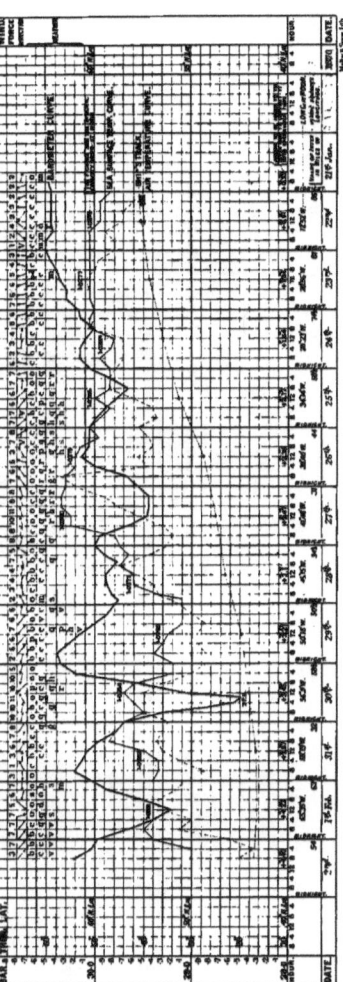

Diagram 1.— Ship's Number on the Charts 37.

S.S. "AUSTRIAN." CAPTAIN JAMES WYLIE, OUTWARD-BOUND TO PORTLAND, MAINE.

Diagram 2.—Ship's Number on the Charts 53
NORTH GERMAN LLOYDS S.S. "WESER", CAPTAIN C. WENKE, HOMEWARD-BOUND TO BREMEN.

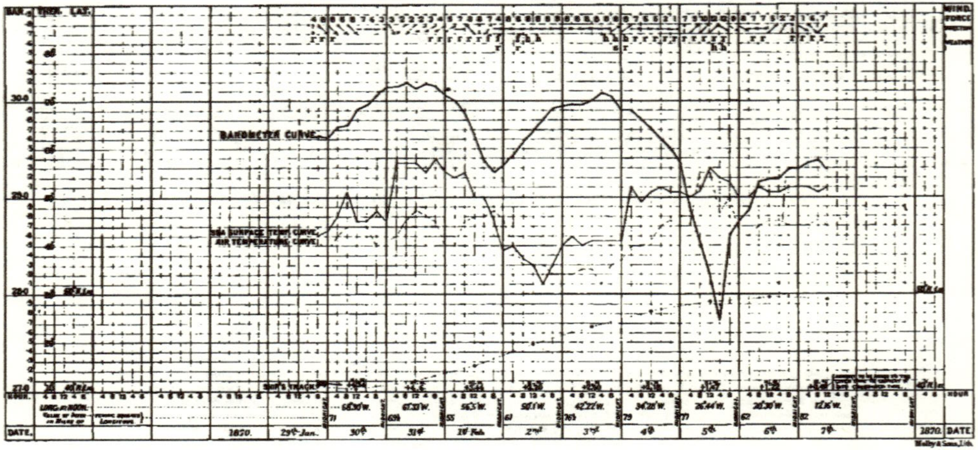

S.S. "TARIFA." CAPTAIN M. MURPHY, OUTWARD-BOUND TO BOSTON.

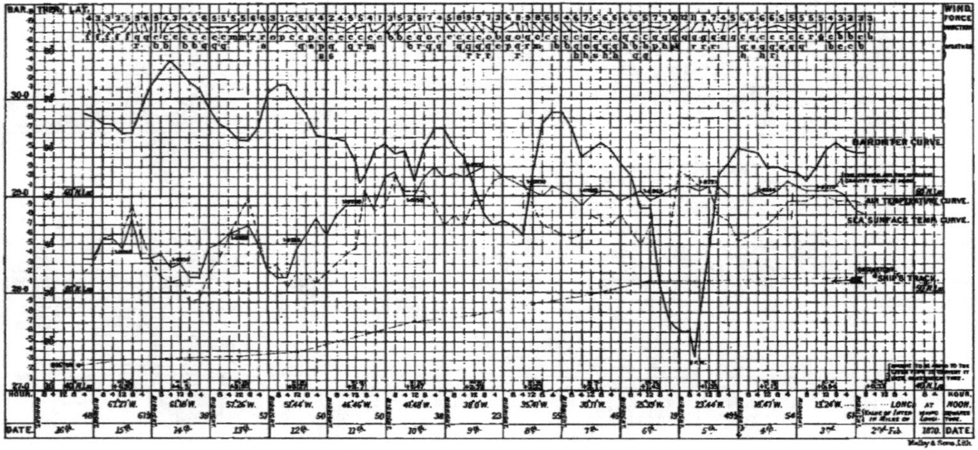

Diagram 3.— Ship's Number on the Charts 35.

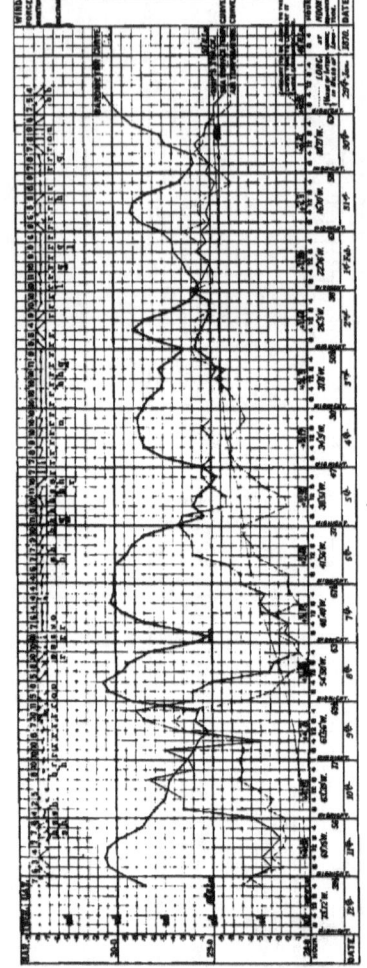

Diagram 4.—Ship's Number on the Charts 33.
NORTH GERMAN LLOYDS S.S. "WESTPHALIA", CAPTAIN TRAUTMANN, OUTWARD-BOUND TO NEW YORK.

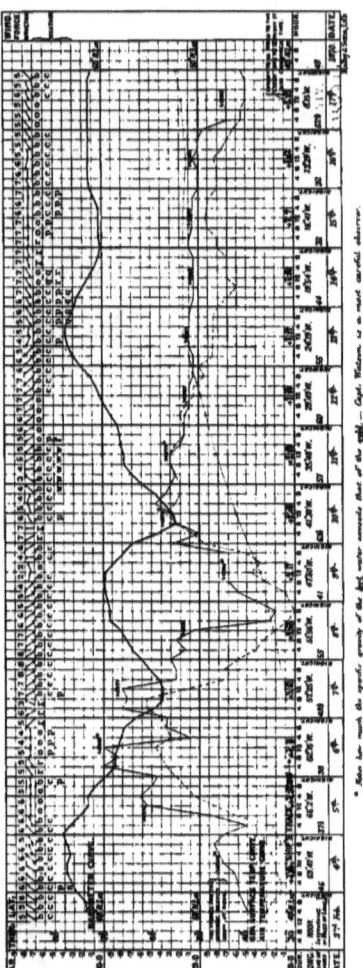

Diagram 5.—Ship's Number on the Charts 36.
R.M.S. "PALMYRA", CAPTAIN W. WATSON, HOMEWARD-BOUND TO LIVERPOOL.